Evolution, Scripture, and Science
Selected Writings

Evolution, Scripture, and Science
Selected Writings

B. B. Warfield

Edited and with an Introduction by

Mark A. Noll & David N. Livingstone

 Baker Books

A Division of Baker Book House Co
Grand Rapids, Michigan 49516

Published by Baker Books
a division of Baker Book House Company
P.O. Box 6287, Grand Rapids, MI 49516–6287

Printed in the United States of America

Library of Congress Cataloging-in-Publication Data

Warfield, Benjamin Breckinridge, 1851–1921.
    Evolution, scripture, and science / selected writings / edited and with
an introduction by Mark A. Noll & David N. Livingstone.
       p.   cm.
    Includes bibliographical references and index.
    ISBN 0-8010-2217-7 (pbk.)
      1. Evolution—Religious aspects—Christianity. 2. Bible and evolution.
3. Religion and science. I. Noll, Mark A., 1946– II. Livingstone,
David N., 1953– III. Title

BT712.W37   2000
231.7′652—dc21   99-058773

For information about academic books, resources for Christian leaders, and all
new releases available from Baker Book House, visit our web site:
http://www.bakerbooks.com

To

William O. Harris

Contents

Warfield on Scripture

Warfield on Evolution and Science

Acknowledgments

In bringing these writings of Warfield to print, the editors are conscious of many debts. They are pleased to be able to acknowledge at least some of them here: to Jim Moore for long-standing inspiration on the project; to Bradley Gundlach for sage advice about Princeton matters; to Bill Harris for many kindnesses in the use of material at Princeton Theological Seminary; to Carmin Ballou, Kathy Lane, Mary Noll, and Lori Willemsen for expert typing; to Peter Wallace, Bryan Bademan, and Estelle Berger whose work on notes and editing was a sine qua non for the book; to Allan Fisher, Jim Weaver, and Ray Wiersma for patient support; to Arthur Rupprecht and Stephen Williams for help with Warfield's knottier Latin quotations; and to the McManis Chair of Wheaton College and a patron of Wheaton's Institute for the Study of American Evangelicals for financial support.

Abbreviations

SSWW = *Selected Shorter Writings of Benjamin B. Warfield,* ed. John E. Meeter, 2 vols. (Nutley, N.J.: Presbyterian and Reformed, 1970 and 1973)

WBBW = *The Works of Benjamin B. Warfield,* 10 vols. (New York: Oxford University Press, 1927–32; Grand Rapids: Baker, 1981 reprint)

Introduction

B. B. Warfield
as a Conservative Evolutionist

The purpose of this book is to introduce and republish the most pertinent theological reflections of Benjamin Breckinridge Warfield (1851–1921) on the relationship between science and Christianity, with special attention to Darwin, Darwinism, and evolution. As will quickly become apparent, for Warfield the latter three subjects were distinct. The reasons why Warfield differentiated among the person of Charles Darwin, Darwin's own opinions about the development of species, and more general considerations concerning evolution link this volume to its predecessor, Charles Hodge's *What Is Darwinism? And Other Writings on Science and Religion.*[1] Of key importance in Warfield's thinking was his willingness throughout a long career to accept the possibility (at times, the probability) of evolution, while always denying Darwinism strictly defined. This introduction will show that the conclusions of these two notable Presbyterian intellectuals, who anchored the faculty of a leading theological seminary for almost a century, were more harmonious than first appears.[2] According to

1. Charles Hodge, *What Is Darwinism?* ed. Mark A. Noll and David N. Livingstone (Grand Rapids: Baker, 1994). The introduction provides historical context for the approach of the nineteenth-century Princeton theologians to questions of science and theology.

2. Hodge taught at Princeton Seminary from 1820 to 1878, Warfield from 1887 to 1921. They were also the major editors of the theological quarterlies associated with the seminary. On Princeton as the nation's premier institution of theological education in the period, see Peter Wallace and Mark Noll, "The Students of Princeton Seminary, 1812–1929," *American Presbyterians* 72 (Fall 1994): 203–15.

Hodge, as he put it at the end of *What Is Darwinism?* in 1874, "We have thus arrived at the answer to our question, What is Darwinism? It is Atheism."[3] Forty-one years later, Warfield included in a lengthy paper on John Calvin's view of creation an opinion that doubtless represented his own view as well: "All that has come into being since [the original creation of the world-stuff]—except the souls of men alone—has arisen as a modification of this original world-stuff by means of the interaction of its intrinsic forces. . . . [These modifications] find their account proximately in second causes, and this is not only evolutionism but pure evolutionism."[4] To grasp the underlying harmony between these two statements, it is necessary to pay strict attention to the distinction between "Darwinism" and "evolution" that Hodge cautiously advanced in his 1874 book and that Warfield developed much more boldly in a series of weighty writings.

More generally, this introduction also demonstrates that the recent perception of a deep, permanent conflict between "naturalistic evolution" and "Christian creation" is mistaken. Warfield's writings on evolution or, more broadly, on science—the last of which appeared in the year of his death, 1921—cannot, of course, pronounce definitively on theological-scientific questions at the beginning of the twenty-first century. They can, however, show that sophisticated theology, nuanced argument, and careful sifting of scientific research can produce a much more satisfactory working relationship between science and theology than does the heated strife that has dominated public debate on this subject since the time of Warfield's passing.[5]

One way of jolting discussion about science and theology out of the fervent, but also intellectually barren, standoffs of recent decades is to note one of the best-kept secrets in American intellectual history: B. B. Warfield, the ablest modern defender of the theologically conservative doctrine of the inerrancy of the Bible, was also an evolutionist.

3. Hodge, *What Is Darwinism?* 156.

4. B. B. Warfield, "Calvin's Doctrine of the Creation," in *WBBW,* 5:304–5 (reprinted in the present volume, pp. 293–314).

5. On the development of that strife, see Ronald L. Numbers, *The Creationists: The Evolution of Scientific Creationism* (New York: Knopf, 1992).

During the late nineteenth century, when critical views of Scripture came to prevail in American universities, Warfield was more responsible than any other American for refurbishing the conviction that the Bible communicates revelation from God entirely without error. Warfield's formulation of biblical inerrancy, in fact, has been a theological mainstay for recent "creationist" convictions about the origin of the earth and its species.[6] Yet Warfield was also a cautious, discriminating, but entirely candid proponent of the possibility that evolution might offer the best way to understand the natural history of the earth and of humankind. On this score his views place him with more-recent thinkers who maintain ancient trust in the Bible while affirming the modern scientific enterprise.[7] Warfield did not simply assert these two views randomly; rather, he sustained them learnedly, as coordinate arguments, in several kinds of writing—theological essays,

6. For direct use of Warfield on the inerrancy of Scripture, see John C. Whitcomb Jr. and Henry M. Morris, *The Genesis Flood: The Biblical Record and Its Scientific Implications* (Philadelphia: Presbyterian and Reformed, 1961), xx; and in a more historical account, Nigel M. de S. Cameron, *Evolution and the Authority of the Bible* (Exeter: Paternoster, 1983), ch. 2, "What *Is* the Bible: The Evangelical Consensus," 19–32, with Warfield at 24–25 and passim. See also the select bibliography in the present volume (pp. 333–36) for numerous works treating Warfield on biblical inerrancy.

7. See, as only some examples, Bernard Ramm, *The Christian View of Science and Scripture* (Grand Rapids: Eerdmans, 1954); Russell L. Mixter, ed., *Evolution and Christian Thought Today* (Grand Rapids: Eerdmans, 1959); D. C. Spanner, *Creation and Evolution: Some Preliminary Considerations* (Grand Rapids: Zondervan, 1968); Malcolm A. Jeeves, ed., *The Scientific Enterprise and Christian Faith* (Downers Grove, Ill.: InterVarsity, 1969); Donald M. MacKay, *The Clockwork Image: A Christian Perspective on Science* (Downers Grove, Ill.: InterVarsity, 1974); Thomas F. Torrance, *Christian Theology and Scientific Culture* (New York: Oxford University Press, 1981); Davis A. Young, *Christianity and the Age of the Earth* (Grand Rapids: Zondervan, 1982); Charles E. Hummel, *The Galileo Connection: Resolving Conflicts between Science and the Bible* (Downers Grove, Ill.: InterVarsity, 1986); J. C. Polkinghorne, *One World: The Interaction of Science and Theology* (Princeton: Princeton University Press, 1986); Howard J. Van Till, *The Fourth Day: What the Bible and the Heavens Are Telling Us about the Creation* (Grand Rapids: Eerdmans, 1986); John Houghton, *Does God Play Dice? A Look at the Story of the Universe* (Grand Rapids: Zondervan, 1988); Richard T. Wright, *Biology through the Eyes of Faith* (San Francisco: Harper & Row, 1989); J. C. Polkinghorne, *Reason and Reality* (London: SPCK, 1991); Philip Duce, *Reading the Mind of God: Interpretation in Science and Theology* (Leicester: Apollos, 1998); and Alister McGrath, *The Foundations of Dialogue in Science and Religion* (Oxford: Blackwell, 1998).

book reviews, lectures, and historical papers. Warfield's convictions on theology and evolution are, thus, as important for commentary on our own era's intellectual warfare as they are for illuminating the historical situation in his own age.[8]

Warfield's Life and Theology

Benjamin Breckinridge Warfield was the most widely known advocate of confessional Calvinism in the United States at the end of the nineteenth and the beginning of the twentieth centuries.[9] Warfield continues to exert an influence today mostly through his defense of biblical inerrancy, although his convictions about the role of reason in apologetics also stimulate some ongoing discussion. More than three-quarters of a century after his death, many of his works remain in print. His opinions continue to count, not only among conservative Presbyterians and modern advocates of inerrancy, where such attention could be expected, but also with Southern Baptists, Wesleyans, some neoorthodox theologians, and others whose interest in Warfield's views might be regarded as a surprise.[10]

Warfield was born on November 5, 1851, at Grasmere, his

8. For the broader theological context within which Warfield's views developed, see Mark A. Noll, "Science, Theology, and Society: From Cotton Mather to William Jennings Bryan," in *Evangelicals and Science in Historical Perspective*, ed. David N. Livingstone, D. G. Hart, and Mark A. Noll (New York: Oxford University Press, 1999), 99–119.

9. This section of the introduction abridges and adapts the chapter on Warfield by Mark A. Noll in *Handbook of Evangelical Theologians*, ed. Walter Elwell (Grand Rapids: Baker, 1993), 26–39.

10. As examples of the former, see Harvie M. Conn and the faculty of Westminster Theological Seminary, *Inerrancy and Hermeneutic* (Grand Rapids: Baker, 1988), 37–39, 67–80; and John H. Gerstner, "Warfield's Case for Biblical Inerrancy," in *God's Inerrant Word*, ed. John Warwick Montgomery (Minneapolis: Bethany, 1974), 115–42. As examples of the latter, see L. Russ Bush (for Southern Baptists), "The Roots of Conservative Perspectives on Inerrancy (Warfield)," in *The Proceedings of the Conference on Biblical Inerrancy, 1987* (Nashville: Broadman, 1987), 273–88; Charles W. Carter, ed., *A Contemporary Wesleyan Theology: Biblical, Systematic, and Practical* (Grand Rapids: Francis Asbury, 1983), 1:289, 296, 301–2; T. F. Torrance, review of *Inspiration and Authority of the Bible*, by B. B. Warfield, *Scottish Journal of Theology* 7 (March 1954): 104–8; and David H. Kelsey, *The Uses of Scripture in Recent Theology* (Philadelphia: Fortress, 1975), 17–24. As of 1997, fifteen separate titles of Warfield's works were still in print.

family's estate in the vicinity of Lexington, Kentucky. His father, William Warfield, a prosperous gentleman farmer, served as a Union officer in the Civil War. It was pertinent for Warfield's later theological conclusions about evolution that his father bred live-stock scientifically and was the author of *The Theory and Practice of Cattle-Breeding* (1889). It is also significant for his later views that Warfield's entrance into the sophomore class at the College of New Jersey (later Princeton University) in 1868 coincided with the installation of James McCosh as president. McCosh had been called to Princeton from his post as professor of logic and meta-physics at the Queen's College, Belfast, in Ireland, where he was one of the last great exponents of the Scottish philosophy of com-mon sense. Even more significantly, McCosh was also an early promoter of compatibility between traditional Christian faith and nonnaturalistic forms of evolution. In both his philosophy and his desire to maintain the harmony between science and faith, Mc-Cosh set out a path that Warfield would follow.

After graduating from college in 1871, traveling in Europe for a year, and serving briefly as an editor for the *Farmer's Home Journal* in Lexington, Warfield entered Princeton Seminary to prepare for the ministry. During his time at the seminary, Warfield was par-ticularly impressed with the piety and theological comprehension of the elderly Charles Hodge. After graduating from the seminary, Warfield married, once again visited Europe, served for a short time as an assistant minister in Baltimore, and then in 1878 ac-cepted a call to teach New Testament at Western Theological Seminary near Pittsburgh. In 1887, upon the death of Archibald Alexander Hodge, son of his own teacher, Warfield returned to Princeton Seminary as professor of didactic and polemic theol-ogy. During thirty-four years in that position, he taught more than twenty-seven hundred students. Warfield died at Princeton late in the evening of February 16, 1921, after meeting his classes earlier that day.

Warfield's incredibly prolific output of books, learned essays, and reviews (which were frequently sophisticated monographs in their own right) was a product of his devotion to the confes-sional standards of Presbyterianism and, behind those standards, to his conception of classic Christian faith. Even in the long line of outstanding conservative theologians from Old Princeton that stretched from Archibald Alexander (the founding professor in 1812) to J. Gresham Machen (who left Princeton Seminary in 1929), Warfield stands out. In that distinguished company, he was the most widely read, had the greatest skill in European languages, displayed the most patience in unpacking arguments, and wrote clearly on the widest range of subjects. Some of Warfield's convictions—especially his conception of the inerrancy of Scripture in its original autographs—have generated a great quantity of polemical attack and defense. Yet despite helpful work by John E. Meeter, Roger Nicole, and a few other industrious scholars, there exists no comprehensive account of Warfield's theology.[11] And there is nothing close to an adequate biography.

One reason for the absence of such work may be directly related to Warfield's conception of his task. He was, in the strictest sense of the terms, a polemical and a conserving theologian. Despite comprehensive learning, he never attempted a full theological statement, primarily because he found Charles Hodge's *Systematic Theology* generally satisfactory for himself and his students. Because he was entirely content with the positions of the Westminster Confession and Catechisms, he devoted an enormous amount of patient writing to explicating their meaning, fending off misreadings, and defending their content against the modernizing, subjective, and naturalistic tendencies of his day.

Warfield was also content with what had been handed down to him by his Princeton predecessors on questions concerning the larger framework of thought. He did not delight in speculation (and so would mildly criticize Jonathan Edwards for his "individualisms," while praising Edwards for being "a convinced defender of Calvinism").[12] Rather, he gave himself wholeheartedly to Princeton's deeply ingrained commitment to theology as a scientific task (with "science" defined in conventional Enlightenment terms). In so doing, he thus shared fully in Princeton's equally long-standing confidence in a philosophy of commonsense realism. That philosophy owed something to its formal statement by

11. See especially John E. Meeter and Roger R. Nicole, *A Bibliography of Benjamin Breckinridge Warfield, 1851–1921* (Nutley, N.J.: Presbyterian and Reformed, 1974).
12. B. B. Warfield, "Edwards and the New England Theology" (1912), in *WBBW*, 9:530–31.

the cautious savants of the Scottish Enlightenment like Thomas Reid and Dugald Stewart.[13] But it owed even more to a concrete, antispeculative turn of mind that the Old Princeton theologians liked to describe as a simple inductivist Anglo-Saxon inheritance. From the perspective of the early twenty-first century, the philosophy of common sense at Princeton looks mostly like a gentlemanly, Victorian, and dignified Presbyterian adaptation of the practical bent so common at all levels in nineteenth-century American culture.

Warfield's stance as an ardent defender of confessional Calvinism, combined with his positions on the issues that engaged Presbyterians around the turn to the twentieth century, has led to a curiosity. Warfield seems to have regarded his work as a coherent effort to maintain the theology of Calvin and the Westminster divines. Later attention, however, has focused more on his exposition of individual topics, like the inerrancy of Scripture, counterfeit miracles, and the place of apologetics in theology. The result has been that, although several of Warfield's positions continue to exert considerable influence among theological conservatives, the defense of Calvinism that loomed large in his own work receives far less attention today. Yet for the sake of his science, Warfield's comprehensive Calvinism was at least as important as his specific views of Scripture.

By the early 1880s, American Presbyterians were being drawn more directly into European debates over the Bible.[14] Presbyterian leaders realized that the new higher-critical proposals touched the heart of their faith as it had developed in Britain and America. They also knew that the controversies raging in Scotland over modern criticism during the 1870s, especially concerning the work of William Robertson Smith of the Free Church, would soon arrive in America. Smith's acceptance of Old Testament higher criticism was especially significant for Princeton Seminary because Princetonians had championed the Free Church since its founding in 1843. So it came about that A. A.

13. For a solid account of their environment, see Richard B. Sher, *Church and University in the Scottish Enlightenment: The Moderate Literati of Edinburgh* (Princeton: Princeton University Press, 1985).

14. See Mark A. Noll, *Between Faith and Criticism: Evangelicals, Scholarship, and the Bible in America,* 2d ed. (Grand Rapids: Baker, 1991), 27–31.

Hodge of Princeton and Charles Briggs of Union Seminary in
New York agreed that the journal they jointly edited, the *Presbyterian Review,* should consider these matters. Briggs, who was pre-
disposed toward the newer opinions, enlisted several colleagues
to write in favor of adjusting traditional views. Hodge too sought
assistance in supporting his conviction that the new views were
mostly a threat to the church. His first recruit was B. B. Warfield,
then still a young New Testament professor at Western Theological Seminary.

The essay, entitled simply "Inspiration," which Hodge and
Warfield published in the April 1881 issue of the *Presbyterian Review,* both recapitulated many of the themes that had been prominent in previous Princeton writing and anticipated most of the
points about the Bible that Warfield would make over the next
forty years in a wealth of publications. What was new about the
doctrine of Scripture in this essay was its precision of statement
and its detailed response to modern theories. The essay's burden
was to show that proper scholarship on Scripture and its background supported, rather than undercut, a high view of verbal inspiration. The doctrine this essay defended was the belief in
"God's continued work of superintendence, by which, his providential, gracious and supernatural contributions having been pre-
supposed, he presided over the sacred writers in their entire work
of writing, with the design and effect of rendering that writing an
errorless record of the matters he designed them to communicate,
and hence constituting the entire volume in all its parts the word
of God to us."[15]

Throughout the essay, as indeed throughout his entire career,
Warfield took great care to qualify the doctrine of plenary verbal
inspiration. Hodge and Warfield stated, almost at the outset, that
this doctrine is not "a principle fundamental to the truth of the
Christian religion" as such, nor is it the case "that the truth of
Christianity depends upon any doctrine of inspiration what-
ever."[16] They also maintained at length that the inspiration of
Scripture did not rule out a full, active participation of the human

15. Archibald A. Hodge and Benjamin B. Warfield, *Inspiration,* ed. Roger R.
Nicole (Grand Rapids: Baker, 1979), 17–18.
16. Ibid., 8.

authors in its production. In fact, the biblical authors "were in large measure dependent for their knowledge upon sources and methods in themselves fallible, and . . . their personal knowledge and judgments were in many matters hesitating and defective, or even wrong."[17] Hodge and Warfield further insisted that the Bible must be interpreted according to the intent of its authors, an intent that often requires careful study to discover. They held that any supposed errors in Scripture must be located in "some part of the original autograph"[18] rather than haphazardly drawn from what might be corrupted transmissions of the text. And they acknowledged that the doctrine of verbal inspiration, which they held to be the plain teaching of many scriptural passages themselves, needed to be confirmed by paying full attention and responding to all possible objections arising from the study of the Bible itself (e.g., questions concerning mistaken history or geography, inaccurate quotations from the Old Testament in the New, internal lack of harmony, and the like). Yet once having made these qualifications, Hodge and Warfield insisted that the Bible is fully inspired. Absolutely without error, it is to be regarded not just as a bearer of the Word of God, but as that Word itself.

As critics responded to this position paper, and as the Princeton theologians themselves fleshed out their conception of biblical inerrancy in scores of works, Warfield made crucial statements about Scripture that would also shape his response to questions of science. Of particular importance was his response to the charge that his view of inspiration amounted to a mechanical view of divine dictation. In reply, Warfield repeatedly argued that he was advocating, not dictation, but what he called *concursus*. For example, in an 1894 article on "The Divine and Human in the Bible," Warfield was at pains to defend the fully human character of the Bible *in addition to* its fully divine character. As he phrased it in this essay, *concursus* meant that "the Scriptures are the joint product of divine and human activities, both of which penetrate them at every point, working harmoniously together to the production of a writing which is not divine here and human there, but at once divine and human in every part, every word and every particu-

17. Ibid., 28.
18. Ibid., 36.

lar."[19] The ramification of this way of thinking for Warfield's scientific views was great. In simple terms, the products of natural history could be the consequence—at the same time—of both natural forces and divine action.

The main points of Warfield's defense of an inerrant Bible, if not necessarily the details of his position, eventually became major guideposts for the American fundamentalist movement.[20] The rise of fundamentalism, however, placed Warfield and other confessional conservatives in an ambiguous situation. While they applauded the fundamentalists' adherence to biblical infallibility and their defense of a supernatural faith, they found fundamentalism theologically eccentric and methodologically suspect. Many later fundamentalists would employ Warfield's formulation of biblical inerrancy as they defined their own beliefs about Scripture, but Warfield himself maintained several important positions that set him apart from fundamentalism. In the first instance, Warfield held that fundamentalist proof-texting represented a retrograde step in studying the Bible.[21] In addition, Warfield was unimpressed by the dispensationalism that became so influential in American fundamentalism. Modern theologies associated with John Nelson Darby, C. I. Scofield, and other promoters of dispensationalism were suspect to Warfield for faulty exegesis, questionable theological construction, and errors on the work of the Holy Spirit.[22] Finally, like his college teacher James McCosh and his senior colleague A. A. Hodge, Warfield found little difficulty in thinking that, if scientific facts called for such a move, it would be a straightforward theological task to align historic confessional Calvinism with nonnaturalistic forms of evolu-

19. B. B. Warfield, "The Divine and Human in the Bible" (1894), in *SSWW*, 2:547 (pp. 51–58 in the present volume).

20. See George M. Marsden, *Fundamentalism and American Culture* (New York: Oxford University Press, 1980); Ernest R. Sandeen, *The Roots of Fundamentalism: British and American Millenarianism, 1800–1930* (Chicago: University of Chicago Press, 1970); George W. Dollar, *A History of Fundamentalism in America* (Greenville, S.C.: Bob Jones University Press, 1973).

21. See, for example, his review of R. A. Torrey's *What the Bible Teaches* (1899), in *Presbyterian and Reformed Review* 39 (July 1899): 562–64.

22. See, for example, B. B. Warfield, "The Millennium and the Apocalypse" (1904), in *WBBW*, 2:643–64.

tion.[23] This, of course, was a move that fundamentalists were unwilling to make.

In his views on dispensationalism, evolution, and the use of the Bible, therefore, Warfield was not a fundamentalist as the label came to be used. A carefully qualified view of biblical inerrancy, like the one Warfield developed, did not necessarily entail the particulars of fundamentalist theology, but could in fact provide a basis for judgments on nature, the character of biblical theology, and approaches to biblical scholarship very different in tone, and substantially different in substance, from what was found among fundamentalists.

Important as Warfield felt it was to contend for the truthfulness of the Bible, he exerted even more energy throughout his long career expounding the truths of the Bible. Warfield, in other words, was concerned to secure the Bible as the ground of theology and to protect reason as a prime theological tool, but he was (at least usually) even more interested in the theology he felt the Bible taught and reason supported.

Warfield was not embarrassed to say what that theology was and where he felt it had been best represented in the history of the church. Time and again throughout his historical, exegetical, and polemical works (and it was never easy to disengage these categories from each other), Warfield defined true Christianity as the pure religion of the Reformation; or, in phrases that to him meant the same thing, as the Augustinian grasp of human sin and divine grace recovered by Luther and especially Calvin; or, even more fully, as the Pauline summation of the biblical gospel passed on especially to Augustine and then renewed by the magisterial Reformers. "Calvinism," he wrote in 1904, "is just religion in its purity. We have only, therefore, to conceive of religion in its purity, and that is Calvinism."[24]

Four years later Warfield spelled out explicitly what he meant by Calvinism—"a profound apprehension of God in his majesty, with the inevitably accompanying poignant realization of the ex-

23. See, for example, A. A. Hodge's review of Asa Gray's *Natural Science and Religion* in *Presbyterian Review* 1 (July 1880): 586–89; or his introduction to Joseph S. van Dyke, *Theism and Evolution* (New York: A. C. Armstrong & Son, 1886), xv–xxiii.

24. B. B. Warfield, "What Is Calvinism?" (1904), in *SSWW*, 1:389.

act nature of the relation sustained to him by the creatures as such, and particularly by the sinful creature." In the same place, Warfield insisted that he was not using "Calvinism" as a narrow label for those holding a certain theological position. Rather, "Calvinism" meant a way of life before God which, in the course of history, had been most satisfactorily described by the Protestant Reformers who recovered an Augustinian understanding of the biblical message. If Warfield's theological labeling was myopic, his conception of what the label denoted was broadly catholic: "He who believes in God without reserve, and is determined that God shall be God to him in all his thinking, feeling, willing—in the entire compass of his life activities, intellectual, moral, spiritual, throughout all his individual, social, religious relations—is, by the force of that strictest of all logic which presides over the outworking of principles into thought and life, by the very necessity of the case, a Calvinist."[25] The comprehensiveness of this kind of Calvinism—its picture of a God who pervades all aspects of existence—was critical for Warfield's view of nature. To him, it was utter nonsense to think that those who studied the earth, the universe, or the history of humankind were not also studying the works of God.

Although Warfield is today better known for his views on the Bible, a solid case can be constructed on the basis of his own works that his commitment to classic Protestantism was deeper and more comprehensive than even his commitment to biblical inerrancy as such. By classic Protestantism Warfield meant commitment to an Augustinian view of God, of the sinful human condition, and of salvation in Christ, but also a broadly open acceptance of the world as the arena of God's creative activity. For Warfield, the heart of both theology and active religion was the glory of God, who rescues sinful humans from self-imposed destruction and who enables them to share his work of the kingdom in every sphere of life, including the natural world.

Even Warfield's defense of biblical inerrancy, which often seems to have been undertaken on behalf of a bare notion of biblical veracity, was a product of his overarching Calvinism. The point of defending traditional views of the Bible was not so much

---

25. B. B. Warfield, "Calvinism" (1908), in *WBBW*, 5:354–56.

the Bible itself as what the Bible taught. When Warfield in 1910 reviewed the autobiography of William Newton Clarke, a Northern Baptist who over the course of a long career moved from believing in the Bible as inerrant revelation from God to considering it a refined record of religious encounter with God, Warfield rehearsed the arguments he had made many times before concerning Jesus' own testimony to the infallibility of Scripture. But in the end the critical matter was not just Scripture: "He who no longer holds to the Bible of Jesus—the word of which cannot be broken—will be found on examination no longer to hold to the Jesus of the Bible." This Jesus, who communicates forgiveness to needy sinners, is the one "to whom [Scripture] bears consentient witness."[26]

Historian L. Russ Bush has made the observation that Warfield's understanding of the Bible follows his more general conception of theology as a whole.[27] The same is true of his conception of nature. The Calvinistic conception of sovereignty that governs Warfield's soteriology—God as initiator and enabler of human repentance and faith—is the same conception that governs his views on Scripture and the physical world. Because of the *concursus* of salvation—God acting in and with humanity—it is also possible to have a *concursus* that yields an infallible Bible, as well as a *concursus* linking nature and providence.

Warfield on Evolution

In 1916, when Warfield was asked to write an article on his undergraduate days at Princeton, he highlighted the arrival of James McCosh to take up the presidency of the College of New Jersey, as Princeton University was then called. McCosh, who left the Queen's College of Belfast to assume the position in 1868, had by then already acquired a substantial international reputation for showing how the workings of nature could reflect God's intimate superintendence. As early as 1851, the Princeton moral philosopher, Lyman Atwater, had warmly commended McCosh's *Method of the Divine Government, Physical and Moral,* for its

26. B. B. Warfield, review of *Sixty Years with the Bible,* by William Newton Clarke, in *Princeton Theological Review* 8 (Jan. 1910): 167.

27. Bush, "Roots of Conservative Perspectives," 280–81.

careful statement of how divine providence could work in and
with the ordinary processes of the world. Atwater knew of "no
work which we would sooner give to a person of cultivated or
thoughtful mind, who had imbibed any of the fashionable prejudices against the fundamental principles of evangelical doctrine."[28] Soon McCosh would come to be regarded as one of the
foremost reconcilers of evolutionary science and Christian theism
amongst Protestant theologians.[29]

Looking back from 1916, Warfield remembered McCosh's arrival particularly clearly; he was "distinctly the most inspiring
force" that Warfield encountered during his student days. In one
sense, though, Warfield made it clear that McCosh's coming had
no influence on him. On the subject of Darwin's theory of evolution, Warfield was already a convinced believer. Even before Mc-
Cosh arrived, that is, Warfield already was, by his own admission, "a Darwinian of the purest water." To be sure, Warfield
would later depart from what he took to be McCosh's Darwinian
orthodoxy, but throughout his career he remained open to the
possibility of evolutionary transformism through a range of
mechanisms besides Darwinian natural selection.[30] The shape of
that openness changed over the course of Warfield's long tenure
at Princeton, but the possibility of reconciling conservative biblical Calvinism and the era's best empirical science remained a constant goal. By pursuing that goal, Warfield also maintained one of
the central convictions of the conservative confessional theolo-

28. Lyman H. Atwater, review of *The Method of the Divine Government, Physical
and Moral*, by James McCosh, *Biblical Repertory and Princeton Review* 23 (1851): 624.

29. The standard biography is J. David Hoeveler Jr., *James McCosh and the Scottish Intellectual Tradition* (Princeton: Princeton University Press, 1981). McCosh's
thinking on evolution is surveyed in Gary S. Smith, "Calvinists and Evolution,
1870–1920," *Journal of Presbyterian History* 61 (1983): 335–52; James R. Moore, *The
Post-Darwinian Controversies: A Study of the Protestant Struggle to Come to Terms with
Darwin in Great Britain and America, 1870–1900* (Cambridge: Cambridge University Press, 1979); David N. Livingstone, *Darwin's Forgotten Defenders: The Encounter
between Evangelical Theology and Evolutionary Thought* (Grand Rapids: Eerdmans;
and Edinburgh: Scottish Academic Press, 1987); and Bradley John Gundlach, "The
Evolution Question at Princeton, 1845–1929" (Ph.D. diss., University of Rochester, 1995).

30. B. B. Warfield, "Personal Reflections of Princeton Undergraduate Life:
IV—The Coming of Dr. McCosh," *Princeton Alumni Weekly* 16.28 (April 19, 1916):
650–53.

gians who made Princeton such a formidable theological force in the nineteenth and early twentieth centuries.[31]

The chronology of Warfield's engagement with evolution is significant. Although his espousal of Darwinism evidently predated the coming of McCosh to Princeton in 1868, Warfield's earliest published statements on evolutionary theory appeared only in 1888, the year after he returned from Western Theological Seminary near Pittsburgh to take up the chair of didactic and polemic theology at Princeton.

Long before 1888, however, Warfield had evidently thought seriously about the development of species, particularly in connection with a long-standing interest he shared with his father in the breeding of shorthorn cattle. Indeed, in 1873, prior to entering Princeton Seminary as a student for the ministry, he served as livestock editor for the *Farmer's Home Journal* of Lexington, Kentucky. Warfield maintained this interest for the remainder of his life and carefully kept a scrapbook of clippings—mostly those of his father—on what he called "Short Horn Culture."[32] It is noteworthy, moreover, that Warfield shared not only his father's interests but also his father's conclusions about the modification of species over time. In the dedication of his own book, *The Theory and Practice of Cattle-Breeding,* William Warfield thanked his son and indicated the unity of their opinions on such matters:

> I wish to take this opportunity to acknowledge the assistance my sons have given me in preparing all my work for the press. Without their aid much—even most—of it could never have been done. . . . Great credit is also due to my elder son, Prof. Benjamin B. Warfield, D.D., now of Princeton, N.J., whose energy and vigor of thought and pen gave me such essential aid in the earlier years of my connection with the press; nor has the pursuit of the more weighty

31. The essential starting part for all considerations of Warfield's views, and on how Warfield's views related to those of his predecessors and successors, is now Gundlach, "The Evolution Question at Princeton."

32. This scrapbook is extant in the Speer Library, Princeton Theological Seminary. Most of the clippings are from the *National Livestock Journal.* The Speer Library also retains a number of books on shorthorn cattle from B. B. Warfield's personal library. For a fuller account of Warfield's cattle-breeding interests as they relate to his views on evolution, see David N. Livingstone, "Situating Evangelical Responses to Evolution," in *Evangelicals and Science,* ed. Livingstone, Hart, and Noll, 209.

things of theology destroyed his capacity for taking an occasional part in the active discussion of cattle matters. The papers which have appeared over my signature have thus to quite a large degree been of family origin.[33]

This affirmation is particularly significant because in the course of his discussion of such key issues as variation, heredity, atavism (or the reappearance of a trait after the lapse of several generations), and reversion to type, William Warfield quoted liberally from Darwin's *Variation of Animals and Plants under Domestication*.[34] Moreover, in this same work he directly endorsed Darwin's theory of evolution by natural selection:

> Nature's method seems to be a wide and general system of selection, in which the strong and vigorous are the winners and the weaker are crushed out. Among wild cattle the more lusty bulls have their choice of the cows in a way that under natural selection insures the best results to the race. . . . If the conditions of life should suddenly change, the result on such wild cattle would be to deteriorate or to improve the average according as the change was for their advantage or disadvantage. It is quite apparent that no question of breeding intrudes itself here. Nature's selection, while always in favor of the maintenance of the animals in the best manner, yet is impartial, and under ordinary circumstances would maintain an average.[35]

Like Darwin himself, B. B. Warfield thus encountered natural selection through an intense study of breeding.[36] This encounter is almost certainly why Warfield could, early in his career, de-

33. William Warfield, *The Theory and Practice of Cattle-Breeding* (Chicago: J. H. Sanders, 1889), dedication page.

34. From the Darwin volumes in B. B. Warfield's personal library, it is clear that the second volume of this work was the first of Darwin's books he purchased. His copy is dated May 1, 1868. Warfield's inscriptions date his personal copies of both *The Origin of Species* and *The Descent of Man* to 1871. In 1872, while in London, he purchased Darwin's *Expression of the Emotions*. We thank William O. Harris for directing our attention to these inscriptions in Warfield's personal copies.

35. William Warfield, *Cattle-Breeding*, 85–86. William Warfield also enthusiastically commended a volume by J. H. Sanders, *Horse-Breeding: Being the General Principles of Heredity Applied to the Business of Breeding Horses* (Chicago: J. H. Sanders, 1885), in which Darwin's evolutionary thinking was promulgated. Warfield particularly endorsed the long first chapter, which dealt with general principles.

36. See James Secord, "Nature's Fancy: Charles Darwin and the Breeding of Pigeons," *Isis* 72 (1981): 163–86.

scribe himself as a pure Darwinian—he had met the theory empirically, in the feedlot, rather than as merely a question of theology or philosophy.

By the time Warfield came to Princeton as a professor and began to publish on evolution, however, he was entertaining serious reservations about the orthodox Darwinian scheme he once had maintained. In December 1888, he prepared a lecture entitled "Evolution or Development." In it he argued that Darwinism did not enjoy anything like the scientific status of the Newtonian system, for there were simply too many unresolved geological, zoological, and paleontological anomalies—anomalies he did not hesitate to itemize. Quite apart from the specifics of Darwinism, moreover, evolutionary theory in general could never attain more than explanatory probability, although its status would be improved if its capacity for explaining a wide range of observational data could be demonstrated. Despite these objections, Warfield was prepared to leave the truth or falsity of the Darwinian theory an open question. As for more narrowly biblical considerations, Warfield was convinced that, save for the narrative dealing with Eve's creation, there was no "general statement in the Bible or any part of the account of creation, either as given in Genesis 1 and 2 or elsewhere alluded to, that need be opposed to evolution." In sum, as he saw the issue in 1888: "The upshot of the whole matter is that there is no *necessary* antagonism of Christianity to evolution, *provided that* we do not hold to too extreme a form of evolution." If the constant supervision of divine providence and the "occasional supernatural interference" of God were retained, then, he concluded, "we may hold to the modified theory of evolution and be Christians in the ordinary orthodox sense. I say we may do this. Whether we ought to accept evolution, even in this modified sense, is another matter, and I leave it purposely an open question."[37] If Warfield's equivocation is evident here in his first general consideration of the subject, so too is the openness of his stance on the whole issue, as is also his willingness to test the theories by their empirical adequacy.

37. B. B. Warfield, "Evolution or Development" (Dec. 1888), Speer Library, Princeton Theological Seminary (the lecture is printed in the present volume, pp. 114–31; the quotations are from pp. 130–31).

Meanwhile Warfield had already issued his own judgment on McCosh's recent volume entitled *The Religious Aspect of Evolution,* the Bedell Lectures delivered the previous year, 1887.[38] This work was a clear declaration of McCosh's enthusiastic acceptance of evolution, albeit in a Neo-Lamarckian guise. Central to this evolutionary system was the idea that acquired characteristics were heritable and could therefore be passed from one generation to the next. Such a schema, stressing as it did the capacity of organisms to adjust themselves and their habits to changing environmental conditions, could be used for teleological interpretations of the sort that Charles Hodge had sought in vain to find in Darwin's own writings. McCosh was thus interpreting evolutionary development as following predetermined paths and so demonstrating, at least to those with eyes to see, the presence of an intelligent designer behind the physical processes of nature. In his review, Warfield commended McCosh's efforts and remarked that his old teacher had indeed demonstrated the inherent compatibility of evolution with Christian theism. Where he and McCosh parted company was *not* on evolution's theological implications, but on what Warfield regarded as its evidential insecurity. Warfield's principal question was not whether evolution could be true, but if carefully verified scientific facts made the postulation of evolution necessary.

That Warfield could so steadfastly maintain the theological neutrality of evolution is, perhaps, all the more remarkable when we recall that during that same summer (1888) he had been reading the lengthy three-volume *Life and Letters of Charles Darwin,* and writing a review of such sensitivity that historian James Moore has described it as an exemplary reading of Darwin's spiritual pilgrimage.[39] Indeed, in his lecture on "Evolution or Development" Warfield noted that the atheism which Charles Hodge detected in Darwin's theory was confirmed in "the history of his own drift away from theism as recorded in the recently published *Life and*

38. B. B. Warfield, review of *The Religious Aspect of Evolution,* by James McCosh, *Presbyterian Review* 9 (1888): 510–11 (reprinted in the present volume, pp. 66–67).

39. James R. Moore, "Of Love and Death: Why Darwin 'Gave Up Christianity,'" in James R. Moore, ed., *History, Humanity, and Evolution: Essays for John C. Greene* (New York: Cambridge University Press, 1989), 224.

Letters of Charles Darwin." In his review-essay of this biography (see
pp. 68–111), Warfield expressed his conviction that the word "agnosticism" best captures the spiritual state of mind into which Darwin progressively fell. Perhaps for that very reason, Warfield found
this detailed record of Darwin's spiritual evolution or—perhaps
better—spiritual atrophy and associated "affective decline," as it
has been called, uncommonly arresting, not least because the individual concerned was one in whom an "unusual sweetness" of
character was to be found.[40] If Darwin was an unbeliever, he was
still, in Warfield's eyes, a noble figure, albeit of an altogether tragic
sort. "On the quiet stage of this amiable life," Warfield mused,
"there is played out before our eyes the tragedy of the death of religion out of a human soul." All of this was certainly to be la-
mented, but Warfield was careful to insist that it did not inevitably
imply that Darwin's theory itself was atheistic. That was a logically
separate issue. As Warfield put it: "We raise no question as to the
compatibility of the Darwinian form of the hypothesis of evolution with Christianity; Mr. Darwin himself says that 'science' (and
in speaking of 'science' he has 'evolution' in mind) 'has nothing to
do with Christ, except in so far as the habit of scientific research
makes a man cautious in admitting evidence.'"

Certainly in Darwin's own case—at least as Warfield understood that case—it was "his doctrine of evolution [that] directly expelled his Christian belief." Darwin, that is, believed that the bringing of species into being by natural law directly contradicted what
he took to be the plain teaching of Genesis that the origin of species
required immediate divine fiat. To Darwin, it seemed that questioning a literalistic reading of Genesis was the same as rejecting
the authority of the Old Testament and thus subverting the entire
Christian faith. But to Warfield, the intellectual dismantling of Darwin's faith hinged even more clearly on his abandonment of the
doctrine of divine design.[41] Warfield subjected Darwin's reasoning

40. See John Angus Campbell, "Nature, Religion and Emotional Response:
A Reconsideration of Darwin's Affective Decline," *Victorian Studies* 18 (1974): 159–
74. Doubts about Darwin's aesthetic atrophy are expressed in Robert E. Fitch, "Darwin and the Saintly Sentiments," *Columbia University Forum* (Spring 1959): 7–11.

41. For a persuasive argument that the death of Darwin's daughter had more
to do with this loss of belief than did any chain of reasoning, see Moore, "Of Love
and Death."

on this point to painstaking philosophical exegesis and urged that
the arguments advanced on this subject by the great naturalist were
substantially incoherent. Darwin's thinking about teleology, or
purpose in the physical universe, displayed a "total misapprehension of the nature of divine providence, and . . . a very crude notion
of final cause." For Warfield, Darwin had—unnecessarily—linked
the issue of species transformation with a naturalistic reading of
evolutionary change. To refute that conjunction of evolution and
antisupernaturalism, Warfield appealed to the work of writers like
W. B. Carpenter and W. H. Dallinger, not to mention Asa Gray (a
contemporary of Hodge who had earlier attempted to construct a
teleological Darwinism), who more acceptably saw evolution as a
method of divine oversight of matter and perceived that explanation by natural law was not incompatible with divine superintendence. Nonetheless, Warfield remained deeply moved by the tragic
tale of Darwin, the naturalist of Down, this "great man" who
drifted "from his early trust into an inextinguishable doubt. . . . No
more painful spectacle can be found in all biographical literature."
Warfield concluded: "We stand at the deathbed of a man whom, in
common with all the world, we most deeply honor. He has made
himself a name which will live through many generations, and
withal has made himself beloved by all who came into close contact with him. True, tenderhearted, and sympathetic, he has in the
retirement of invalidism lived a life which has moved the world."

These early diagnoses of Warfield clearly display that even if
he had, by this stage, departed from the Darwinian orthodoxy of
his mentor, McCosh, his mind was far from closed on the issue of
evolutionary change. Indeed, it seems as though Warfield was
more concerned with the question of the mechanisms involved in
evolution than with whether evolution was compatible with biblical faith.

Warfield was, nevertheless, evidently concerned lest Darwin's
profession of teleological skepticism should engender the suspicion that science was antagonistic to classical Christian faith. And
so late that same year (1888) he summarized his detailed, techni-
cal argument from the *Presbyterian Review* for the more popular
audience of the *Homiletic Review*. This essay on "Darwin's Arguments against Christianity and against Religion" appeared in the
January 1889 issue (see pp. 132–41 in the present volume). In a

day when more and more observers were perceiving a war between science and religion,[42] Warfield tried to explain why such an unwarranted perception was rising: the spread of scientific materialism, the spiritually stultifying effects of mundane empiricism, a naive social-scientific progressivism, and "the crude mode in which religion is presented to men's minds, in these days of infallible popes and Salvation Armies, which insults the intelligence of thoughtful men and prevents their giving to the real essence of faith the attention which would result in its acceptance." Given the era's blooming, buzzing confusion, it was a pleasure for Warfield to study Darwin's personal story, which afforded the opportunity to scrutinize spiritual decline in calm detail. Warfield now repeated much of the substance of his earlier review and used Darwin's arguments as a foil for presenting his own views on mechanism, design, and miracle. All brought him to the conclusion that in Darwin's "case the defection of a scientific man from religion was distinctly due to an atrophy of mental qualities by which he was unfitted for the estimation of any kind of evidence other than that derived from the scalpel and the laboratory, and no longer could feel the force of the ineradicable convictions which are as 'much a part of man as his stomach or his heart.'"

During the nineteenth century's last decade, Warfield continued to comment on evolution but mostly through the medium of book reviews. This strategy enabled him to keep abreast of vicissitudes in current scientific theory as well as interventions by Christian intellectuals whether scientist or theologian. George John Romanes' posthumously published *Darwin and After Darwin* and A. A. W. Hubrecht's *Descent of the Primates,* for example, assured an up-to-date acquaintanceship with the latest theories. In the same period Warfield also reviewed the work of the distinguished anti-Darwinian naturalist, J. W. Dawson, in which he found much of value. By contrast, he found less convincing Charles Warring's harmonizing attempts to read the Genesis narrative in scientific detail. Warfield commended efforts by Scottish

---

42. E.g., John William Draper, *History of the Conflict between Religion and Science* (London: Henry S. King, 1875); and Andrew Dickson White, *A History of the Warfare of Science with Theology in Christendom,* 2 vols. (New York: D. Appleton, 1896). For Warfield's assessment of White's argument, see pp. 179–82 in the present volume.

Presbyterian James Iverach to defend a teleological evolution, but not without reservation.

The dawning of the new century witnessed the fullest expression of Warfield's reservations about the scientific credibility of evolution. No doubt this situation reflected, at least in part, his distaste for the efforts of some to "evolutionize" theology as well as the machinations of those allowing full rein to untrammeled speculation. Writing on "Creation, Evolution, and Mediate Creation" for *The Bible Student* in 1901 (pp. 197–210), for example, Warfield reviewed the "scientific theology" of Otto Pfleiderer which, on inspection, revealed a wholesale importation of evolutionism into theological reflection. What Pfleiderer's project amounted to was—ultimately—a denial of God's creative intervention by an overemphasis on providential superintendence. Pfleiderer's conclusions prompted Warfield to insist that "when we say 'evolution,' we definitely deny creation; and when we say 'creation,' we definitely deny evolution. Whatever comes by the one process by that very fact does not come by the other. Whatever comes by evolution is not created; whatever is created is not evolved." Evolution and creation were mutually exclusive categories; to Warfield evolution meant modification of previously existing material, while creation referred to origination *ex nihilo*. The significance of this distinction, however, was not what it has since become. Warfield did not simply rule out evolution as antithetical to Christianity, but was appealing for a careful use of words to distinguish between different modes of God's care over the world.

Despite his growing frustration with the casual confusion of evolution and creation, Warfield still admitted the possibility of theistic evolution, even if he queried just how Christian it really could be. His reason for this judgmental equivocation lay in his conviction that theistic evolution "confines the creative operations of God to the origination of the primal world-stuff. Everything subsequent to that is withdrawn from the sphere of creation, i.e., is explained as a mere modification of the primal world-stuff by means of its intrinsic forces. The providential guidance of God need not be excluded, to be sure; the theist will readily allow that God directs the evolution. But all origination, all production of what is really new, is necessarily excluded throughout the whole process of evolution. And this is the definite exclusion of all creation." Remarkably, Warfield eventually came to view the substance of what he here in 1901 labeled theistic evolution as precisely the mechanism by which a Calvinist should think about the development of forms, species, and structures in the natural world!

This 1901 essay was Warfield's most articulate presentation yet of a crucial distinction he was drawing between three modes of divine action or superintendence of the physical world. Warfield saw them as methods that God used to generate physical forms, species, and individuals. First was theistic evolution, or the providentially controlled unfolding of nature. Second was creation *ex nihilo,* or out of nothing. Warfield's third category was the most complicated and the one that least resembles schemes developed since his time. This was the category of mediate creation—in effect, a via media between evolution and creation *ex nihilo* that he developed from hints in earlier Reformed theologians. By mediate creation Warfield meant that God acted, or intervened, with already existing material to bring something new into existence that could not have developed from the forces latent in the material itself. Like creation *ex nihilo,* mediate creation required a direct act of God. Like evolution, mediate creation featured already existing material.

These subtle distinctions may well be of considerable theological and metaphysical significance. Among other advantages, the threefold division enabled Warfield to enter fully into scientific researches while maintaining full confidence in the intervening activity (as well as the providential superintendence) of God. For Warfield, holding to the doctrine of mediate creation certainly did not rule out species transformation or a developmental account of natural history. It simply reserved space for a variety of explanatory mechanisms to account for the history of the universe. Methodological pluralism was what Warfield sought to preserve. Reductionism—whether of a naturalistic, anti-Christian sort or a supernaturalistic, antiscientific type—was what he wanted to prevent. Thus Warfield concluded his survey in 1901 with the assertion that "the Christian man has as such no quarrel with evolution when confined to its own sphere as a suggested account of the method of the divine providence. What he needs to insist on is that providence cannot do the work of creation and is not to be permitted to intrude itself into the sphere of creation, much less to crowd creation out of the recognition of man, merely because it puts itself forward under the new name of evolution."

Although Warfield was theologically tentative about the evolution question at the very beginning of the twentieth century, during the succeeding decade he came to adopt a decidedly more favorable stance. The depth of evolutionary penetration into his thinking as the first decade of the twentieth century wore on is particularly evident in his views on two issues of burning concern, namely, the origin and the unity of the human species. As his lecture on "Evolution or Development" had already made plain, Warfield (like McCosh) saw no need for *ex nihilo* divine intervention to produce the human *physical* form. Certainly he insisted on the need for an act of divine intervention in the origin of humanity, although it is not clear in his 1903 essay "The Manner and Time of Man's Origin" (pp. 211–29) whether he had mediate creation or *ex nihilo* creation in mind, or even if he still retained the distinctions he had worked so hard to develop in 1901. He did, however, make clear to readers of *The Bible Student,* where the 1903 essay appeared, that neither the evolutionist who insisted that the "ascent to man" had been "accomplished by the blind action of natural forces," nor the biblicist who asserted "that the creation of man by the divine fiat must have been immediate in such a sense as to exclude all process, all interaction of natural forces," was warranted in his extreme assertions. For Warfield himself, the need for divine intervention to create the *imago dei* was in itself no "denial of the interaction of an evolutionary process in the production of man."[43]

In 1906, a review of James Orr's *God's Image in Man* (see pp. 230–36) afforded Warfield the opportunity to spell out his own thinking in more detail. In this book Orr had argued for the entirely supernatural origin of the first human on the grounds that the complex physical organization of the brain—necessary, he believed, for human consciousness—made it impossible to postulate an evolutionary origin of the body while holding to a special creation of the mind. In Warfield's view, however, Orr's argument

43. B. B. Warfield, "The Manner and Time of Man's Origin," *Bible Student* 8 (1903): 243 (pp. 213, 215 in the present volume).

could effectively be undermined by the idea of evolution *per saltum* (that is, evolution by mutation). In place of Orr's formulation, Warfield proposed again his combination of evolution and some form of creation to account for the origin of humanity. As he put it: "If under the directing hand of God a human body is formed at a leap by propagation from brutish parents [that is, *per saltum* evolution], it would be quite consonant with the fitness of things that it should be provided by his creative energy with a truly human soul." Again, whether Warfield had mediate or *ex nihilo* creation in mind when speaking of divine creative energy is not clear.

By 1906, in other words, Warfield had clearly accepted the theological legitimacy of an evolutionary account of the human body. He also was taking pains to show how carefully elaborated mechanistic theories of explanation were compatible with Christian orthodoxy. This stance is particularly evident in his lengthy review from 1908 of Vernon Kellogg's *Darwinism Today* (pp. 237–51). In this extended critique, Warfield lavishly praised Kellogg for his expository skill and critical judgment; readers interested in biological theory, he averred, "cannot do better than to resort to his comprehensive and readable volume." Yet on one key point Warfield made it clear that he and Kellogg parted company, namely, on the issue of teleology. "Some lack of general philosophical acumen must be suspected," Warfield insisted, "when it is not fully understood that teleology is in no way inconsistent with—is, rather, necessarily involved in—a complete system of natural causation. Every teleological system implies a complete causo-mechanical explanation as its instrument." To Warfield, then, mechanistic accounts of scientific phenomena could be at the same time teleological explanations. Here his idea of *concursus* as applied to scientific explanation fully manifests itself. Clearly Warfield was every bit as willing as his old teacher McCosh to locate divine design in the orderly and regulative laws of nature.

The possibility of a human evolutionary history combined with a theologically permissible materialism was, to Warfield, entirely consistent with his self-perception as an orthodox Calvinist. Nowhere is this stance more dramatically displayed than in his 1915 exposition of "Calvin's Doctrine of the Creation" for the *Princeton Theological Review* (pp. 293–314). In this article Warfield made much of Calvin's insistence that the term "creation" should be strictly reserved for the initial creative act. For the subsequent creations were—technically speaking—*not* creations as such, but were, rather, modifications of the primeval "indigested mass . . . by means of the interaction of its intrinsic forces." The human soul was the only exception, for Calvin held to the creationist (as opposed to the traducianist) theory that every soul throughout the history of human propagation was an immediate creation out of nothing. To Warfield, then, Calvin's doctrine opened the door to a controlled materialist explanation of natural history—including the human physical form—in terms of the operation of secondary causes. These, to be sure, were directed by the guiding hand of divine providence; but this conviction did not prevent Warfield from asserting that Calvin's account of the physical world actually turned out to be "a very pure evolutionary scheme."

Warfield's reading of Calvin's theology of creation has not gone uncontested: John Murray, for example, rejected it in 1954,[44] and Richard Stauffer, writing in 1973, thought that Murray probably had a better reading of Calvin than did Warfield.[45] But the accuracy of Warfield's interpretation of Calvin is not what is at stake here. What *is* important are the lengths to which Warfield was prepared to go in order to establish that Reformed orthodoxy could readily embrace evolutionary change.

In this path Warfield has been followed by several important evangelical thinkers of the twentieth century. James I. Packer, for instance, once wrote that in the early chapters of Genesis, which he defended as inerrant Scripture, he could not see anything that "bears on the biological theory of evolution one way or the other." Moreover, Packer went on to say that as a nonexpert he was willing to follow the Princeton theologian: "I recall that B. B.

44. John Murray, "Calvin's Doctrine of Creation," *Westminster Theological Journal* 17 (1954): 21–43, esp. 40–41.

45. Richard Stauffer, "L'Exégèse de Genèse 1, 1–3 chez Luther et Calvin," in *In principio: Interprétations des premiers versets de la Genèse* (Paris: Etudes Augustiniennes, 1973), 245–66, esp. 260–61. For echoes of Murray's rejection of Warfield's argument, see Henri Blocher, *In the Beginning: The Opening Chapters of Genesis*, trans. David G. Preston (Downers Grove, Ill.: InterVarsity, 1984), 223; and John D. Woodbridge, "Some Misconceptions of the Impact of the 'Enlightenment' on the Doctrine of Scripture," in *Hermeneutics, Authority, and Canon*, ed. D. A. Carson and John D. Woodbridge (Grand Rapids: Zondervan, 1986), 260, 417.

Warfield was a theistic evolutionist. If on this count I am not an evangelical, then neither was he."[46]

It is crucial to underscore that Warfield's architectonic defense of biblical inerrancy did not prevent him from adopting a non-literal interpretation of the early Genesis narratives. Thus, while acknowledging that Calvin himself had understood the days of creation as six literal days, Warfield still contended that Calvin believed that Moses, "writing to meet the needs of men at large, accommodated himself to their grade of intellectual preparation, and confined himself to what met their eyes." Now in the early twentieth century Warfield suggested that in order to perpetuate the spirit of Calvin's hermeneutic genius "these six days would have to be lengthened out into six periods—six ages of the growth of the world. Had that been done, Calvin would have been a precursor of the modern evolutionary theorists. As it is, he forms only a point of departure for them to this extent—that he teaches, as they teach, that by the instrumentality of second causes—or as a modern would put it, of intrinsic forces—the original world-stuff was modified into the varied forms which constitute the ordered world."

It is important to recall that Warfield penned these words in 1915, or at about the time he was reminiscing on his student days under McCosh. In those reminiscences he observed that he later abandoned the Scotsman's Darwinian orthodoxy. In light of his essay on Calvin's doctrine of creation, it becomes readily clear that for Warfield to depart from classical Darwinism did not mean abandoning evolutionary transformism.

Although Warfield wrote extensively on human origins, he believed that the issue of the antiquity of the human race was theologically neither interesting nor significant. He had already insisted that there were no biblical data for providing a precise estimate of the age of the earth.[47] In this insistence, he relied on the work of his Princeton colleague William Henry Green, who had shown to Warfield's satisfaction that biblical genealogies

46. J. I. Packer, *The Evangelical Anglican Identity Problem* (Oxford: Latimer House, 1978), 5. For recent confirmation that "Packer followed Warfield at this point," see McGrath, *Foundations of Dialogue in Science and Religion*, 129–30.

47. See his November 1903 essay for *The Bible Student* (pp. 211–29 in the present volume).

could not be relied upon to give precise chronological dating—
that it was, in any case, not the purpose of those genealogies to
supply that kind of information.[48] To be sure, Warfield was fully
aware of the much reduced estimates of the age of the physical
earth that Lord Kelvin had put forward—geophysical evidence
that Darwin himself held to constitute a serious criticism of his
theory of natural selection—and Warfield did not hesitate to con-
vey to his readers either these facts or the various efforts at refutation.[49] But all of these matters constituted only intramural feuds
between scientific speculators and left theology entirely un-
touched. As he put it: "Theology as such has no concern in this
conflict and may stand calmly by and enjoy the fuss and fury of
the battle."

Of far greater importance to Warfield was the ideologically
laden controversy over the unity of the human species.[50] On this
subject he was uncompromising. Both Scripture and science, he
believed, taught the organic solidarity of all human stock. The
racist undercurrents in much of the era's polygenist polemic,
which implied that humankind comprised several distinct biological species, Warfield unhesitatingly attributed to an ugly, if deep-
seated, racial pride.[51] To him the specific unity of humankind was
a prerequisite for biblical soteriology; it was also supported by the
monogenetic implications of evolutionary biology. "The preva-

48. For example, William Henry Green, "Primeval Chronology," *Bibliotheca
Sacra* 47 (April 1890): 285-303.

49. The criticisms of Kelvin and others are surveyed in Joe D. Burchfield, *Lord
Kelvin and the Age of the Earth* (New York: Science History, 1975); Peter J. Vorzim-
mer, *Charles Darwin: The Years of Controversy. The* Origin of Species *and Its Critics
1859–1882* (Philadelphia: Temple University Press, 1975); and David Hull, *Darwin
and His Critics: The Reception of Darwin's Theory of Evolution by the Scientific Community* (Cambridge, Mass.: Harvard University Press, 1973).

50. See the discussions in William Stanton, *The Leopard's Spots: Scientific Attitudes toward Race in America, 1815–59* (Chicago: University of Chicago Press, 1960);
John S. Haller Jr., *Outcasts from Evolution: Scientific Attitudes of Racial Inferiority, 1859–
1900* (Urbana: University of Illinois Press, 1971).

51. Warfield's straightforward support of monogenesis carried over into at-
tacks on racism that were rare at the time for Kentuckians of his class. See, for example, his essays "A Calm View of the Freedman's Case" (1887) and "Drawing the
Color Line" (1888), as reprinted in *SSWW* 2:735–42, 743–50, as well as the poem
"Wanted—A Samaritan," in Warfield, *Four Hymns and Some Religious Verse* (Philadelphia: Westminster, 1910), 11.

lence of the evolutionary hypotheses," he wrote in the *Princeton Theological Review* for 1911 (pp. 279–80 in the present volume), "has removed all motive for denying a common origin to the human race." On this issue, evidently, evolutionary science and scriptural orthodoxy spoke with one voice.[52]

By the early twentieth century Warfield had, by his own admission, departed from Darwinism narrowly construed, but he had by no means discounted evolutionary theses about organic change, provided that such schemes were not construed to oppose teleology and design. Thus when in 1916 he reviewed J. N. Shearman's *Natural Theology of Evolution*—a book long overdue but "bound to come"—he was pleased to announce that the author was an "evolutionary Paley." To Warfield, Shearman was doing for the scientific worldview of organic evolutionary development what William Paley had done for the worldview of static mechanical organization—which was to show the necessity of a divine mind behind what the day's best scientific thinking had concluded to be the workings of the universe.

The last word in this discussion of Warfield's non-Darwinian, but still evolutionary views is to note the spread of a diverse range of non-Darwinian evolutionary theses precisely during the early years of the twentieth century. Their significance for Warfield lay in their proposal of many different mechanisms *within* the evolutionary paradigm that could explain the way in which God's providence actively engaged the world. When Warfield was making his full statements in 1911 on the human race and in 1915 on Calvin's view of creation, Darwinism as an explanation for evolutionary development was in eclipse among scientists. The problems of inheritance, which the rediscovery of Gregor Mendel's experiments had brought to light, cast classical Darwinism in the shade until the Neo-Darwinian synthesis of the 1930s. In the interim, evolutionary theses of various kinds flourished—including Neo-Lamarckism, orthogenesis (or evolution proceeding along predetermined paths), the theory of Hugo de Vries concerning large-scale mutations. Most of them played down the gradualism

52. Ironically, some later evangelicals would reverse Warfield's judgment and see evolutionary theory as a support *for* racism; for example, Francis A. Schaeffer, *How Should We Then Live?* (Old Tappan, N.J.: Revell, 1976), 151; and E. H. Andrews, *Is Evolution Scientific?* (Herts, Eng.: Evangelical, 1977), 6.

and the central significance of natural selection which Darwin's disciples had promulgated.[53]

Warfield was thoroughly apprised of these most recent departures, for in his 1908 review of George Paulin's rejection of Darwinism (pp. 252–56), he castigates the author for assuming originality in doubting the all-sufficiency of natural selection and the struggle for existence. To the contrary, Warfield states that anyone "unaware of the widespread revolt from these conceptions among recent scientific investigators should read at least the three chapters on 'Darwinism Attacked' in Professor Vernon L. Kellogg's *Darwinism Today.*" By departing from Darwinian orthodoxy in the decades prior to the advent of the Neo-Darwinian or synthetic theory, Warfield was thereby declaring his preference for the newest evolutionary orthodoxies on the scientific horizon.

The Shape of Warfield's Evolutionism

In the course of his career, both Warfield's positions and his vocabulary shifted on the question of evolution. But they shifted only within the constraints of a fairly narrow range. What remained constant was his adherence to a broad Calvinistic conception of the natural world—of a world that, even in its most material, physical aspects, reflected the wisdom and glory of God—and his commitment to the goal of harmonizing a sophisticated conservative theology and the most securely verified conclusions of modern science. Another way of describing the constancy of his position is to say that while Warfield consistently rejected naturalistic, reductionistic, or ateleological explanations for natural phenomena (explanations that he usually associated with Darwinism), Warfield just as consistently entertained the possibility that other kinds of evolutionary theses, which avoided Darwin's rejection of design, could satisfactorily explain the physical world.

In several of his writings Warfield carefully distinguishes three ways in which God has worked in and through the physical world. Warfield felt that each of these concepts, if properly applied to the developments in natural history and in the history of

53. See the discussion in Peter J. Bowler, *The Eclipse of Darwinism: Anti-Darwinian Evolution Theories in the Decades around 1900* (Baltimore: Johns Hopkins University Press, 1983).

salvation, was compatible with the theology he found in an inerrant Bible. "Evolution" meant developments arising out of forces that God had placed inside matter at the original creation of the world-stuff and also directed to predetermined ends by his providential superintendence of the world. At least in writings toward the end of his life, Warfield held that evolution in this sense was fully compatible with biblical understandings of the production of the human body. "Mediate creation" meant the action of God upon matter to bring something new into existence that could not have been produced by forces or energy latent in matter itself. Warfield did not apply the notion of mediate creation directly in his last, most mature writings on evolution, but it may be that he had expounded the concept as much to deal with miracles and other biblical events as for developments in the natural world.[54] The last means of God's action was "creation *ex nihilo*," which Warfield consistently maintained was the way that God made the original stuff of the world. It also seems that, in his 1915 article on Calvin, when he considered the soul of every human, Warfield held that God created each soul directly *ex nihilo*.

Throughout Warfield's career, the concept of *concursus* was especially productive for both theology and science. Just as the authors of Scripture were completely human in writing the Bible, even as they enjoyed the full inspiration of the Holy Spirit, so too could all living creatures develop fully (with the exception of the original creation and the human soul) through natural means. The key for Warfield was a doctrine of providence that saw God working in and with, instead of as a replacement for, the processes of nature. Late in his career, this stance also grounded Warfield's opposition to faith healing. In his eyes, physical healing through medicine and the agency of physicians was as much a result of God's action (if through secondary causes) as were the cures claimed as a direct result of divine intervention.[55] For his views on evolution, *concursus* was as important, and as fruitful, as it was for his theology as a whole. It was a principle he felt the

54. Warfield deploys a similar vocabulary in a discussion of miracles that he published at about the same time; see "The Question of Miracles," in *The Bible Student* 7.3–6 (March–June 1903), as reprinted in *SSWW* 2:167–204.

55. See *Counterfeit Miracles* (New York: Scribner, 1918).

Scriptures provided for approaching the natural world fearlessly and for doing so to the greater glory of God.

Warfield's commitment to solid empirical science and to the *concursus* of divine and natural action gave him extraordinary balance in sifting his era's difficult questions of science and faith. One of the reasons that many in subsequent decades have failed to retain his equipoise on this subject may be that they have abandoned one or both of these commitments.

Texts and Apparatus

The documents reprinted in this volume were, with one exception, published during Warfield's lifetime. That exception is his lecture from December 1888 on "Evolution or Development," which is reprinted here with the permission of the Office of Archives and Special Collections of Princeton Theological Seminary. The introduction to each text identifies the original source of the writing and, where applicable, its location in *WBBW* or *SSWW*.

All editorial insertions, translations, identifications, and annotations are enclosed in brackets. On the very few occasions where Warfield inserted his own editorial additions to quotations, his initials are added within the brackets. Notes without brackets are Warfield's originals. Minor alterations in Warfield's original punctuation, capitalization, and spelling have been made silently to conform to modern usage; in addition, a few alterations in his original wording are aimed at clarifying the meaning for today's readers. A biographical annotation is provided wherever Warfield first mentions an individual; for subsequent references the index provides access to that annotation.

We have tried to reprint all of Warfield's writings of any significance on evolution, along with several of his more general reflections on science. Warfield, however, referred fleetingly to scientific concerns in many other places in his writings. A partial list of those other works includes:

1888   Article, "Christian Evidences: How Affected by Recent
        Criticisms," in *Homiletic Review* 16:107–12
1889   Review of J. I. D. Hinds, *Charles Darwin,* in *Presbyterian
        Review* 10:513–14

1889   Review of James L. Martin, *Dr. Girardeau's Anti-Evolution,*
        in *Presbyterian Review* 10:687

1892   Review of Robert Watts, *Dr. Briggs' Biblical Theology
        Traced to Its Organific Principle,* in *Presbyterian and Re-
        formed Review* 3:373

1892   Review of G. G. Stokes, *Natural Theology,* vol. 1, in *Pres-
        byterian and Reformed Review* 3:585–86

1894   Review of Charles Marsh Mead, *Some Current Notions con-
        cerning Dogmatic Theology,* in *Presbyterian and Reformed
        Review* 5:543

1894   Review of Prof. Marais, *Darwinism,* in *Presbyterian and Re-
        formed Review* 5:543–44

1894   Review of Emory Miller, *The Evolution of Love,* in *Presbyte-
        rian and Reformed Review* 5:546–47

1895   Review of G. G. Stokes, *Natural Theology,* vol. 2, in *Pres-
        byterian and Reformed Review* 6:365

1895   Review of J. William Dawson, *The Meeting-place of Geol-
        ogy and History,* in *Presbyterian and Reformed Review*
        6:391

1896   Review of John Laidlaw, *The Bible Doctrine of Man,* in *Pres-
        byterian and Reformed Review* 7:174–75

1896   Review of Charles Gore, *Dissertations on Subjects Con-
        nected with the Incarnation,* in *Presbyterian and Reformed
        Review* 7:175–76

1896   Review of George John Romanes, *Mind and Motion, and
        Monism,* in *Presbyterian and Reformed Review* 7:383

1896   Review of John H. Denison, *Christ's Idea of the Supernatu-
        ral,* in *Presbyterian and Reformed Review* 7:746–47

1897   Article, "Christian Supernaturalism," in *Presbyterian and
        Reformed Review* 8:58–74

1897   Review of Hugh Mortimer Cecil, *Pseudo-Philosophy at the
        End of the Nineteenth Century,* in *Presbyterian and Re-
        formed Review* 8:776–77

1898   Review of Andrew Lang, *The Making of Religion,* in *Pres-
        byterian and Reformed Review,* 9:744–49

1899   Review of Emily Lovira Gregory, *A Scientist's Confession of
        Faith,* in *Presbyterian and Reformed Review* 10:150

1899   Review of George John Romanes, *Darwin and After Darwin,* vol. 2, in *Presbyterian and Reformed Review* 10:583–84

1899   Review of J. William Dawson, *Relics of Primeval Life,* in *Presbyterian and Reformed Review* 10:584

1901   Review of L. Kessler, *Ueber Offenbarung und Wunder* (Concerning revelation and miracle), in *Presbyterian and Reformed Review* 12:295–96

1902   Review of Andrew Lang, *Magic and Religion,* in *Presbyterian and Reformed Review* 13:457–59

1902   Review of George Campbell, *A Revolution in the Science of Cosmology,* in *Presbyterian and Reformed Review* 13:673

1903   Review of H. Bavinck, *De Zekerheid des Geloofs* (The security of faith), in *Princeton Theological Review* 1:138–48

1904   Review of Greville Macdonald, *The Religious Sense in Its Scientific Aspects,* in *Princeton Theological Review* 2:327–30

1904   Review of H. H. Kuyper, *Evolutie of Revelatie* (Evolution or revelation), in *Princeton Theological Review* 2:668–70

1916   Review of James Hastings, ed., *Encyclopaedia of Religion and Ethics,* vol. 8, in *Princeton Theological Review* 14:649–56

Warfield
on
Scripture

May 3, 1894
Presbyterian Journal
(reprinted from *SSWW* 2:542–48)

The Divine and Human in the Bible

In this short essay Warfield summarizes for a popular audience many of the themes on Scripture he had been emphasizing for more than twenty years.[1] In several ways this essay also provides a theological baseline for Warfield's many writings on science and evolution. It reflects Warfield's commitment to the inerrancy of the Bible, but also to a view of biblical inerrancy that affirms the full *human* character of Scripture. Most importantly, the essay concludes with a careful statement concerning the principle of *concursus,* or the acting together by two forces or causes in the creation of one entity or event. This article shows that Warfield's thinking on *concursus* in the natural world, where material and divine explanations may both prove satisfactory, was rooted in his convictions about *concursus* in the process of revelation itself.

There is probably no problem more prominently before the minds of Bible students of today than the one which concerns the relation between the divine and human elements in the Bible. Recent discussion of the authenticity, authorship, integrity, and structure of the several biblical books has called men's attention, as possibly it has never before been called, to the human element in the Bible. Even those who were accustomed to look upon their Bible as simply divine, never once thinking of the human agents through whom the divine Spirit spoke, have had their eyes opened to the

1. [Many of Warfield's most important articles on Scripture are collected in *WBBW,* vol. 1, *Revelation and Inspiration* (New York: Oxford University Press, 1927), and *The Inspiration and Authority of the Bible* (Philadelphia: Presbyterian and Reformed, 1948). There is much overlap between the two volumes.]

fact that the Scriptures are human writings, written by men, and bearing the traces of their human origin on their very face. In many minds the questions have become quite pressing: How are the two factors, the divine and the human, to be conceived as related to each other in the act of inspiration? And, how are the two consequent elements in the product, the divine and human, to be conceived to be related to each other in the Scriptures?

It would be a mistake to suppose such questions as these of little practical importance. It is true enough that Christian men are more concerned with the effects of inspiration than with its nature or mode. But men will not rest in their belief in effects which are not congruous with their conception of the nature and mode of inspiration. Inadequate or positively false conceptions of the nature and mode of inspiration are being continually suggested, and wherever they are in any degree accepted, they bring forth their natural fruit in a modified view of the effects of inspiration. Men are continually striving to be rid of the effects which are ascribed to inspiration in the Scriptures and the formularies of the church; their plea is that inspiration is not to be so conceived as to require these effects. The question of how inspiration is to be conceived having been thus raised, it becomes of very serious importance to go at least so far into it as to exhibit the untenableness of those theories which, when accepted, wholly overthrow the biblical conception of the effects of inspiration. It is a matter, then, of importance, and not merely of curious interest, to ask, How are the two factors, the divine and human, to be conceived to be related to each other in the act of inspiration? And how are the two consequent elements in the Bible, the divine and human, to be conceived to be related to each other in the product of inspiration?

1. In the first place, we may be sure that they are not properly conceived when one factor or element is so exaggeratingly emphasized as to exclude the other altogether.

At one time there arose in the church, under the impulse of zeal to assert and safeguard the divinity of Scripture, a tendency toward so emphasizing the divine element as to exclude the human. The human writers of Scripture were conceived as mere implements in the hands of the Holy Ghost, implements by which (rather than through whom) he wrote the Scriptures. Men were not content to call the human authors of Scripture merely the penmen, the amanuenses of the Holy Spirit, but represented them as simply his pens. Inspiration, in this view, was conceived as a simple act of dictation; and it was denied that the human writers contributed any quality to the product, unless, indeed, it might be their handwriting. This, properly so-called, mechanical theory of inspiration was taught by a number of seventeenth-century divines in all Protestant communions alike—by Quenstedt, Calov, and Hollaz among the Lutherans; by Heidegger and Buxtorf among the Reformed; by Richard Hooker among the Anglicans; and by John White among the Puritans.[2] The obvious marks of human authorship in the biblical books, however, prevented the mechanical theory from becoming dominant in its extreme form. Recognition of these marks of human authorship— as, for example, differences in vocabulary, style, and the like— was recognition of a human element in the Bible; and involved, in the place of the strict theory of sole divine authorship, the substitution of a theory of coauthorship by God and man for the Scriptures. In this form alone has the theory of dictation persisted in the church, and in this form it no longer belongs to the class of theories under discussion. Probably no one today so emphasizes the divine element in Scripture as to exclude the human altogether.

The opposite fault, however, is exceedingly common today. Nothing, indeed, is more common than such theories of the origin and nature of the Scriptures as exclude the divine factor and element altogether, and make them purely human in both origin and character. Historically, this mode of thought is an outgrowth of rationalism, but it takes every form which is required by a change of philosophical basis. A Hegelian, like Dr. Whiton,

2. [Johannes Andreas Quenstedt (1617–88), Abraham Calov or Calovius (1612–86), and David Hollaz (1648–1713) were leaders among the orthodox Lutheran theologians of the seventeenth century. John Henry Heidegger (1633–98), a Reformed theologian from Zurich, was a key figure in drawing up the Formula Consensus Helvetica of 1675. Two Johann Buxtorfs, father (1564–1629) and son (1599–1664), were Hebrew and rabbinical scholars at Basel. Richard Hooker (1553–1600), Anglican theologian, is noted for his *Laws of Ecclesiastical Polity,* which defended a conservative Episcopacy wedded with Augustinian theology. John White (1574–1648), one of the divines who formulated the Westminster Confession, was also a great-grandfather of John and Charles Wesley.]

adapts himself to it as readily as does a deist; a mystic like R. F. Horton as readily as does a vulgar rationalist.[3] The modes of statement given to it are very various, but they all agree in holding the Bible to be a purely human book. They differ only as to whether there has been any divine preparation for the book at all, or, if this be allowed, whether this divine preparation included a revelation which men have recorded in this book, or whether it was only gracious or indeed only providential. The book market is flooded at present with treatises teaching this hopelessly one-sided theory. Dr. Washington Gladden's *Who Wrote the Bible?* [1891] is a very crude instance in point.[4] To him God had the same sort of care over the production of the Bible that he has over the growth of an old apple tree. Dr. John DeWitt's recent book *What Is Inspiration?* [1893] is another crude instance.[5] According to him the prophet was left to express himself in human language "as well as he could." A slightly higher conception is taken by T. George Rooke in his *Inspiration and Other Lectures* [1893]; and a higher one still by a recent German writer, Leonard Stählin, who thinks that God specifically prepared the biblical writers for their task, but left them, when prepared, to execute their task in a manner so "free" as to be without continued divine guidance.[6] Throughout all these modifications the germinal conception persists that it was man and man alone who made the Bible, and that it is, therefore, a purely human book, although it may contain a human report of divine deeds and words.

2. We may be equally sure that the relation of the divine and human in inspiration and in the Bible is not properly conceived

3. [James Morris Whiton (1833–1920) was a Congregational minister who sided with the progressive forces in his denomination. Robert Forman Horton (1855–1934) was the author of *Inspiration and the Bible: An Inquiry* (1888).]

4. [Washington Gladden (1836–1918), a Congregational minister who served in New York, Massachusetts, and Ohio, endorsed the social gospel and considered theology per se to be subordinate to ethics.]

5. [John DeWitt (1821–1906) was a Dutch Reformed minister who became a professor of Greek and New Testament at Rutgers University.]

6. [The book by Thomas George Rooke (1837–90) that Warfield mentions here was published posthumously in Edinburgh by T. & T. Clark. Leonhard Stählin published *Kant, Lotze, and Ritschl* (1889) and *Über den Ursprung der Religion* (On the origin of religion) (1905).]

when they are thought of as elements in the Bible that lie over against each other and divide the Bible between them, or as factors in inspiration that strive against and exclude each other so that where one enters the other is pushed out. This hopelessly crude conception seems to have become extraordinarily common in recent years. It is this point of view which underlies the remark, now heard very frequently, that the human element in the Bible is coming to be recognized as larger than we had supposed—with the implication that, therefore, the divine element must be acknowledged to be smaller than we had supposed. Even so thoughtful a writer as Dr. Sanday falls into this mode of speech: "The tendency of the last 50 or 100 years of investigation," he tells us, "is to make it appear that this human element is larger than had been supposed."[7] So, too, Prof. Kirkpatrick says: "In the origin of Scripture there has been a large human element, larger than there was at one time supposed."[8] The underlying conception is that what is human cannot also be divine, and that wherever the human enters, there the divine disappears. Thus Dr. Sanday speaks of his thesis as an apparent contention "for an encroachment of the human element upon the divine," and Dr. G. T. Ladd even speaks of the chief difficulty in the matter being the determination of "the exact place where the divine meets the human and is limited by it."[9]

On such a conception it is easy to see that every discovery of a human trait in Scripture is a disproving of the divinity of Scripture. If, then, it be discovered that the whole fabric of the Bible is human—as assuredly is true—men who start with this concep-

7. *The Oracles of God* [1891], 161. [William Sanday (1843–1920), professor of theology at Oxford, viewed the Bible on the analogy of body and soul, but with the two often, if not usually, blended together.]

8. *The Divine Library of the Old Testament* [1891], 53. [Alexander Francis Kirkpatrick (1849–1940), Anglican theologian, asserted the unique truth of Christianity and held that Scripture possesses both human and divine aspects. Unlike Warfield, Kirkpatrick held that the human authors could err in matters of science or history.]

9. *What Is the Bible?* [1888], 437. [George Trumbull Ladd (1842–1921), professor of philosophy at Yale University, insisted that neither natural science nor biblical science should try to force the other side into agreement; rather, they could coexist in separate spheres. The Bible's creation account was for him religiously true, but not a scientific fact.]

tion in mind must end with denying that the whole fabric of the Bible is divine. As a preliminary stage we shall expect to meet with efforts to go through the Bible and anxiously to separate the divine and human elements. And if these elements are really so related to one another that when one enters the other is pushed out, this task will not seem a hopeless one. We may be warned, as Dr. Sanday does warn us, that it is "a mistake to attempt to draw a hard and fast line between the two elements." But some will feel that, on this conception of their relation to each other, it is a greater mistake not to make such an attempt. How shall we consent to leave confused such very diverse elements? We need not be surprised, therefore, that men like Horton and Gess have made the attempt.[10] Nor need we who perceive the folly of the underlying conception of the mechanical relation of the two elements to each other feel surprised over the destructive nature of their results. They do not fail to find the human element entering almost everywhere, and therefore the divine element almost nowhere.

3. Justice is done to neither factor of inspiration and to neither element in the Bible, the human or the divine, by any other conception of the mode of inspiration except that of *concursus,* or by any other conception of the Bible except that which conceives of it as a divine-human book in which every word is at once divine and human.

The philosophical basis of this conception is the Christian idea of God as immanent as well as transcendent in the modes of his activity. Its idea of the mode of the divine activity in inspiration is in analogy with the divine modes of activity in other spheres—in providence, and in grace wherein we work out our own salvation with fear and trembling, knowing that it is God who is working in us both the willing and the doing according to his own good pleasure. The biblical basis of *concursus* is found in the constant scriptural representation of the divine and human coauthorship of the biblical commandments and enunciations of truth, as well as in the constant scriptural ascription of Bible passages to both the divine and the human authors, and in the constant scrip-

10. [Wolfgang Friedrich Gess (1819–91) was a German pastor and theologian of liberal views who taught at Basel and Göttingen.]

tural recognition of Scripture as both divine and human in quality and character.

The fundamental principle of this conception is that the whole of Scripture is the product of divine activities which enter it, not by superseding the activities of the human authors, but by working confluently with them, so that the Scriptures are the joint product of divine and human activities, both of which penetrate them at every point, working harmoniously together to the production of a writing which is not divine here and human there, but at once divine and human in every part, every word and every particular. According to this conception, therefore, the whole Bible is recognized as human, the free product of human effort, in every part and word. And at the same time the whole Bible is recognized as divine, the Word of God, his utterances, of which he is in the truest sense the Author.

The human and divine factors in inspiration are conceived of as flowing confluently and harmoniously to the production of a common product. And the two elements are conceived of in the Scriptures as the inseparable constituents of one single and uncompounded product. Of every word of Scripture is it to be affirmed, in turn, that it is God's word and that it is man's word. All the qualities of divinity and of humanity are to be sought and may be found in every portion and element of the Scripture. While, on the other hand, no quality inconsistent with either divinity or humanity can be found in any portion or element of Scripture.

On this conception, therefore, for the first time full justice is done to both elements of Scripture. Neither is denied because the other is recognized. And neither is limited to certain portions of Scripture so that place may be made for the other, nor is either allowed to encroach upon the other. As full justice is done to the human element as is done by those who deny that there is any divine element in the Bible, for of every word in the Bible it is asserted that it has been conceived in a human mind and written by a human hand. As full justice is done to the divine element as is done by those who deny that there is any human element in the Bible, for of every word in the Bible it is asserted that it is inspired by God and has been written under the direct and immediate guidance of the Holy Spirit. And full justice being done to both elements in the Bible, full justice is done also to human needs. "The Bible," says Dr. Westcott, "is authoritative, for it is the Word of God; it is intelligible, for it is the word of man."[11] Because it is the word of man in every part and element, it comes home to our hearts. Because it is the Word of God in every part and element, it is our constant law and guide.

---

11. [Brooke Foss Westcott (1825–1901), traditional Anglican New Testament scholar and textual critic, was responsible with his colleague F. J. A. Hort (1828–92) for a masterful edition of the Greek New Testament published in 1881.]

Warfield
on Evolution
and Science

April 1888
Presbyterian Review 9:335

Review of George Matheson,
T. W. Fowle, George W. Cox,
[Alfred Williams] Momerie,
[Charles] Chapman, P. W. Darnton,
J. Matthews, W. F. Adeney,
A. F. Muir, and J. J. Murphy,
Christianity and Evolution:
Modern Problems of the Faith,
Nisbet's Theological Library
(New York: T. Whittaker, 1887)

Warfield's comments on Robert Watts's *Reign of Causality* in the
same issue of the *Presbyterian Review* were more substantial than
this brief notice. But it was significant as one of Warfield's first published statements on the subject. Its plea to ground reasoning about
science in solid theology would be repeated in a variety of ways for
more than thirty years. The book under review was a collection of articles that appeared during 1886 and 1887 in the British publication
Homiletic Magazine. Its contributors came primarily from Broad
Church and liberal backgrounds and shared the editors' conviction
that "acceptance of the ascertained facts of Evolution is not incompatible with a genuine, intelligent Christian Faith" [from the preface,
v–vi].

Unevenness of execution is the natural vice of books of the "symposium" class, and this volume forms no exception to the rule. Of the dozen papers here collected, less than half can be, with any justice, called able, while only two are of permanent value—the two really masterly papers by Professor Chapman on "Evolution and the Biblical Doctrine of Sin and Redemption," and "Evolution and the Biblical Representations of God." Mr. J. J. Murphy pleads ably for the inclusion of mind under the law of evolution, but renders it only the more plain that in order to do so we must give up the natural immortality of the soul and transmute the doctrine of life after death into the one formula of *"God will raise the dead"*—an inevitable result, as Dr. Dallinger has already taught us in his Fernley Lecture.[1] Is theology ready to make this sacrifice? To judge by the general tone of the present volume, theology is ready for any sacrifices, if, indeed, the crude driftage which passes for theology here can be called by that name. Nothing is so characteristic of the volume as the unsettled, unreasoned, uninstructed attitude of the writers, as a body, toward theology.

---

1. [On W. H. Dallinger, see Warfield's "Charles Darwin's Religious Life" and his review of Dallinger's *The Creator, and What We May Know of the Method of Creation*," both of which were published in October 1888 and are reprinted in the present volume; see pp. 68–111 and 112–13].

April 1888
Presbyterian Review 9:340–41

Review of Robert Watts,
The Reign of Causality:
A Vindication of the Scientific
Principle of Telic Causal Efficiency
(Edinburgh: T. & T. Clark, 1888)

Robert Watts (1820–95) was one of many Irish Presbyterian students who had come to Princeton Theological Seminary for study under Charles Hodge. After returning to Ireland, Watts gained renown (or notoriety, depending on point of view) by challenging the speeches that John Tyndall (whom Warfield here calls Tyndale) and T. H. Huxley presented at the 1874 Belfast gathering of the British Association for the Advancement of Science. Those speeches championed an anti-religious materialism and were sharply rebuked in Watts's defense of a Christian basis for all science.[1] Watts continued to write on such matters until his essays were eventually collected in the book reviewed here. Warfield's review is noteworthy for its approval of Watts's defense of design in nature, since even while he cautiously approved various evolutionary schemes, Warfield always held firmly (as had his mentor Charles Hodge) to God's direction of all natural processes. Extant correspondence between Warfield and Watts testifies to the firm links between Irish and American Presbyterianism.

By the phrase "a vindication of the scientific principle of telic causal efficiency" Dr. Watts means that the fundamental assumption of all science and philosophy that "every effect must have a cause" involves, first, that we must assign an adequate cause for

1. See David N. Livingstone, "Darwinism and Calvinism: The Belfast-Princeton Connection," *Isis* 83 (1992): 408–28.

every effect, that is, "a cause that will account for the *production of all* the phenomena under investigation in the particular instance"; and, secondly, that we shall find "that within the sphere of the phenomena with which science has to do, adequate Causality is invariably telic"—that is to say, that a thorough analysis of all the phenomena reveals adaptations of means to ends, and conducts the investigator back behind the phenomena and the ordered array of ends and means to an antecedent presiding intelligence. With this simple wand of an adequate cause, he proposes to exorcise all the demons of recent unbelieving thinking.

The main point which Watts insists upon and admirably illustrates from the writings of Professor Huxley, Dr. Tyndale, Mr. Spencer, Mr. Mill, etc., is that scientific theory can be made antagonistic to Christian truth only "at the modest cost" of stifling what Dr. Tyndale has happily termed "the questioning impulse"; that materialistic and agnostic thinkers, in a word, avoid reaching theistic conclusions only by resting satisfied with causes which the constitution of the human mind assures us are insufficient to account for the phenomena under investigation.[2] They consider themselves, for instance, to have accounted for a crystal when they have laid bare the immediate and proximate causes of its formation, whereas the "questioning impulse" is not satisfied until the crystal is made to give as full an account of itself as is an Egyptian pyramid. It will not do to stop with the discovery of the forces used in crystal building, to rest in the slaves without the architect; we must still ask why these blind slaves build so deftly, on so exquisite a plan, and with such perfect results; nor can we believe that the more perfect the result and the more exquisite the

2. [Thomas Henry Huxley (1825–95), a zoologist and paleontologist, was one of Darwin's closest friends. Although he doubted whether Darwin's theory of natural selection adequately explained the transmutation of species, he so zealously defended *The Origin of Species* that he became known as "Darwin's bulldog." By "Tyndale" Warfield means John Tyndall (1820–93), a prolific younger Darwinist who published in a number of scientific fields and also, as at the 1874 Belfast convention of the British Association, argued against the idea of design in nature. Herbert Spencer (1820–1903), the philosopher and evolutionary theorist, was an extreme liberal individualist, an ardent proponent of social evolution, and a firm believer in the progress of Western society. John Stuart Mill (1806–73) was the influential promoter of utilitarian ethics whose antimetaphysical and antireligious arguments counted for a great deal in the mid-nineteenth century.]

agency, the less need is there for supposing the intervention of mind. So again it gratifies but does not satisfy the mind to be told that Kepler's laws[3] are referred to the principle of gravitation; it still asks, "Whence this principle of gravitation? How comes it that matter is possessed of this marvelous gravity?"

Dr. Watts writes with adequate learning and vigor, and fairly carries his point, showing that all the fashionable antitheistic forms of reasoning are alike sinners against the scientific fundamental on the acknowledgment of which alone can any science or philosophy exist. The book is made up of a number of essays written at intervals during the last fourteen years, and suffers somewhat in continuity and unity in consequence. It must be read, therefore, more as a cumulative than as a continuous argument; but every chapter is made to bear witness to the correctness of the key position, and everywhere the clear and trenchant style and telling illustrations conduct us over agreeable paths to the one ever more and more certain goal.

3. [Johannes Kepler (1571–1630) continues to attract interest both for his astronomical work on the regularity of the planets' elliptical orbits and for his belief that God's wisdom is manifest in the design of the universe.]

July 1888
Presbyterian Review 9:510–11

Review of James McCosh,
The Religious Aspect of Evolution
(New York and London: Putnam, 1888)

James McCosh (1811–94) arrived as the new president of the College of New Jersey in 1868, the same year Warfield matriculated as a student. As one of his era's leading reconcilers of evolution and traditional Christianity, McCosh was following through on principles of harmonizing religion and science that he had learned as a student in his native Scotland from the influential Thomas Chalmers (1780–1847) and that he had taught as a renowned professor of logic and metaphysics at the Queen's College of Belfast.[1] By 1888 Warfield had abandoned the Darwinism that he had brought with him from Kentucky to Princeton. As this review shows, he had also come to rely on empirical procedure as the key issue in judging the adequacy of various evolutionary theories. With McCosh his teacher, Warfield could be confident of the compatibility of evolution, carefully defined, with theism. Unlike later in his career, however, in 1888 he was less certain than McCosh that the results of scientific research justified the conclusions of evolutionary theory.

D r. McCosh has deserved well of our generation, for which he has been the defender, through many strifes, of all that we hold true in philosophy and of much that we hold precious in faith. Nothing that comes from him can come without a welcome or can be received without gain. Always in the forefront of the battle in defense of fundamental truth, he appears here once more to defend and commend the Christian doctrine of God. Heartily ac-

1. See the solid biography by J. David Hoeveler Jr., *James McCosh and the Scottish Intellectual Tradition: From Glasgow to Princeton* (Princeton: Princeton University Press, 1981).

cepting the evolutionary hypothesis as true science, he has written this little book to show, for the benefit of his cobelievers in
that doctrine, and for the relief of the many who are prejudiced
against it, that it is thoroughly consistent with Christian theism.
In this he has been entirely successful; the position that he has
taken up, which looks upon evolution as a proved fact, yet not as
a sufficient account of the phenomena of the organic world, but
only as opening to us the method through which the true force or
cause works, is not only consistent with but even presuppositive
of theism. The present reviewer cannot, however, accord with his
revered preceptor in adopting language (pp. 39f.) which speaks of
the fact of evolution as "completely made out," "proved," "demonstrated" (although not "mathematically," p. 45), but must still
take his seat alongside of those who look upon it as a more or less
probable or more or less improbable conjecture of scientific workers as to the method of creation, which is at present on its probation, and which has not yet been shown to be able to account for
the facts, much less to be the true theory to assume in order to account for them. Professor Flint's remarks on the difference in kind
between the inductive process applicable to the discovery of the
law of gravitation and the inductive process applicable to cases
like the present (in the *Encyclopaedia Britannica,* 23:266a) may be
profitably read in this connection.[2]

2. [Robert Flint (1838–1910), a Scottish philosopher and theologian, was the
Stone Lecturer at Princeton in 1880. He contributed articles on "Theism" and
"Theology" to the ninth edition of the *Encyclopaedia Britannica.*]

October 1888
Presbyterian Review 9:569–601

Charles Darwin's Religious Life: A Sketch in Spiritual Biography

Warfield's essay on the three-volume *Life and Letters of Charles Darwin* (1888) combined a sensitive reading of Darwin's biography with a statement of principles that would guide much of Warfield's later writing on evolution. The essay uses the *Life* to chart Darwin's loss first of Christian belief, then of confidence in theistic natural theology, and finally of belief in the uniqueness of human moral consciousness. As was characteristic of the Princeton polemical style he had learned from Charles Hodge, Warfield quoted Darwin, the object of his criticism, at length and wrote with considerable appreciation for certain aspects of his life and work.

Warfield assesses Darwin's spiritual pilgrimage as an unnecessary tragedy. It was a tragedy because of Darwin's gradual loss of confidence in the possibility of Christian truth. It was unnecessary because of Darwin's faulty reasoning about connections between nature and God. In particular, Warfield scored Darwin for picturing divine design as an all-or-nothing situation: God was either absent from nature or active with the kind of single-minded intent displayed by breeders of pigeons or dogs. Against Darwin's view, which Warfield called a "deistic conception," he urged his Christian notion of *concursus* (twice in the essay he uses the word "concause"), an approach that views God as working in, with, and through the natural processes of the physical world. To remedy Darwin's narrow conception of design, Warfield distinguishes between design as willed action toward one specific end and design as a general "contrivance" of the entire physical realm. By featuring the latter over the former, Warfield felt he overcame Darwin's simplistic objections to design in nature.

Beyond its treatment of Darwin's own life, this essay was also significant for outlining Warfield's more general stance on scientific questions. Without going into detail, Warfield maintained that just because Darwin was led by his own theories first away from Christianity and then from natural religion, there was no reason to conclude that theories of evolutionary natural selection had to move others in the same direction. To Warfield, it remained a possibility that Darwin's use of his own theory to overthrow Christianity was "an illogical train of reasoning" and not "inevitable." Rather, Warfield argued that Darwin was led to reject Christianity because he thought his own theory was incompatible with an overly restricted view of natural theology, a view derived from William Paley, and because he interpreted the early chapters of Genesis with an unnecessary literalism. Warfield thus suggested the lines of inquiry he would follow in his own careful consideration of empirical evidence for evolutionary theories and, eventually, his own embrace of certain kinds of evolution.

Warfield concluded this essay by contrasting the spiritually bleak end of Darwin's life with the spiritual serenity marking the death of Charles Hodge, Warfield's theological mentor and predecessor at Princeton Theological Seminary. A minor irony is hidden in that comparison since in the course of his essay Warfield refers often, and with approval, to the way that the American naturalist Asa Gray had interpreted Darwin's natural selection as fully compatible with Christian orthodoxy. The irony is that in *What Is Darwinism?* (1874) Hodge, while open to the development of species over time and even the possibility of natural selection as a means of that development, had stoutly resisted Gray's effort to interpret Darwin's own writings as compatible with teleology.

Since the Second World War, knowledge about Darwin's life and thought has proceeded well beyond the three-volume biography Warfield reviewed. Recent works drawing upon Darwin's notebooks and correspondence suggest, for example, that the death of Darwin's daughter in 1851 (to which Warfield refers in passing) probably had more to do with his alienation from traditional Christianity than did any scientific conclusion.[1] Despite advances in biographical knowledge, however, this early assessment by Warfield remains an unusually significant effort to provide a sympathetic, a Christian, and an intellectually sophisticated interpretation of that unusually significant life.

There was a great deal of discussion in the newspapers, about the time of Mr. Darwin's death, concerning his religious opinions. This discussion was provoked in part by the publication of a letter written by him in 1879 to a Jena student in reply to inquiries as to

1. See especially James R. Moore, "Of Love and Death: Why Darwin 'Gave Up Christianity,'" in Moore, ed., *History, Humanity and Evolution: Essays for John C. Greene* (New York: Cambridge University Press, 1989), 195–229.

his views with reference to a revelation and a future life,[2] and in part by a report published by Drs. Aveling and Büchner of an interview which they had had with him during the last year of his life.[3] Of course the appearance of the elaborate *Life and Letters* by his son has now put an end to all possible doubt as to so simple a matter.[4] Mr. Darwin describes himself as living generally, and more and more as he grew older, in a state of mind which, with much fluctuation of judgment from a cold theism down the scale, never reaching, however, a dogmatic atheism, would be best described as agnosticism.[5] But the *Life and Letters* does far more for us than merely determine this fact. "In the three huge volumes which are put forth to embalm the philosopher's name," as *Blackwood* somewhat flippantly expresses it, "he is observed like one of his own specimens under the microscope, and every peculiarity recorded, for all the world as if a philosopher were as important as a mollusc, though we can scarcely hope that a son of Darwin's would commit himself to such a revolutionary view."[6]

The result of this excessively minute description, and all the more because it is so lacking in proportion and perspective, is that we are put in possession of abundant material for tracing the evolution of his life and opinions with an accuracy and fullness of detail seldom equaled in the literature of biography. For example, although the book was not written in order to depict Mr. Darwin's "inward life," it is quite possible to arrange out of the facts it gives a fairly complete history of his spiritual changes. And this proves

2. First published in the *Deutsche Rundschau,* then in the separate edition of Professor Haeckel's paper "Die Naturanschauung von Darwin, Goethe und Lamarck," 60 n. 17. Afterward also in English journals; see *The Academy* 22 (1882), nos. 545, 546, 547, 548. [Ernst Haeckel (1834–1919) was a leading promoter of Darwin in German-speaking regions. His own views of evolution, ironically, were more Neo-Lamarckian than Darwinian.]

3. *The National Reformer* for October 29, 1882. [Edward Bibbins Aveling (1851–98) and Ludwig Büchner (1824–99) were militant Marxists who claimed that Darwin was a secular prophet and was indirectly promoting the decline of Christianity.]

4. *The Life and Letters of Charles Darwin, Including an Autobiographical Chapter.* Edited by his son, Francis Darwin. In three volumes. London: John Murray, 1888. Revised. All references in the present paper are to this edition. [Francis Darwin (1848–1925), son of Charles Darwin, was an English botanist who investigated plant movement and response to stimuli.]

5. *Life and Letters,* 1:304 (written in 1879).

6. *Blackwood's Edinburgh Magazine* 143 (1888): 105.

unexpectedly interesting. Such men as Bunyan and Augustine and St. Paul himself have opened to us their spiritual growth from darkness into light, and made us familiar with every phase of the struggle by which a spirit moves upward to the hope of glory. Such a writer as Rousseau lifts for us a corner of the veil that hides from view the depths of an essentially evil nature. But we have lacked any complete record of the experiences of an essentially noble soul about which the shades of doubt are slowly gathering. This it is that Mr. Darwin's *Life* gives us.

No one who reads the *Life and Letters* will think of doubting the unusual sweetness of Mr. Darwin's character. In his schooldays he is painted by his fellow students as "cheerful, good-tempered, and communicative."[7] At college, we see him, through his companions' eyes, as "the most genial, warm-hearted, generous, and affectionate of friends," with sympathies alive for "all that was good and true," and "a cordial hatred for everything false, or vile, or cruel, or mean, or dishonorable"—in a word, as one "pre-eminently good, and just, and lovable."[8] A colaborer with him in the high studies of his mature life sums up impressions of his whole character in equally striking words:

> Those who knew Charles Darwin most intimately are unanimous in their appreciation of the unsurpassed nobility and beauty of his *whole* character. In him there was no "other side." Not only was he the Philosopher who has wrought a greater revolution in human thought within a quarter of a century than any man of our time— or perhaps of *any* time— . . . but as a Man he exemplified in his own life that true *religion* which is deeper, wider, and loftier than any Theology. For this not only inspired him with the devotion to Truth which was the master-passion of his great nature, but made him the most admirable husband, brother, and father; the kindest friend, neighbour, and master; the genuine lover, not only of his fellow-man, but of every creature.[9]

7. Rev. John Yardley, in the *Modern Review,* July 1882, p. 504.

8. *Life and Letters,* 1:166.

9. Dr. W. B. Carpenter, in the *Modern Review,* July 1882, pp. 523–24. [William B. Carpenter (1813–85), physician, physiologist, and naturalist, lectured in medicine at the University of London. From a Unitarian theological position he came to accept natural selection as an explanation for what he took to be a divinely ordered creation.]

Mr. Darwin himself doubted whether the religious sentiment was ever strongly developed in him,[10] but this opinion was written in his later years, and the context shows that there is an emphasis upon the word "sentiment." There was, on the other hand, a truly religious coloring thrown over all his earlier years, and the fruits of religion never left his life. But, nevertheless, there gradually faded out from his thought all purely religious concepts, and there gradually died out of his heart all the higher religious sentiments, together with all the accompanying consolations, hopes, and aspirations. On the quiet stage of this amiable life there is played out before our eyes the tragedy of the death of religion out of a human soul. The spectacle is none the less instructive that it is offered in the case of one before whom we gladly doff our hats in true and admiring reverence.

The first clear glimpse which we get of the future philosopher is a very attractive one. As a child he seems to have been sweet-tempered, simple-hearted, conscientious, not without his childish faults, but with a full supply of childish virtues. Here is a pretty picture. Being sent, at about the age of nine years, to Mr. Butler's school, situated about a mile from his home, he often ran home "in the longer intervals between the callings over and before locking up at night. . . . I remember in the early part of my school life," he writes, "that I often had to run very quickly to be in time, and from being a fleet runner was generally successful; but when in doubt I prayed earnestly to God to help me, and I well remember that I attributed my success to the prayers and not to my quick running, and marvelled how generally I was aided."[11]

Thus, heaven lay about Darwin in his infancy. But he does not seem to have been a diligent student, and his school life was not altogether profitable; his subsequent stay at Edinburgh was no more so, and before he reached the age of twenty it seemed clear that his heart was not in the profession of medicine to which he had been destined. In these circumstances, his father, who was a nominal member of the Church of England, took a step which seemed from his point of view, no doubt, quite natural: he pro-

10. *Life and Letters,* 1:311 (1876).
11. *Life and Letters,* 1:31.

posed that his son should become a clergyman.[12] "He was very properly vehement," the son writes, "against my turning into an idle sporting man"—as if this was a sufficient reason for the contemplated step. The son himself was, however, more conscientious. "I asked for some time to consider," he writes, "as from what little I had heard or thought on the subject I had scruples about declaring my belief in all the dogmas of the Church of England, though otherwise I liked the thought of being a country clergyman. Accordingly I read with care 'Pearson on the Creed,'[13] and a few other books on divinity; and as I did not then in the least doubt the strict and literal truth of every word in the Bible,[14] I soon persuaded myself that our Creed must be fully accepted."[15]

This step led to residence at Cambridge, where, however, again the time was mostly wasted. The influences under which he there fell, moreover, were not altogether calculated to quicken his reverence for the high calling to which he had devoted himself. "The way in which the service was conducted in chapel shows that the dean, at least, was not over zealous. I have heard my father tell [it is Mr. Francis Darwin who is writing—BBW] how at evening chapel the dean used to read alternate verses of the Psalms, without making even a pretense of waiting for the congregation to take their share. And when the Lesson was a lengthy one, he would rise and go on with the Canticles after the scholar had read fifteen or twenty verses."[16] Nor were Darwin's associates at Cambridge always all that could be desired: from his passion for sport he "got into a sporting set, including some dissipated low-minded young men" with whom he spent days and evenings of which (he says) he should have felt ashamed.[17]

Fortunately, he had other companions also, of a higher stamp,[18] and among them preeminently Professor Henslow, who

12. Ibid., 1:45.

13. [John Pearson (1613–86) was Anglican lord bishop of Chester and author of the influential *An Exposition of the Creed* (1659).]

14. An interesting indication that in Mr. Darwin's mature judgment the Bible does teach the doctrines of the Creed.

15. *Life and Letters,* 1:45.

16. Ibid., 1:165.

17. Ibid., 1:48.

18. Ibid., 1:49.

united in his own person the widest scientific learning and the deepest piety, and with whom Darwin happily became quite intimate, gaining from him, as he says, "more than I can express."[19] Best of all, Henslow was accustomed to let his light shine, and talked freely "on all subjects, including his deep sense of religion."[20] Accordingly, as we are not surprised to learn, it was with him that Mr. Darwin wished to read divinity.[21]

Not that he was even now ready to enter with spirit upon his preparation for his future work. A touching letter written in 1829 on the occasion of the death of the sister of his friend William Fox shows that Darwin's heart at this time knew something of the consolations of Christianity.[22] "I feel most sincerely and deeply for you," he writes, "and all your family; but at the same time, as far as any one can, by his own good principles and religion, be supported under such a misfortune, you, I am assured, will know where to look for such support. And after so pure and holy a comfort as the Bible affords, I am equally assured how useless the sympathy of all friends must appear, although it be as heartfelt and sincere as I hope you believe me capable of feeling."[23] But he still had conscientious scruples about taking orders. A fellow student writes (1829): "We had an earnest conversation about going into Holy Orders; and I remember his asking me, with reference to the question put by the Bishop in the ordination service, 'Do you trust that you are inwardly moved by the Holy Spirit, etc.,' whether I could answer in the affirmative, and on my saying I could not, he said, 'Neither can I, and therefore I cannot take Orders.'"[24]

Certainly the lines of Darwin's intellectual interest were cast elsewhere. Only under the pressure of his approaching examinations was he led to anything like professional study. On such

19. Ibid., 1:188 [John Stevens Henslow (1795–1861) was an English botanist and Anglican clergyman who at Cambridge taught students to be diligent in research and respectful of God as the author of nature.]

20. Ibid., 1:188.

21. Ibid., 1:171.

22. [William Darwin Fox was a cousin with whom Darwin maintained a regular correspondence on matters religious and scientific for many years. He introduced Darwin to entomology at Cambridge.]

23. *Life and Letters,* 1:177–78.

24. Ibid., 1:171.

occasions, however, he showed that his mind was open to impression:

> In order to pass the B.A. examination, it was also necessary to get up Paley's *Evidences of Christianity* and his *Moral Philosophy.*[25] This was done in a thorough manner, and I am convinced that I could have written out the whole of the *Evidences* with perfect correctness, but not of course in the clear language of Paley. The logic of this book and, as I may add, of his *Natural Theology* gave me as much delight as did Euclid. The careful study of these works, without attempting to learn any part by rote, was the only part of the academical course which, as I then felt and as I still believe, was of the least use to me in the education of my mind. I did not at that time trouble myself about Paley's premises; and taking these on trust, I was charmed and convinced by the long line of argumentation.[26]

Despite such occasional pleasure in his work, when the offer of a place in the *Beagle* expedition came,[27] and his father objected to his interrupting his clerical studies, Josiah Wedgwood[28] was able to argue: "If I saw Charles now absorbed in professional

25. [William Paley (1734–1805) was an English theologian and moral philosopher. His *Natural Theology, or Evidences of the Existence and Attributes of the Deity* (1802) established a benchmark for later natural theology. It was especially renowned for arguing that humans can clearly and unambiguously discern the conscious activity of God in the visible workings of nature. In his famous analogy, Paley suggested that if a traveler found a watch on a barren heath, the traveler would quite naturally assume the existence of a watchmaker. So also with the universe, which Paley thought was much more obviously constructed than a watch. Paley's kind of self-confident, everything-in-its-place natural theology was what Darwin eventually rejected. Whether a more subtle natural theology, where more attention was paid to human limitations in understanding God's ways in nature, would have cushioned Darwin's reaction against Paleyite Christianity is one of the great imponderables of nineteenth-century intellectual history.]

26. *Life and Letters,* 1:47.

27. [Darwin went as a companion to Captain Fitzroy on the *Beagle's* survey of the South American coasts and islands, including the Galapagos, from December 1831 to October 1836. The observations that he made on this expedition were a significant factor in the development of his evolutionary theory of natural selection.]

28. [Josiah Wedgwood (1769–1843), Darwin's uncle, continued to operate the renowned pottery works that his father had founded at Etruria. Wedgwood's sister Susannah was Darwin's mother.]

studies, I should probably think it would not be advisable to interrupt them; but this is not, and, I think, will not be the case with him. His present pursuit of knowledge is in the same track as he would have to follow in the expedition."[29] By this representation his father's consent was obtained, although, with that long-sighted wisdom which his son always regarded as his distinguishing characteristic, he "considered it as again changing his profession."[30]

And so, indeed, it proved. Mr. Darwin's estimate of the sacredness of a clergyman's office improved somewhat above what it was when, if only he could sign the Creed, he was ready to undertake the office because the life of a country clergyman offered advantages in a sporting way.[31] He writes in 1835 to his friend Fox, almost sadly: "I dare hardly look forward to the future, for I do not know what will become of me. Your situation is above envy: I do not venture even to frame such happy visions. To a person fit to take the office, the life of a clergyman is a type of all that is respectable and happy."[32] But though, perhaps because, his feeling toward the clerical office had grown to be so high, he no longer thought of entering it. He writes in his autobiography that this intention was never "formally given up, but died a natural death when, on leaving Cambridge, I joined the *Beagle* as naturalist."[33]

The 1835 letter to Fox is a sufficient indication that it was not Darwin's Christian faith, but only his intention of taking orders that was dying out during the course of his five years' cruise. Other like indications are not lacking.[34] We are, therefore, not surprised to read: "Whilst on board the *Beagle* I was quite orthodox, and I remember being heartily laughed at by some of the officers (though themselves orthodox) for quoting the Bible as an unanswerable authority on some point of morality."[35] Nevertheless, his defection from Christianity was during these years si-

29. *Life and Letters,* 1:199.
30. Ibid., 1:197.
31. Ibid., 1:45.
32. Ibid., 1:262.
33. Ibid., 1:45.
34. See his words of appreciation of missionary work, ibid., 1:264; see also 1:246.
35. Ibid., 1:307–8.

lently proceeding through the ever increasing completeness of his absorption in scientific pursuits, which left little time for or interest in other things.

And on his return to England, the working up of the immense mass of material which he had collected during his voyage claimed his attention even more exclusively than its collection had done. Thus he was given occasion to occupy himself so wholly with science that there was not only no time left to think of his former intention of entering the ministry, but there was also little time left to remember that there was a soul within him or a future life beyond the grave. Readers of the sad account which Mr. Darwin appended at the very end of his life (1881) to his autobiographical notes, of how at about the age of thirty or thereabouts his higher aesthetic tastes began to show atrophy, so that he lost his love for poetry, art, and music, and his mind more and more began to take upon itself the character of a kind of machine for grinding general laws out of large collections of facts,[36] will not be able to resist the suspicion that this exclusive direction to one type of thinking was really, as he himself believed, injurious to his intellect as well as enfeebling to his emotional nature, and lay at the root of his subsequent drift away from religion.

It was an ominous conjunction that, simultaneously with the early progress of this "curious and lamentable loss of the higher aesthetic tastes," another influence that was destined most seriously to modify his thought on divine things was entering his mind. "In July [1837]," he tells us, "I opened my first note-book for facts in relation to the Origin of Species, about which I had long reflected."[37] The change that was passing over his views as to the manner in which species originate is illustrated by the fact that a passage from his manuscript journal (1834) that freely speaks of "creation" was omitted from the printed journal, the proofs of which were completed in 1837. This omission "harmonizes with the change we know to have been proceeding in his views."[38]

We raise no questions as to the compatibility of the Darwinian form of the hypothesis of evolution with Christianity; Mr. Dar-

36. Ibid., 1:100ff.
37. Ibid., 1:68.
38. Ibid., 2:1.

win himself says that "science" (and in speaking of "science" he has "evolution" in mind) "has nothing to do with Christ, except in so far as the habit of scientific research makes a man cautious in admitting evidence."[39] But if we confine ourselves to Mr. Darwin's own personal religious history, it is very clear that, whether on account of a peculiarity of constitution or by an illogical train of reasoning or otherwise, as he wrought out his theory of evolution, he gave up his Christian faith—nay, his doctrine of evolution directly expelled his Christian belief.

How it operated in so doing is not difficult dimly to trace. Darwin was thoroughly persuaded (like Mr. Huxley)[40] that, in its plain meaning, Genesis teaches creation by immediate, separate, and sudden fiats of God for each distinct species. And as he more and more convinced himself that species, on the contrary, originated according to natural law and through a long course of gradual modification, he felt ever more and more that Genesis "must go." But Genesis is an integral part of the Old Testament, and with the truth and authority of the Old Testament the truth and authority of Christianity itself is inseparably bound up. Thus the doctrine of evolution, once heartily adopted, gradually undermined his faith, until he cast off the whole of Christianity as an unproved delusion.

The process was neither rapid nor unopposed. Darwin speaks of his unwillingness to give up his belief and of the slow rate at which unbelief crept over him, although it became at last complete.[41] Drs. Büchner and Aveling report him as assigning the age of forty years (1849) as the date of the completion of the process.[42] Of course, to strengthen him in his new position, other arguments came gradually to the support of the original disturbing cause, until his former acceptance of Christianity became almost incredible to him. His autobiography gives a deeply interesting account of the whole process. "During these two years," he says—meaning the years when his theory of evolution was taking shape in his mind—"I was led to think much about religion. . . . I had gradually come by this time, i.e., 1836 to 1839,

39. Ibid., 1:307.
40. Ibid., 2:181.
41. Ibid., 1:308–9.
42. *National Reformer* 40 (1882): 292.

to see that the Old Testament was no more to be trusted than the sacred books of the Hindoos. The question then continually rose before my mind and would not be banished—is it credible that if God were now to make a revelation to the Hindoos, he would permit it to be connected with the belief in Vishnu, Siva, etc., as Christianity is connected with the Old Testament? This appeared to me to be utterly incredible."[43]

Here is the root of the whole matter. Darwin's doctrine of evolution had antiquated for him the Old Testament record, and Christianity is too intimately connected with the Old Testament to stand as divine if the Old Testament be fabulous. Certainly, if the premises are sound, the conclusion is inevitable. But both conclusion and premises must shatter themselves against the fact of the supernatural origin of Christianity. Once Darwin reached the conclusion, however, bolstering arguments, pressing directly against Christianity, did not fail to make their appearance: the difficulty of proving miracles, their antecedent incredibility, the credulity of the age in which they are declared to have been wrought, the unhistorical character of the Gospels, their discrepancies, man's proneness to religious enthusiasm[44]—arguments, all of them, drawn from a sphere in which Mr. Darwin was not a master, and all of them, in reality, afterthoughts called in to support the doubts which were already dominating him.

How impervious to evidence he at last became is naively illustrated by the words with which he closes his account of how he lost his faith. He says he feels sure that he gave up his belief unwillingly: "For I can well remember often and often inventing day-dreams of old letters between distinguished Romans, and manuscripts being discovered at Pompeii or elsewhere, which confirmed in the most striking manner all that was written in the Gospels. But I found it more and more difficult, with free scope given to my imagination, to invent evidence which would suffice to convince me."[45] When a man has reached a stage in which no conceivable historical evidence can convince him of the actual oc-

currence of a historical fact, we may cease to wonder that the almost inconceivable richness of the actual historical evidence of
Christianity is insufficient to retain his conviction. He ceases to be
a judge of the value of evidence. That he has resisted it, however,
is no proof that it is resistible; it is only an evidence of such indu-
ration [i.e., hardening] of his believing tissue that it is no longer
capable of responding to the strongest reagents.

Here, then, approximately at the age of forty, is the end of one
great stage of Mr. Darwin's spiritual development. He was no
longer a Christian; he no longer believed in a revelation. We see the
effect in the changed tone of his speech. According to Mr. J. Brodie
Innes,[46] Darwin claimed that he did not attack Moses, and that he
could not remember that he had ever published a word directly[47]
against religion or the clergy.[48] But in his private letters of this later
period he certainly speaks with scant respect for Genesis[49] and the
clergy,[50] if not also for religion,[51] and he even gradually grew somewhat irreverent in his use of the name of God.

We see the effect still more sadly in Darwin's loss of the consolations of religion. It is painful to compare his touching, if somewhat formal and shallow, letter of condolence to his friend Fox,
which was written in 1829 and which we have already quoted,
with the hopeless grief of later letters. When in 1851 Darwin lost
his beloved daughter, his "only consolation" was "that she passed
a short, though joyous life."[52] When Fox lost a child in 1853, Darwin's only appeal was to the softening influence of the passage of
time. "As you must know," he wrote, "from your own most painful
experience, time softens and deadens, in a manner truly wonderful,
one's feelings and regrets. At first it is indeed bitter. I can only hope
that your health and that of poor Mrs. Fox may be preserved, and

46. [J. Brodie Innes, a friend of Darwin and an Anglican minister, became
vicar of Darwin's parish (Down) in 1846. Believing that science "should be pursued without reference to the Bible" because nature and Scripture both come
from God, he maintained cordial relations with Darwin. The two of them rarely
agreed on religious matters, but nevertheless remained close friends.]
47. Note the word "directly."
48. *Life and Letters,* 2:288–89.
49. Ibid., 2:152.
50. Ibid., 1:340.
51. Ibid., 2:143.
52. Ibid., 1:380.

that time may do its work softly, and bring you all together, once again, as the happy family which, as I can well believe, you so lately formed."[53] What a contrast with "the pure and holy comfort afforded by the Bible"! Already he was learning the grief of those who "sorrow as the rest who have no hope." Whether his habitual neglect of the Sunday rest and of the ordinances of religion was another effect of the same change it is impossible to say, given our ignorance of his habits previous to the loss of his Christian faith. But throughout the whole period of his life at Down, we are told, "week-days and Sundays passed by alike, each with their stated intervals of work and rest," while his visits to the church were confined to a few rare occasions of weddings and funerals.[54]

But the loss of Christianity did not necessarily mean the loss of religion. As a matter of fact, in yielding up revelation Mr. Darwin retained a strong hold upon natural religion. There were yet God, the soul, the future life. The theory which he had elaborated as a sufficient account of the differences that exist between the several kinds of organic beings, including man, was, however, destined to work havoc in his mind with even the simplest tenets of natural religion. Again we raise no question as to whether this drift was inevitable; it is enough for our present purpose that in Mr. Darwin's case it was actual.[55] To understand how this was so,

53. Ibid., 1:388; see 3:39 n. ‡, written in 1863.

54. Ibid., 1:127–28.

55. In the case of many others it has not proved inevitable, as, e.g., in the case of Dr. W. B. Carpenter, whose opinion is worth quoting here, because his general conception of the relation of God to the universe seems to be very similar to what Mr. Darwin's originally was. "To myself," he writes, in an interesting paper on "The Doctrine of Evolution in Its Relations to Theism" (*Modern Review,* October 1882, p. 685), "the conception of a continuity of action which required no departure to meet special contingencies, because the plan was all-perfect in the beginning, is a far higher and nobler one than that of a succession of interruptions. . . . And in describing the process of evolution in the ordinary language of Science as due to 'secondary causes,' we no more dispense with a First Cause than we do when we speak of those Physical Forces which, from the Theistic point of view, are so many diverse modes of manifestation of one and the same Power. Nor do we in the least set aside the idea of an original Design when we regard these adaptations which are commonly attributed to special exertions of contriving power and wisdom, as the outcome of an all-comprehensive Intelligence which foresaw that the product would be 'good,' before calling into existence the germ from which it would be evolved."

it is necessary for us to remember only that he had laid hold upon natural selection as the *vera causa* and sufficient account of all organic forms. His basic premises were that every form may vary indefinitely in all directions, and that every variation which is a gain to the form in adaptation to its surroundings is necessarily preserved by that very fact through the simple reaction of the surroundings upon the struggle for existence. Any divine guidance of the direction of the variation seemed to him as much opposed to the one premise of the theory as any divine interference with the working of natural selection seemed to be opposed to the other premise, and he included all organic phenomena, mental and moral as well as physical, in the scope of this natural process. Thus to him God became an increasingly unnecessary and therefore an increasingly incredible hypothecation.

The seriousness of this drift of thought makes it worthwhile to illustrate it somewhat in detail. During the whole time occupied in collecting material for and in writing the *Origin of Species* Mr. Darwin was a theist,[56] or, as he expressed it on one occasion: "Many years ago, when I was collecting facts for the 'Origin,' my belief in what is called a personal God was as firm as that of Dr. Pusey himself."[57] The rate at which this firm belief passed away was slow enough for the process to occupy several years. He tells us that his thought on such subjects was never profound or long-continued.[58] This was certainly not the fault, however, of his friends, for from the first publication of his development hypothesis they plied him with problems that forced him to face the great questions of the relation of his views to belief in God and his modes of activity.

We get the first glimpse of this in Darwin's correspondence with Sir Charles Lyell.[59] That great geologist had suggested that

56. *Life and Letters,* 1:313.
57. Ibid., 3:236 (1878). [Edward Bouverie Pusey (1800–1882), theologian and professor at Oxford, was the best-known leader of the High Church, Tractarian, traditionalist party in the Church of England.]
58. See, e.g., ibid., 1:305–6 (1871).
59. [Charles Lyell (1797–1875) was an eminent geologist who believed that geological change took place at a uniform rate in time. In the last edition of his *Principles of Geology,* under the personal as well as professional influence of Darwin, Lyell accepted a modified version of the transmutation of species.]

we must "assume a primeval creative power" acting throughout the whole course of development, though not uniformly, if we are to account for the supervening, say, of man at the end of the series. To this Mr. Darwin replied with a decided negative:

> We must, under present knowledge, assume the creation of one or of a few forms in the same manner as philosophers assume the existence of a power of attraction without any explanation. But I entirely reject, as in my judgment quite unnecessary, any subsequent addition "of new powers and attributes and forces," or of any "principle of improvement," except in so far as every character which is naturally selected or preserved is in some way an advantage or improvement; otherwise it would not have been selected. If I were convinced that I required such additions to the theory of natural selection, I would reject it as rubbish. . . . If I understand you, the turning point in our difference must be that you think it impossible that the intellectual powers of a species should be much improved by the continued natural selection of the most intellectual individuals. To show how minds graduate, just reflect how impossible everyone has yet found it to define the difference in mind of man and the lower animals; the latter seem to have the very same attributes in a much lower stage of perfection than the lowest savage. I would give absolutely nothing for the theory of Natural Selection if it requires miraculous additions at any one stage of descent. I think Embryology, Homology [i.e., study of the likenesses between different organisms thought to derive from the same evolutionary ancestor], Classification, etc., show us that all vertebrata have descended from one parent; how that parent appeared we know not. If you admit in ever so little a degree the explanation which I have given of Embryology, Homology and Classification, you will find it difficult to say, "Thus far the explanation holds good, but no further; here we must call in 'the addition of new creative forces.'"[60]

A few days later he wrote again: "I have reflected a good deal on what you say on the necessity of continued intervention of creative power. I cannot see this necessity; and its admission, I think, would make the theory of Natural Selection valueless. Grant a simple Archetypal creature, like the Mudfish or Lepidosi-

60. *Life and Letters,* 2:210–11 (written Oct. 11, 1859).

ren,[61] with the five senses and some vestige of mind, and I believe
natural selection will account for the production of every vertebrate animal."[62]

Let us weigh well the meaning of Mr. Darwin's strong assertions of the competency of natural selection to "account" for every distinguishing characteristic of living forms. It meant to him,
first, the assimilation of the human mind, in its essence, with the
intelligence of the brutes; and this meant the elimination of what
we ordinarily mean by "the soul." He needed to have given only
"the five senses and some vestige of mind" such as exists, for instance, in the mudfish to enable him by natural selection alone,
with the exclusion of all "new powers and attributes and forces,"
to account for the mental power of Newton, the high imaginings
of Milton, the devout aspirations of a Bernard [of Clairvaux].
How early he consciously formulated the extreme form of this
conclusion it is difficult to say, but we find him in 1871 thanking
Mr. Tylor[63] for giving him new standing ground for it: "It is wonderful how you trace animism from the lower races up to the religious belief of the highest races. In the future it will make me
look at religion—a belief in the soul, etc.—from a new point of
view."[64] Accordingly, the new view was incorporated into the
Descent of Man, published that same year.[65] Dr. Robert Lewins[66]
seems quite accurately to sum up the ultimate opinion which
Darwin attained on this subject:

> Before concluding I may, without violation of any confidence,
> mention that, both *viva voce* and in writing, Mr. Darwin was much
> less reticent to myself than in this letter to Jena. For, in an answer

61. [The *Lepidosiren,* or Brazilian mudfish, is a genus of eel-shaped fishes inhabiting the swamps of the Amazon and La Plata Rivers. It was of particular interest because it has a lung or air bladder, representing a possible intermediate
evolutionary development.]

62. *Life and Letters,* 2:174.

63. [Sir Edward Burnett Tylor (1832–1917), English anthropologist, attempted
to apply evolutionary theory to all human activities and became the first professor
of anthropology at Oxford.]

64. *Life and Letters,* 3:151.

65. *The Descent of Man,* 1:62ff.

66. [Robert Lewins was the author of *Life and Mind, on the Basis of Materialism*
(1873) and *Autocentricism; or, The Brain Theory of Life and Mind* (1888).]

to the direct question I felt myself justified, some years since, in addressing to that immortal expert in Biology, as to the bearing of his researches on the existence of an *"Anima,"* or "Soul" in Man, he distinctly stated that, in his opinion, a vital or "spiritual" principle, apart from inherent somatic energy, had no more *locus standi* [standing] in the human than in the other races of the Animal Kingdom—a conclusion that seems a mere corollary of, or indeed a position tantamount with, his essential doctrine of human and bestial identity of Nature and genesis.[67]

It was but a corollary to loss of belief in a soul, secondly, to lose belief also in immortality. If we are one with the brutes in origin, why not also in destiny? Mr. Darwin thought it "base" in his opponents to "drag in immortality" in objection to his theories,[68] but in his own mind he was allowing his theories to push immortality out. His final position as to the future of man he gives in an interesting passage in the autobiographical notes written in 1876. He speaks there of immortality as a "strong and almost instinctive belief," but also of the "intolerableness" of the thought that the more perfect race of the future years shall be annihilated by the gradual cooling of the sun, pathetically adding: "To those who fully admit the immortality of the human soul, the destruction of our world will not appear so dreadful."[69] Accordingly, when writing to the Jena student in 1879, after saying that he did not believe that "there ever had been any revelation," he adds: "As for a future life, every man must judge for himself between conflicting vague probabilities."[70]

Thirdly, his settled conviction of the sufficiency of natural selection to account for all differentiations in organic forms deeply affected Mr. Darwin's idea of God and of his relation to the world. Darwin's notion at this time (1859), while theistic, appears to have been somewhat crassly deistic. He seems never to have been able fully to grasp the conception of divine immanence, but from the opening of his first notebook on species[71] to the end of

67. *Journal of Science* 19 (1882): 751–52.
68. *Life and Letters,* 2:228.
69. Ibid., 1:312.
70. Ibid., 1:307.
71. Ibid., 2:9 (1837).

his days he gives ever repeated reason to the reader to fear that the sole conceptions of God in his relation to the universe which were possible were that God either should do all things without second causes, or, having ordained second causes, should sit outside and beyond them and leave them to do all things without him. Beginning with this deistic conception, which pushed God out of his works, it is perhaps not strange that Darwin could never be sure that he saw God in his works; and when he could trace effects to a "natural cause" or group a body of phenomena under a "natural law," this seemed to him equivalent to disproving the connection of God with them.[72] The result was that the theistic proofs gradually grew more and more meaningless to him, until, at last, no one of them carried conviction to his mind.

Sir Charles Lyell was not left alone in his efforts to clarify Mr. Darwin's thinking on such subjects; soon Dr. Asa Gray took his place by Lyell's side and became at once the chief force in the en-

72. We have seen that Dr. W. B. Carpenter [note 55] refuses to be held in Mr. Darwin's logic, although with him holding to a somewhat deistic conception of the divine relation to the process of development. "Attach what weight we may to the *physical* causes which have brought about this Evolution," he insists, "I cannot see how it is possible to conceive of any but a Moral Cause for the endowments that made the primordial germ susceptible of their action" ("Doctrine of Evolution," 680). "And in the so-called *laws* of Organic Evolution, I see nothing but the orderly and continuous working-out of the original intelligent Design" (p. 681). Dr. W. H. Dallinger also begins with a similar conception (comparing God's relation to the universe to the relation to his work of a machinist who constructs a calculating machine to throw numbers of one order for a given time and then introduce suddenly a new series "by prevised and preordained arrangement"), and yet refuses the conclusion. "Evolution," he argues, "like gravitation, is only a method; and the self-adjustments demonstrated in the 'origin of species' only make it, to reason, the clearer, that variation and survival is a method that took its origin in mind. It is true that the egg of a moth, and the eye of a dog-fish, and the forearm of a tiger *must* be what they are to accomplish the end of their being. But that only shows, as we shade our mental eyes, and gaze back to the beginning, the magnificence of the design that was *in*volved in nature's beginning, so as to be *e*volved by the designed rhythm of nature's methods." See the whole passage in his eloquent Fernley Lecture for 1887: *The Creator, and What We May Know of the Method of Creation* (London: T. Woolmer, 1887), 61–62. [W. H. Dallinger (1842–1909), British Methodist and microscopist, studied one-celled organisms and the formation of heat-resistant spores. See pp. 112–13 for Warfield's review.]

deavor.[73] Nevertheless, Mr. Darwin outlines already in a letter to
Lyell in 1860[74] the arguments by which he stood unto the end:

I must say one more word about our quasi-theological controversy
about natural selection. . . . Do you consider that the successive
variations in the size of the crop of the pouter pigeon,[75] which
man has accumulated to please his caprice, have been due to "the
creative and sustaining powers of Brahma"? In the sense that an
omnipotent and omniscient Deity must order and know everything, this must be admitted; yet, in honest truth, I can hardly admit it. It seems preposterous that a maker of a universe should care
about the crop of a pigeon solely[76] to please man's silly fancies. But
if you agree with me in thinking such an interposition of the Deity
uncalled for, I can see no reason whatever for believing in such interpositions in the case of natural beings where strange and admirable peculiarities have been naturally selected for the creature's
own benefit. Imagine a pouter in a state of nature wading into the
water, and then, being buoyed up by its inflated crop, sailing about
in search of food. What admiration this would have excited—adaptation to the laws of hydrostatic pressure, etc. For the life of me
I cannot see any difficulty in natural selection producing the most
exquisite structure, *if such structure can be arrived at by gradation,* and
I know from experience how hard it is to name any structure towards which at least some gradations are not known. . . . P.S. The
conclusion at which I have come, as I have told Asa Gray, is that

73. [Asa Gray (1810–88), America's leading botanist of the nineteenth century
and a longtime professor at Harvard, was among Darwin's earliest and most per-
ceptive advocates in America. He was also a trinitarian Congregationalist of traditional theological views who felt that Darwin's conclusions could fit into a teleological picture of the universe. On differences between Gray and Charles Hodge
as to whether Darwin's theories could be compatible with traditional trinitarian
Christianity, see Charles Hodge, *What Is Darwinism? And Other Writings on Science
and Religion* (Grand Rapids: Baker, 1994), 159–69.]
    74. *Life and Letters,* 2:303–4.
    75. [The pouter is a domestic pigeon with an erect body and dilatable crop
that was intentionally bred for size. Darwin divided doves, or pigeons, into four
groups, one being the pouters.]
    76. How much of the argument depends on this word! [Warfield here draws
attention to the fact that Darwin's notion of design follows William Paley's perfect "adaptionism" in supposing that every aspect of nature is not only designed
by God, but also designed in such a way that its benefit for humans is entirely
clear in every respect.]

such a question, as is touched on in this note, is beyond the human intellect, like "predestination and free will," or the "origin of evil."

There is much confused thought in this letter, but it concerns us now only to note that Mr. Darwin's difficulty arises on the one side from his inability to conceive of God as immanent in the universe and his consequent total misapprehension of the nature of divine providence, and on the other from a very crude notion of final cause which posits a single extrinsic end as the sole purpose of the Creator. No one would hold to a doctrine of divine "interpositions" such as appears to him here as the only alternative to divine absence. And no one would hold to a teleology of the raw sort which he here has in mind—a teleology which finds the end for which a thing exists in the misuse or abuse of it by an outside selecting agent.

Mr. Darwin himself felt a natural mental inability for dealing with such themes, and accordingly wavered long as to the attitude he ought to assume toward the evidences of God's hand in nature. Thus he wrote in May 1860 to Dr. Gray:

> With respect to the theological view of the question. This is always painful to me. I am bewildered. I had no intention to write atheistically. But I own that I cannot see as plainly as others do, and as I should wish to do, evidence of design and beneficence on all sides of us.[77] There seems to me too much misery in the world. I cannot persuade myself that a beneficent and omnipotent God would have designedly created the Ichneumonidae[78] with the express intention of their feeding within the living bodies of caterpillars, or that a cat should play with mice. Not believing this, I see no necessity in the belief that the eye was expressly designed. On the other hand, I cannot anyhow be contented to view this wonderful universe, and especially the nature of man, and to conclude

77. [Darwin's stress on his inability to see the "beneficence" of design is a response to Paley, who held that God oversees all nature in such manner as to promote human happiness. Darwin's awareness of misery in the world actually opened him to a more Christian notion of divine providence, in which the cross of Christ played a much more important part than it ever did for Paley, but this was an opening that Darwin did not enter. Warfield soon will turn to address Darwin's restricted sense of "beneficence."]

78. [Ichneumonidae are a family of insects whose larvae are usually internal parasites of other insect larvae, especially of caterpillars.]

that everything is the result of brute force. I am inclined to look at everything as resulting from designed laws, with the details, whether good or bad, left to the working out of what we may call chance. Not that this notion *at all* satisfies me. I feel most deeply that the whole subject is too profound for the human intellect. A dog might as well speculate on the mind of Newton. Let each man hope and believe what he can. Certainly I agree with you that my views are not at all necessarily atheistical. The lightning kills a man, whether a good one or bad one, owing to the excessively complex action of natural laws. A child (who may turn out an idiot) is born by the action of even more complex laws, and I can see no reason why a man, or other animal, may not have been aboriginally produced by other laws, and that all these laws may have been expressly designed by an omniscient Creator, who foresaw every future event and consequence. But the more I think, the more bewildered I become, as indeed I have probably shown by this letter.[79]

The reasoning of this extract, which supposes that the fact that a result is secured by appropriate conditions furnishes ground for regarding it as undesigned, is less suitable to a grave thinker than to a redoubtable champion like Mr. Allan Quatermain, who actually makes use of it.[80] "At last he was dragged forth uninjured, though in a very pious and prayerful frame of mind," he is made to say of a negro whom he had saved by killing an attacking buffalo; "his 'spirit had certainly looked that way,' he said, "or he would now have been dead. As I never like to interfere with true piety, I did not venture to suggest that his spirit had deigned to make use of my eight-bore [rifle] in his interest."[81]

Dr. Gray appears to have rallied Darwin in his notion of an omniscient and omnipotent Creator, foreseeing all future events and consequences, and yet not responsible for the results of the laws which he ordains. At all events, Mr. Darwin writes him again in July of the same year:

79. *Life and Letters,* 2:311–12.
80. [Allan Quatermain was a fictional character developed by H. Rider Haggard in *King Solomon's Mines* and other stories.]
81. Dr. Flint seriously refutes this strange reasoning, which he justly speaks of as "irrational" and explicable in "sane minds" only from the exigencies of foregone conclusions; see his "Theism," lecture 6, 3d ed., pp. 189–90.

One word more on "designed laws" and "undesigned results." I see
a bird which I want for food, take my gun and kill it—I do this *designedly*. An innocent and good man stands under a tree and is
killed by a flash of lightning. Do you believe (and I really should
like to hear) that God *designedly* killed this man? Many or most
people do believe this; I can't and don't. If you believe so, do you
believe that when a swallow snaps up a gnat God designed that
that particular swallow should snap up that particular gnat at that
particular instant? I believe that the man and the gnat are in the
same predicament. If the death of neither man nor gnat is designed, I see no good reason to believe that their *first* birth or production should be necessarily designed.[82]

We read such words with almost as much bewilderment as
Mr. Darwin says he wrote them. It is almost incredible that he
should have so inextricably confused the two senses of the word
"design"—so as to confound the question of intentional action
with that of the evidences of contrivance, the question of the existence of a general plan in God's mind, in accordance with which
all things come to pass, with that of the existence of marks of his
hand in creation arising from intelligent adaptation of means to
ends. It is equally incredible that he should present the case of a
particular swallow snapping up a particular gnat at a particular
time as (to use his own words) "a poser," when he could scarcely
have already forgotten that all Christians have long since learned
to understand that the care of God extends as easily to the infinitely little as to the infinitely great, that the very hairs of our
head are numbered, and not one sparrow falls to the ground
unnoted by our heavenly Father. Yet this seems to him so self-
evidently unbelievable that he rests his case against God's direction of the line of development—for this is really what he is arguing against here—on its obvious incredibility.

Darwin found it impossible to shake himself free from his confusion. In November of the same year he wrote again to Dr. Gray:

I grieve to say that I cannot honestly go as far as you do about design. I am conscious that I am in an utterly hopeless muddle. I cannot think that the world, as we see it, is the result of chance; and

82. *Life and Letters,* 1:314–15.

yet I cannot look at each separate thing as the result of design. To take a crucial example, you lead me to infer . . . that you believe "that variation has been led along certain beneficent lines." I cannot believe this, and I think you would have to believe that the tail of the fantail was led to vary in the number and direction of its feathers in order to gratify the caprice of a few men. Yet if the fantail had been a wild bird, and had used its abnormal tail for some special end, as to sail before the wind, unlike other birds, everyone would have said, "What a beautiful and designed adaptation." Again, I say I am, and shall ever remain, in a hopeless muddle.[83]

The reader is apt to ask in wonder if we would not be right in thinking the fantail's tail a "beautiful and designed adaptation" under the circumstances supposed. Mr. Darwin actually falls here into incredible confusion: as an argument against the designed usefulness of the laws of nature in fitting animals to their environment, he adduces a perversion of those laws by which man makes an animal unfit for its environment. We might as well argue that Jael's nail was not designedly made because it was capable of being adapted to so fearful a use, or that the stylets of Caesar's assassins could not have been manufactured with a useful intention.

Nevertheless, in June 1861 Mr. Darwin writes again to Dr. Gray: "I have been led to think more on this subject of late, and grieve to say that I come to differ more from you. It is not that designed variation makes, as it seems to me, my deity of 'Natural Selection' superfluous; rather, from studying, lately, domestic variation, I have come to see what an enormous field of undesigned variability there is ready for natural selection to appropriate for any purpose useful to each creature."[84]

And a month later he writes to Miss Julia Wedgwood:[85]

Owing to several correspondents I have been led lately to think, or rather to try to think over some of the chief points discussed by you. But the result has been with me a maze—something like thinking on the origin of evil, to which you allude. The mind re-

83. Ibid., 2:353–54.
84. Ibid., 2:373.
85. [Julia Wedgwood was Charles Darwin's cousin. She authored a work on John Wesley and the evangelical revivals.]

fuses to look at this universe, being what it is, without having been designed; yet, where one would most expect design, viz. in the structure of a sentient being, the more I think on the subject, the less I can see proof of design. Asa Gray and some others look at each variation, or at least at each beneficial variation (which A. Gray would compare with the raindrops which do not fall on the sea, but on the land to fertilize it)[86] as having been providentially designed. Yet when I ask him whether he looks at each variation of the rock pigeon, by which man has made by accumulation a pouter or fantail pigeon, as providentially designed for man's amusement, he does not know what to answer; and if he, or anyone, admits [that] these variations are accidental as far as purpose is concerned (of course not accidental as to their cause or origin), then I can see no reason why he should rank as providentially designed the accumulated variations by which the beautifully adapted woodpecker has been formed. For it would be easy to imagine the large crop of the pouter, or tail of the fantail, as of some use to birds, in a state of nature, having peculiar habits of life. These are the considerations which perplex me about design; but whether you will care to hear them, I know not.[87]

The most careless reader of this letter cannot fail renewedly to feel that while what was on trial in Mr. Darwin's thought was not the argument "from design" so much as general providence, yet he falls here again into the confusion of confining to the most proximate result his view of God's possible purpose in directing any course of events, as if the most proximate result were the indications of design in a given organism which he was investigating. If, however, we are inquiring into the existence of a general and all-comprehending plan in God's mind, for the working out of which he directs and governs all things, the ever recurring ar-

86. Mr. Francis Darwin indicates in a note that Dr. Gray's metaphor occurs in the essay "Darwin and his Reviewers" (*Darwiniana,* 157): "The whole animate life of a country depends absolutely upon the vegetation, the vegetation upon the rain. The moisture is furnished by the ocean, is raised by the sun's heat from the ocean's surface, and is wafted inland by the winds. But what multitudes of raindrops fall back into the ocean—they are as much without a final cause as the incipient varieties which come to nothing! Does it therefore follow that the rains which are bestowed upon the soil with such rule and average regularity were not designed to support vegetable and animal life?"

87. *Life and Letters,* 1:313–14.

gument from the pouter and fantail pigeons is irrelevant, proceeding as it does on the unexpressed premise that God's direction of their variations can be vindicated only if these variations can be shown to be beneficial to the pigeons themselves and that in a state of nature. It is apparently an unthought thought with Mr. Darwin that the abundance of variations capable of misdirection on man's part for his pleasure or profit, while of absolutely no use to the bird in a state of nature, and liable to abuse for the bird and for man in the artificial state of domestication, may yet be a link in a great chain which in all its links is preordained for good ends—whether morally, mentally, or even physically, whether in this world or in the next. This narrowness of view, which confined his outlook to the immediate proximate result, played so into the hands of his confusion of thought about the word "design" as from the outset fatally to handicap his progress to a reasoned conclusion.

The history of Darwin's yielding up Christianity because, as he said, "it is not supported by evidence"[88]—that is, because its appropriate evidence, being historical, is of a kind which lay outside of his knowledge or powers of estimation—was therefore paralleled by his gradual yielding up of his reasoned belief in God because all the evidences of his activities are not capable of being looked at in the process of a dissection under the simple microscope. We have seen Darwin at last reaching a position in which no evidence which he could even imagine would suffice to prove the historical truth of Christianity to him. He was fast drifting into a similar position about design. He writes to Dr. Gray, apparently in September 1861: "Your question what would convince me of design is a poser. If I saw an angel come down to teach us good, and I was convinced from others seeing him that I was not mad, I should believe in design. If I could be convinced thoroughly that life and mind was in an unknown way a function of other imponderable force, I should be convinced. If man was made of brass or iron and no way connected with any other organism which had ever lived, I should perhaps be convinced. But this is childish writing."[89]

88. *National Reformer*, October 29, 1882.
89. *Life and Letters*, 2:377.

And so indeed it is, and in a sense in which Mr. Darwin scarcely intended. But such words teach us very clearly where the real difficulty lay in his own mind. Life and mind with him were functions of matter; and, other than the natural forces employed in the natural process of reproduction, he could not see that any concause [i.e., coordinate cause following the principle of *concursus*] in bringing new births into the world could be witnessed to by the nature of the results. He believed firmly that indiscriminate variation, reacted upon through natural laws by the struggle for existence, was the sufficient account of every discrimination in organic nature—was the *vera causa* of all forms which life took; and believing this, he could see no need of God's additional activity to produce the very same effects, and could allow no evidence of its working.

"I have lately," he continues in the letter to Dr. Gray just quoted,

> been corresponding with Lyell, who, I think, adopts your idea of the stream of variation having been led or designed. I have asked him (and he says he will hereafter reflect and answer me) whether he believes that the shape of my nose was designed. If he does I have nothing more to say. If not, seeing what fanciers have done by selecting individual differences in the nasal bones of pigeons, I must think that it is illogical to suppose that the variations which natural selection preserves for the good of any being have been designed. But I know that I am in the same sort of muddle (as I have said before) as all the world seems to be in with respect to free will, yet with everything supposed to have been foreseen or preordained.[90]

And again, a few months later, still laboring under the same confusion, he writes to the same correspondent: "If anything is designed, certainly man must be: one's 'inner consciousness' (though a false guide) tells one so; yet I cannot admit that men's rudimentary mammae . . . were designed. If I was to say I believed this, I should believe it in the same incredible manner as the orthodox believe the Trinity in unity. You say that you are

90. Ibid., 2:378.

in a haze; I am in thick mud; . . . yet I cannot keep out of the question."[91]

One wonders whether Mr. Darwin, in examining a door knocker carved in the shape of a face, would say that he believed the handle was designed, but could not admit that the carved face was designed. Nevertheless, an incised outline on a bit of old bone, though without obvious use, or a careless chip on the edge of a flint, though without possible use, would at once be judged by him to be designed—that is, to be evidence, if not of obvious contrivance, yet certainly of intentional activity. Why he could not make a similar distinction in natural products remains a standing matter of surprise.

The years ran on, however, and his eyes were still holden [i.e., blinkered]; he never advanced beyond even the illustrations he had grasped at from the first to support his position. In 1867 his *Variation of Animals and Plants under Domestication* appeared, and on February 8th of that year he wrote to Sir Joseph Hooker:[92] "I finish my book . . . by a single paragraph, answering, or rather throwing doubt on, in so far as so little space permits, Asa Gray's doctrine that each variation has been specially ordered or led along a beneficial line. It is foolish to touch such subjects, but there have been so many allusions to what I think about the part which God has played in the formation of organic beings, that I thought it shabby to evade the question."[93] In writing his autobiography in 1876, he looks back with pride upon this "argument" as one which "has never, as far as I can see, been answered."[94] It has a claim, therefore, to be considered something like a classic in the present discussion, and although it does not advance one step either in force or form beyond the earlier letters to Dr. Gray and Sir Lyell, we feel constrained to transcribe it here in full:

91. Ibid., 2:382.

92. [Sir Joseph Dalton Hooker (1817–1911) was an English botanist whose work encouraged Darwin to publish *On the Origin of Species*. Rigorously scientific, he cautiously began to agree with Darwin in the 1850s—that is, *prior* to publication of *The Origin*—as his own botanical research seemed to confirm Darwin's theories.]

93. *Life and Letters,* 3:62.

94. Ibid.,1:309.

An omniscient Creator must have foreseen every consequence which results from the laws imposed by Him. But can it be reasonably maintained that the Creator intentionally ordered, if we use the words in the ordinary sense, that certain fragments of rock should assume certain shapes so that the builder might erect his edifice? If the various laws which have determined the shape of each fragment were not predetermined for the builder's sake, can it with any greater probability be maintained that He specially ordained for the sake of the breeder each of the innumerable variations in our domestic animals and plants—many of these variations being of no service to man, and not beneficial, far more often injurious, to the creatures themselves? Did He ordain that the crop and tail feathers of the pigeon should vary in order that the fancier might make his grotesque pouter and fantail breeds? Did He cause the frame and mental qualities of the dog to vary in order that a breed might be formed of indomitable ferocity, with jaws fitted to pin down the bull for man's brutal sport? But if we give up the principle in one case—if we do not admit that the variations of the primeval dog were intentionally guided in order that the greyhound, for instance, that perfect image of symmetry and vigor, might be formed—no shadow of reason can be assigned for the belief that variations, alike in nature and the result of the same general laws, which have been the groundwork through natural selection of the formation of the most perfectly adapted animals in the world, man included, were intentionally and specially guided. However much we may wish it, we can hardly follow Professor Asa Gray in his belief "that variation has been led along certain beneficial lines" like a stream "along definite and useful lines of irrigation." If we assume that each particular variation was from the beginning of all time preordained, the plasticity of organization, which leads to many injurious deviations of structure, as well as that redundant power of reproduction which inevitably leads to a struggle for existence, and, as a consequence, to the natural selection or survival of the fittest, must appear to us superfluous laws of nature. On the other hand, an omnipotent and omniscient Creator ordains everything and foresees everything. Thus we are brought face to face with a difficulty as insoluble as is that of free will and predestination.[95]

95. *Variation of Animals and Plants under Domestication,* authorized edition (1868), 2:515–16.

We read with an amazement which is akin to amusement the string of queries with which Mr. Darwin here plies his readers, as if no answer were possible to conception but the one which would drive "the omnipotent and omniscient Creator" into impotency and ignorance, if not into nonexistence. An argument which has never been answered! Why should it be answered? Is not any man competent to string like questions together ad infinitum with an air of victory? "Did the omnipotent and omniscient Creator intentionally order that beetles should vary to so extreme an extent in form and coloration solely in order that Mr. Darwin might in his enthusiastic youth arrange them artistically in his cabinet? Did he cause the blackthorn to grow of such strong and close fiber in order that Pat might cut his shillalah from it and break his neighbor's head? Did Mr. Darwin himself write and print these words in order that his fellows might wonder why and how he was in such a muddle?" But there is really no end to it, unless we are ready to confess that an object may be put to a use which was not "the end of its being," that there may be intentions possible beyond the obvious proximate one, and that there is a distinction between an intentional action and a contrivance. The fallacy of Mr. Darwin's reasoning here ought not to have been hidden from him, as he tells us repeatedly that he early learned the danger of reasoning by exclusion; and yet that is exactly the process employed here.

Dr. Gray did not delay long to point out some of the confusion under which his friend was laboring.[96] And Mr. Wallace[97] shortly afterward showed that there was no more difficulty in tracing the divine hand in natural production, through the agency of natural selection, than there is in tracing the hand of man in the formation of the races of domesticated animals through artificial selection. In

96. With reference to the first simile of the extract Dr. Gray pointedly urged: "But in Mr. Darwin's parallel, to meet the case of nature according to his own view of it, not only the fragments of rock (answering to variation) should fall, but the edifice (answering to natural selection) should rise, irrespective of will or choice!" Mr. Darwin (*Life and Letters,* 3:84) calls this "a good slap," but thinks it does not essentially meet the point. Mr. F. Darwin *(loc. cit.)* answers it lamely by observing that according to his father's parallel natural selection should be the *architect,* not the *edifice.* Do architects get along without "will or choice"?

97. [Alfred Russel Wallace (1823–1913), with Darwin the codiscoverer of natural selection, had no difficulty aligning his view of evolutionary natural selection with a distinctive form of spirituality.]

neither case does there confront the outward eye other than a series of forms produced by natural law, and in the one case as little
as the other is the selecting concause of the outside agent excluded
by the unbroken traceableness of the process of descent.[98] But Mr.
Darwin was immovable. One of the odd circumstances of the case
was that he still felt able to express pleasure in being spoken of as
one whose great service to natural science lay "in bringing back to
it Teleology."[99] Yet this did not mean that he himself believed in teleology, and in his autobiography written in 1876 he sets aside the
whole teleological argument as invalid.[100]

Nor was the setting aside of teleology merely the discrediting
of one theistic proof in order to clear the way for others. The
strong acid of Mr. Darwin's theory of the origin of man ate into
the very heart of the other proofs as surely, though not by the
same channel, as it had eaten into the fabric of the argument from
design. We have already seen him speaking of the demand of the
mind for a sufficient cause for the universe and its contents as
possessing great weight with him; and he realized the argumen-
tative value of the human conviction, arising from the feelings of
dependence and responsibility, that there is one above us on
whom we depend and to whom we are responsible. But both
these arguments were, in his judgment, directly affected by his
view of the origin of man's mental and moral nature as a development, by means of the interworking of natural laws alone, from
the germ of intelligence found in brutes. We have seen how un-
compromisingly he denied to Lyell the need or propriety of postulating any additional powers or any directing energy for the
production of man's mental and moral nature. In the same spirit
he writes complainingly to Mr. Wallace in 1869: "I can see no necessity for calling in an additional and proximate cause in regard
to man."[101] This being so, he felt that he could scarcely trust
man's intuitions or convictions. And thus he was able at the end
of his life (1881) to acknowledge his "inward conviction . . . that

98. *Life and Letters,* 3:116.
99. Ibid., 3:189: "What you say about Teleology pleases me especially, and I
do not think that anyone else has ever noticed the part." This was written June 5,
1874. See also 3:255 and 2:201.
100. Ibid., 1:309–10.
101. Ibid., 3:116.

the Universe is not the result of chance," and at once to add: "But then with me the horrid doubt always arises whether the convictions of man's mind, which has been developed from the mind of the lower animals, are of any value or at all trustworthy. Would anyone trust in the convictions of a monkey's mind, if there are any convictions in such a mind?"[102]

It is illustrative of Mr. Darwin's strange confusion of thought on metaphysical subjects that he does not appear to perceive that this doubt, if valid at all, ought to affect not only the religious convictions of men, but all their convictions; and that it, therefore, undermines the very theory of man's origin because of which it arises within him. There is not a whit more reason to believe that the processes of physical research and the logical laws by means of which inferences are drawn and inductions attained are trustworthy, than that these higher convictions, based on the same mental laws, are trustworthy; and the origin of man's mind from a brutish source, if fatal to trust in one mental process, is fatal to trust in all others, throwing us, as the result of such a plea, into sheer intellectual suicide.[103]

In discussing these human convictions Mr. Darwin draws a sharp distinction between those which appeared to him to rest on feeling and that which springs from the instinctive causal judgment and demands a sufficient cause for the universe, and which, as he judged it to be "connected with reason and not with the feelings," "impressed him as having much more weight." To the argument from our Godward emotions he allows but little value, although he looks back with regret upon the time when the grandeur of a Brazilian forest stirred his heart with feelings not only of wonder and admiration but also of devotion, and filled and elevated his mind.[104] He sadly confesses that the grandest scenes would no longer awaken such convictions and feelings within him, and acknowledges that he is become like a man who is color-blind and

---

102. Ibid., 1:316.

103. [In these paragraphs Warfield is presenting in a general way the principle of commonsense reasoning that had been a mainstay at Princeton Theological Seminary since its founding. That principle treated human conscience as a sense analogous to human sensations of the physical world.]

104. This paragraph is a report of what Mr. Darwin says in his autobiography in 1876; see *Life and Letters,* 1:311–12.

whose failure to see is of no value as evidence against the universal belief of men. But after he makes this remark, he immediately endeavors to rob it of its force. He urges that all men of all races do not have this inward conviction "of the existence of one God,"[105] and then attempts to confound the conviction which accompanies the emotions which he has described, or more properly which quickens them, and to the reality and abidingness of which they are undying witnesses, with the emotions themselves, as if all "the moving experiences of the soul in the presence of the sublimer aspects of nature" were resolvable "into moods of feelings."[106]

He does more; he attempts to resolve all such moods of feeling essentially into the one "sense of sublimity," and then assumes that this sense must be itself resolvable into still simpler constituents, by which it may be proved to be a composite of bestial elements, and to witness to nothing beyond our brutish origin.[107]

105. Mr. Darwin writes more guardedly here than in his *Descent of Man* (1871), 1:63, where he declares, chiefly on Sir John Lubbock's authority, that there are "numerous races" who have no idea of "one or more gods, and who have no words in their language to express such an idea." Professor Flint, in his "Antitheistic Theories," lecture 7, with its appropriate appendixes, has sifted this question of fact, with the result of showing the virtual universality of religion. [Sir John Lubbock (1834–1913), also Lord Avebury, British biologist and friend of Darwin, was influential in providing an evolutionary framework for human cultural development. Besides his scientific work, he was a popularizer of Darwinianism in Britain.]

106. See this criticism properly pressed by Dr. Noah Porter, in *New Englander and Yale Review,* March 1888, p. 207. [Noah Porter (1811–1892) attempted during his tenure as Yale's president to fuse the college's heritage of commonsense philosophy and Christian belief with a cautious acceptance of the new sciences.]

107. The elements which in his view unite to form a religious emotion are enumerated for us in the *Descent of Man,* 1:65: "The feeling of religious devotion is a highly complex one, consisting of love, complete submission to an exalted and mysterious superior, a strong sense of dependence, fear, reverence, gratitude, hope for the future, and perhaps other elements." How, in these circumstances, he can speak of his state of mind, involving "feelings of wonder, admiration, and devotion" (*Life and Letters,* 1:311), as one which "did not essentially differ from that which is often called the sense of sublimity," is somewhat mysterious. But we must remember that even this complex of emotions was, in Mr. Darwin's view, distantly approached by certain mental states of dogs and monkeys. Nevertheless, the whole drift of the passage in the *Descent of Man* is to credit the results of man's reasoning faculties as he progressed more and more in the power to use them, while the drift of the present passage is to discredit them.

"The state of mind," he writes, "which grand scenes formerly excited in me, and which was intimately connected with a belief in God, did not essentially differ from that which is often called the sense of sublimity; and however difficult it may be to explain the genesis of this sense, it can hardly be advanced as an argument for the existence of God, any more than the powerful though vague and similar feelings excited by music."[108] Here is reasoning! Is it then a fair conclusion that because the sense of sublimity no more than other similar feelings is itself a proof of divine existence, therefore the firm conviction of the existence of God, which is "intimately connected with" a feeling similar to sublimity, is also without evidential value? It is as if one should reason that because the sense of resentment which is intimately connected with the slap that I feel tingling upon my cheek does not essentially differ from that which is often called the sense of indignation, which does not any more than other like feelings always imply the existence of human objects, therefore the tingling slap is no evidence that a man to give it really exists!

How strong a hold this odd illusion of reasoning had upon Mr. Darwin's mind is illustrated by an almost contemporary letter to Mr. E. Gurney,[109] which discusses the origin of capacity for enjoyment of music and closes with the following words: "Your simile of architecture seems to me particularly good; for in this case the appreciation almost must be individual, though possibly the sense of sublimity excited by a grand cathedral may have some connection with the vague feelings of terror and superstition in our savage ancestors when they entered a great cavern or gloomy forest. I wish," he adds, semipathetically, "someone could analyze the feeling of sublimity."[110] He seems to think that to analyze this feeling would be tantamount to letting our conviction of God's existence escape in a vapor.

Darwin ascribed much more weight to the conviction of the existence of God that arises from our causal judgment, and it was chiefly under pressure of this instinct of the human mind, by

108. *Life and Letters*, 1:312.
109. [Edmund Gurney (1847–88) was the author of *The Power of Sound* (1880), which tried to provide scientific analysis for the psychologial effects of music. He supported Darwin's theories in the realm of music and aesthetics.]
110. *Life and Letters*, 3:186 (written July 8, 1876).

which we are forced to assign a competent cause for all becoming, that he was continually being compelled "to look to a First Cause having an intelligent mind in some degree analogous to that of man," and so "to deserve to be called a Theist." But as often "the horrid doubt . . . arises whether the convictions of man's mind," any more than those of a monkey's mind from something similar to which it has been developed, "are of any value or at all trustworthy."[111]

The growth of such doubts in his mind is not traceable in full detail, but some record of it is left in the letters that have been preserved for us. For example, in 1860 he wrote to Dr. Gray: "I cannot anyhow be contented to view this wonderful universe, and especially the nature of man, and to conclude that everything is the result of brute force."[112] Again, "I cannot think that the world, as we see it, is the result of chance."[113] Again, in 1861 he writes to Miss Wedgwood: "The mind refuses to look at this universe, being what it is, without having been designed."[114] At this time he deserved to be called a theist. In 1873 he writes, in reply to a query by a Dutch student: "I may say that the impossibility of conceiving that this grand and wondrous universe, with our conscious selves, arose through chance, seems to me the chief argument for the existence of a God"; but he immediately adds: "But whether this is an argument of real value, I have never been able to decide."[115] And in 1876, after speaking of "the extreme difficulty or rather impossibility of conceiving this immense and wonderful universe, including man with his capacity of looking far backwards and far into futurity, as the result of blind chance or necessity," he immediately adds: "But then arises the doubt, can the mind of man, which has, as I fully believe, been developed from a mind as low as that possessed by the lowest animals, be trusted when it draws such grand conclusions?"[116] Nearly the same words, as we have seen, were repeated in 1881.[117] And he

111. Ibid., 1:316 (written in 1881).
112. Ibid., 2:312.
113. Ibid., 2:353.
114. Ibid.,1:313–14.
115. Ibid., 1:306.
116. Ibid., 1:312–13.
117. Ibid., 1:316.

appears to have had this branch of the subject in his mind rather than teleology when in 1882 the Duke of Argyll[118] urged that it was impossible to look upon the contrivances of nature without seeing that they were the effect and expression of mind. Darwin, shaking his head vaguely and looking hard at him, said: "Well, that often comes over me with overwhelming force; but at other times it seems to go away."[119]

What, then, became of his instinctive causal judgment amid these crowding doubts? It was scarcely eradicated. Darwin could write to Mr. Graham[120] as late as 1881: "You have expressed my inward conviction . . . that the Universe is not the result of chance."[121] But "inward conviction" with Mr. Darwin did not mean "reasoned opinion" which is to be held and defended, but "natural and instinctive feeling" which is to be corrected. And he certainly allowed his causal judgment gradually to fall more and more into abeyance. In his letter to the Dutch student in 1873, he added to his avowal that he felt the impossibility of conceiving of this grand universe as causeless: "I am aware that if we admit a first cause, the mind still craves to know whence it came, and how it arose."[122] Thus he did what he could to throw doubt on the theistic inference. He also spoke as if the agnostic inference were reasonable and philosophical, everywhere maintaining his right to assume living forms to begin with, as a philosopher assumes gravitation.[123] As he is careful to explain, he does not mean that these forms (or this form) have been "created" in the usual sense of that word, but "only that we know nothing as yet [of] how life originates."[124] And as late as 1878 he wrote, "As to the

118. [George Campbell, eighth Duke of Argyll (1823–1900), was a Scottish nobleman and British statesman who wrote several popular books on science and religion. They interpreted contemporary scientific findings within the framework of traditional religious beliefs.]

119. *Life and Letters,* 1:316.

120. [W. Graham (1839–1911) was the author of *Creed of Science* (1881), with which Darwin took issue because Graham argued that natural laws imply purpose.]

121. *Life and Letters,* 1:316.

122. Ibid., 1:306–7.

123. E.g., ibid., 2:210.

124. Ibid., 2:251.

eternity of matter, I have never troubled myself about such insoluble questions."[125]

Nevertheless, it is perfectly certain that neither Mr. Darwin nor anyone else can reject both creation and noncreation, both a first cause and the eternity of matter. As Professor Flint truly points out, "we may believe either in a self-existent God or in a self-existent world, and must believe in one or the other; we cannot believe in an infinite regress of causes."[126] When Mr. Darwin threw doubt on the philosophical consistency of the assumption of a first cause, he was bound to investigate the hypothesis of the eternity of matter; and until this latter task was completed, he was bound to keep silence on a subject on which he had so little right to speak. Where his predilection would carry him is plain from the pleasure with which he read of Dr. Bastian's[127] *Archebiosis* in 1872: he wished that he could "live to see" it "proved true."[128] We are regretfully forced to recognize in his whole course of argument a desire to eliminate the proofs of God's activity in the world; "he did not like to retain God in his knowledge."

Further evidence of this trend may be observed in the tone of the addition to the autobiographical notes which he made, with especial reference to his religious beliefs, in 1876, and in which he, somewhat strangely, included a full antitheistic argument, developed in so orderly a manner that it may stand for us as a complete exhibit of his attitude toward the problem of divine existence. In this remarkable document[129] he first discusses the

125. Ibid., 3:236.
126. "Theism," 3d ed., p. 120; see also p. 390 n. xxii: "Creation is the *only* theory of the *origin* of the universe. Evolution assumes either the creation or the self-existence of the universe. The evolutionist must choose between creation and non-creation. They are opposites. There is no intermediate term. The attempt to introduce one—the Unknowable—can lead to no result; for unless the Unknowable is capable of creating, it can account for the origin of nothing." The whole note should be read.
127. [Henry Charlton Bastian (1837–1915), British neurologist who founded the discipline in England. Denying that there is a strict boundary between organic and inorganic life, he promoted the doctrine of spontaneous generation. Hence his belief in "archebiosis": living things arise from inorganic matter or dead animal or plant tissue.]
128. *Life and Letters,* 3:169.
129. Ibid., 1:307–13.

argument from design, concluding that the "old argument from design in Nature, as given by Paley, which formerly seemed to me so conclusive," fails "now that the law of natural selection has been discovered." He adds that "there seems to be no more design in the variability of organic beings, and in the action of natural selection, than in the course in which the wind blows," and refers the reader to the "argument" given at the end of *Variation of Animals and Plants under Domestication* as one which has never been answered.

Having set this more detailed teleology aside, he next examines the broader form of the argument from design, which rests on the general beneficent arrangement of the world, and he concludes that the great fact of suffering is opposed to the theistic inference, while the prevailing happiness, in conjunction with "the presence of much suffering, agrees well with the view that all organic beings have been developed through variation and natural selection."

Next he discusses the "most usual argument" of the present day "for the existence of an intelligent God," that "drawn from the deep inward conviction and feelings which are experienced by most persons." He speaks sadly of his own former firm conviction of the existence of God, and describes how feelings of devotion welled up within him in the presence of grand scenery; but he sets the argument summarily aside as invalid.

Finally, in a passage which has already been quoted, he adduces the demands of the causal judgment, but discards it, too, with an expression of doubt as to the trustworthiness of such grand conclusions when drawn by a brute-bred mind like man's. His conclusion is formulated helplessness: "The mystery of the beginning of all things is insoluble by us, and I for one must be content to remain an Agnostic." It was out of such a reasoned position that he wrote in 1879: "In my most extreme fluctuations I have never been an Atheist in the sense of denying the existence of God. I think that generally (and more and more as I grow older), but not always, an Agnostic would be the more correct description of my state of mind."[130] Nor can we help carrying over the light thus gained to aid us in explaining the words written to Jena the same year: Mr. Darwin "considers that the theory of Evo-

130. Ibid., 1:304.

lution is quite compatible with the belief in a God, but that you must remember that different persons have different definitions of what they mean by God."[131] It would be an interesting question what conception Mr. Darwin, who began with a deistic conception, had come to when he reached the agnostic stage and spoke familiarly of "what is called a personal God."[132]

By such stages as these did this great man drift from his early trust into an inextinguishable doubt whether such a mind as man's can be trusted in its grand conclusions, and by such reasoning as this did he support his suicidal results. No more painful spectacle can be found in all biographical literature, no more startling discovery of the process by which even great and good men can come gradually to a state of mind in which, despite their more noble instincts, they can but

> Judge all nature from her feet of clay,
> Without the will to lift their eyes to see
> Her Godlike head, crowned with spiritual fire,
> And touching other worlds.

The process that we have been observing, as has been truly said,[133] is not that of an *ejectment* of reverence and faith from the system (as, say, in the case of Mr. Froude),[134] or of an *encysting* of them (as, say, with Mr. J. S. Mill), but simply of an *atrophy* of them, as they dissolve painlessly away. In Mr. Darwin's case this atrophy was accompanied by a similar deadening of his higher emotional nature, by which he lost his power of enjoying poetry, music, and to a large extent scenery, and stood like some great tree of the forest with broad-reaching boughs beneath which men may rest and refresh themselves, but with decay already

131. Ibid., 1:307.

132. Ibid., 3:236 (1878).

133. F. W. H. Myers, in the *Fortnightly Review,* January 1888, p. 103. [Frederic William Henry Myers (1843–1901), poet and essayist, spent the last twenty years of his life in psychical research with particular interest in telepathy. Along with Edmund Gurney, Myers cofounded the Society for Psychical Research in 1882.]

134. [James Anthony Froude (1818–94) was an English writer, fellow of Oxford, and biographer of Thomas Carlyle. Originally intent upon the Anglican ministry, he experienced a spiritual crisis through Carlyle's writings, after which he abandoned Christianity for a less defined spirituality.]

marking it as its own, as evidenced by the deadness of its upper branches. He was a man dead at the top.

It is more difficult to trace the course of Darwin's personal religious life during this long-continued atrophying of his religious conceptions. He was not permitted to enter upon this development without a word of faithful admonition. When the *Origin of Species* was published in 1859, his old friend and preceptor, Professor A. Sedgwick,[135] appears to have foreseen the possible driftage of his thought, and wrote him the following touching words:

> I have been lecturing three days a week (formerly I gave six a week) without much fatigue, but I find by the loss of activity and memory, and of all productive powers, that my bodily frame is sinking slowly towards the earth. But I have visions of the future. They are as much a part of myself as my stomach and my heart, and these visions are to have their antitype in solid fruition of what is best and greatest. But on one condition only—that I humbly accept God's revelation of himself both in his works and in his word, and do my best to act in conformity with that knowledge which he only can give me, and he only can sustain me in doing. If you and I do all this, we shall meet in heaven.[136]

The appeal had come too late to aid his old pupil to conserve his Christian faith; it was already long since he had believed that God had ever spoken in word, and he was fast drifting to a position from which he could only with difficulty believe that God had spoken in his works.

It is not a pleasant letter that Darwin wrote to Mrs. Boole in 1866, in reply to some very respectfully framed inquiries as to the relation of his theory to the possibility of belief in inspiration and a personal and good God who exercises moral influence on man, to which he is free to yield. The way in which Darwin avoids replying to these questions seems to be almost irritable,[137] and is

135. [Adam Sedgwick (1785–1873) was an English geologist and teacher of Darwin at Cambridge. Convinced that voluntaristic mechanisms could never account for new species, he insisted on the necessity of design and believed that Darwin's denial of teleology would eventually destroy the idea of a "moral" realm.]

136. *Life and Letters,* 2:250.

137. Ibid., 3:63–64.

possibly an index to his feelings toward the matters involved. Nevertheless, his sympathy with suffering and his willingness to lend his help toward the elevation of his fellow men remained; he even aided the work of Christian missions by contributions in money,[138] although he no longer shared the hopes by which those were nerved who carried the civilizing message to their degraded fellow beings.

Why, indeed, Darwin should have trusted the noble impulses of his conscience, and been willing to act upon them, when he judged that the brutish origin of man's whole mental nature vitiated all its grand conclusions, might puzzle a better metaphysician than he laid claim to be; but his higher life seems to have taken this direction, and it is characteristic of him to close the letter to the Dutch student, written in 1873, with such words as these: "The safest conclusion seems to be that the whole subject is beyond the scope of man's intellect, but man can do his duty."[139]

But when there is no one to show us any truth, who is there to show us duty? If our conscience is but the chance growth of the brute mind, hemmed in by its environment and squeezed into a new form by the pressure of a fierce and unmoral struggle for existence, what moral imperative deserves the high name of "duty"?[140] Certainly the argument is as valid here as there. But by

138. Ibid., 3:127–28.
139. Ibid., 1:307.
140. What Mr. Darwin actually taught as to the moral sense may be conveniently read in the third chapter of the *Descent of Man* (1871). "This sense," he says, "as Mackintosh remarks, 'has a rightful supremacy over every other principle of human action'; it is summed up in that short but imperious word 'ought,' so full of high significance" (1:67). But what gives this "imperious word 'ought'" so rightful a supremacy? Mr. Darwin teaches that "the moral sense is fundamentally identical with the social instincts" (pp. 93f.), and that "the imperious word 'ought' seems merely to employ the consciousness of the existence of a persistent instinct, either innate or partly acquired," so that "we hardly use the word 'ought' in a metaphorical sense when we say hounds ought to hunt, pointers to point, and retrievers to retrieve their game" (p. 88). He has, indeed, "endeavored to show that the social instincts—the prime principle of man's moral constitution—with the aid of active intellectual powers and the effects of habit, naturally lead to the golden rule, 'As ye would that men should do to you, do ye to them likewise'; and this lies at the foundation of morality" (pp. 101–2). But this is not because the golden rule is any more truly "moral" than any other rule. "Any animal whatever,

the power of so divine an inconsistency, Mr. Darwin was enabled as citizen, friend, husband, and father to do his duty. He had no sharp sense of sin;[141] but so far as duty lay before him he retained a tender conscience. And thus, as he approached the end of his long and laborious life, he felt able to say: "I feel no remorse from having committed any great sin, but have often and often regretted that I have not done more direct good to my fellow creatures."[142] Again, as the end came on, "he seemed to recognize the approach of death, and said, 'I am not the least afraid to die.'"[143] And thus he went out into the dark without God in all his thoughts, with no hope for immortality, and with no keenness of regret for all the high and noble aspirations and all the elevating imaginings which he had lost out of life.

That we may appreciate how sad a sight we have before us, let us look back from the end to the beginning. We stand at the deathbed of a man whom, in common with all the world, we most deeply honor. He has made himself a name which will live through many generations, and withal has made himself beloved by all who came into close contact with him. True, tender-hearted, and sympathetic, he has in the retirement of invalidism lived a life which has moved the world. But is his death the death

---

endowed with well-marked social instincts, would inevitably acquire a moral sense or conscience as soon as its intellectual powers had become as well developed, or nearly as well developed, as in man" (pp. 68–69), but not necessarily "exactly the same moral sense as ours" (p. 70). For instance, bees so developing a moral sense would develop one which required it as a duty to murder their brothers and fertile daughters. Thus the moral law has no more sanction than arises from its being the best mode of conserving the common good, as it is known in present conditions; and its very opposite might be as moral and as imperious under changed conditions. Mr. Darwin's own tender conscience was thus, in his own eyes, nothing more than the dissatisfaction that arose from an unsatisfied inherited instinct (p. 69)! [Sir James Mackintosh (1765–1832), utilitarian philosopher, relative of Darwin, and close friend to Jeremy Bentham, influenced Darwin by means of his writings.]

141. How inevitable this was may be seen from John Tulloch's temperate discussion ("The Christian Doctrine of Sin," lecture 1) of the relation of naturalistic evolution to the sense of sin. [John Tulloch (1823–86), Presbyterian theologian and historian at St. Andrew's University, was considered one of the most prominent Scottish churchmen of his day.]

142. *Life and Letters,* 3:359 (1879).

143. Ibid., 3:358.

we should expect from one who had once given himself to be an ambassador of the Lord? When we turn from what he has done to what he has become, can we say that, in the very quintessence of living, he has fulfilled the promise of that long-ago ingenuous youth who suffered something like remorse when he beat a puppy, and as he ran to school "prayed earnestly to God to help him"?

Let us look upon Darwin in the light of a contrast. There was another Charles, living in the world with him, but a few years his senior, whose childhood, too, was blessed with a vivid sense of the nearness of heaven. He, too, has left us some equally simple-hearted and touching autobiographical notes; and from them we learn that his, too, was a praying childhood. "As far back as I can remember," he writes, "I had the habit of thanking God for everything I received, and asking him for everything I wanted. If I lost a book, or any of my playthings, I prayed that I might find it. I prayed walking along the streets, in school and out of school, whether playing or studying. I did not do this in obedience to any prescribed rule. It seemed natural. I thought of God as an everywhere-present being, full of kindness and love, who would not be offended if children talked to him. I knew he cared for sparrows."[144]

Thus Charles Hodge and Charles Darwin began their lives on a somewhat similar plane.[145] And both write in their old age of their childhood's prayer with something like a smile. But how different the quality of these smiles! Charles Darwin's smile is almost a sneer: "When in doubt," he writes, "I prayed earnestly to God to help me, and I well remember that I attributed my success to the prayers and not to my quick running, and marvelled how generally I was aided."[146] Charles Hodge's smile is the pleasant smile of one who looks back on small beginnings from a well-won height. "There was little more in my prayers and praises," he writes, "than in the worship rendered by the fowls of the air. This mild form of natural religion did not amount to much."[147] Dar-

144. *The Life of Charles Hodge,* by his son A. A. Hodge (1880), p. 13.
145. [For an introduction to the life of Charles Hodge (1797–1878) and a consideration of his interests in science, see the introduction to Hodge, *What Is Darwinism?*]
146. *Life and Letters,* 1:31.
147. *Life,* 13.

win's praying childhood was his highest religious attainment; Hodge's praying childhood was but the inconsiderable seed out of which were marvelously to unfold all the graces of a truly devout life. Starting from a common center, these two great men, with much of natural endowment in common, trod opposite paths; and when the shades of death gathered around them, one could but face the depths of darkness in his greatness of soul without fear, and yield like a man to the inevitable lot of all; the other, bathed in a light not of the earth, rose in spirit upon his dead self to higher things, repeating to his loved ones about him the comforting words of a sublime hope: "Why should you grieve? To be absent from the body is to be with the Lord, to be with the Lord is to see the Lord, to see the Lord is to be like him."[148] The one conceived that he had reached the end of life, and looked back upon the little space that had been allotted to him without remorse, indeed, but not without a sense of its incompleteness; the other, contemplating all that he had been enabled to do through the many years of rich fruitage which had fallen to him, reckoned it but childhood's preparation for the true life which in death was but dawning upon him.[149]

148. Ibid., 582.
149. Since this paper was put into type, a new letter of Mr. Darwin's on his religious views has come to light, which adds, indeed, nothing to what we already knew, but which is so characteristic as to deserve insertion here. It is dated March 11, 1878, and runs as follows: "Dear Sir: I should have been very glad to have aided you in any degree if it had been in my power. But to answer your question would require an essay, and for this I have not the strength, being much out of health. Nor, indeed, could I have answered it distinctly and satisfactorily with any amount of strength. The strongest argument for the existence of God, as it seems to me, is the instinct or intuition which we all (as I suppose) feel that there must have been an intelligent beginner of the Universe; but then comes the doubt and difficulty whether such intuitions are trustworthy. I have touched on one point of difficulty in the two last pages of my *Variation of Animals and Plants under Domestication,* but I am forced to leave the problem insoluble. No man who does his duty has anything to fear, and may hope for whatever he earnestly desires.— Yours faithfully, Ch. Darwin." (See *The British Weekly* for August 3, 1888.)

October 1888
Presbyterian Review 9:680

Review of W. H. Dallinger,
The Creator, and What We May Know of the Method of Creation
(London: T. Woolmer, 1887)

William Henry Dallinger (1842–1909) was both a Wesleyan minister
and a prominent biologist and microscopist. In this brief review,
Warfield commends him for successfully refuting Herbert Spencer's
mechanistic evolutionary philosophy, but is less pleased with
Dallinger's apparently deistic, "watchmaker" (and so Paleyite) view
of the relationship between God and nature.

The purpose of this eloquent discourse is, negatively, to refute
the Spencerian philosophy of mechanical evolution and, positively, to commend a doctrine of creation by law in the sense of a
theistic evolution. The former work is admirably done. The conception of the method of creation which is commended is illustrated by a calculating machine "which shall continue for a number of motions, without necessary limit, according to primal law,
but which by prevised and preordered arrangement would suddenly, at the required point of time, undergo a change and operate
henceforth under a law entirely new" (p. 42). "Could not infinite
power, infinite wisdom, the originator of all that we call natural
phenomena," Dallinger asks, "have prevised and preordered, in
the impenetrable mystery of 'the beginning,' that the creative
laws of evolution for an inorganic world should, as they brought
about the completion of their perfect purpose, have carried with
them from that 'beginning' preordered potentialities that should

112

by the primal volition of the Creator emerge as an inevitable and orderly sequence into the operation of higher activities and new laws?" Thus life might have originated, and even the soul, "physical laws" being caused so to act "as to give origin to consciousness, thought, and moral faculties" (p. 81). Dr. Dallinger's philosophy is not always of the best, and his notion of God in his relation to the universe has a crassly deistic look.

Evolution or Development

Hard on the heels of his first publications on Darwin and questions concerning evolution, Warfield prepared a lecture for his students at Princeton Seminary on the subject "Evolution or Development." This lecture represented Warfield at his most skeptical about evolutionary theory. Compared to his early infatuation with Darwin's own account of development and his later efforts (after about 1900) to define a Calvinistic way of accommodating to certain types of evolution, this lecture was more cautious. In it Warfield discriminated among three general meanings of "evolution": (1) a total philosophy of life, which he rejected; (2) a demonstrated fact explaining how species come into existence, which he questioned; and (3) a hypothesis with varying potential for explaining the different natural phenomena, which he was willing to consider.

The bulk of the lecture is taken up with Warfield's careful consideration of what he believed, by the inductivist standards of his time, constituted proof of the sort needed to demonstrate that a scientific theory is true. He assesses the evidence as it existed in the late 1880s for evolutionary theories, and he suggests ways in which deistic, theistic, and fully Christian (to Warfield, biblical) conceptions could be aligned with the evolutionary theories of his day. Objections occupy much of this discussion, so it is all the more remarkable that Warfield ends by affirming that, if proper qualifications are made, nothing should prejudge whether there *can be* a Christian conception of evolution. His lifelong desire to respect properly stated results of research is well illustrated by the words that close the lecture: "I say we may do this [that is, define a Christian form of modified evolution]. Whether we ought to accept it, even in this modified sense, is another matter, and I leave it purposely an open question."

The lecture was written (or presented) on December 12, 1888. For the next few years Warfield added new notations in his own hand (as interpolations or, more extensively, on the reverse side of

This lecture is published with the permission of the Office of Archives and Special Collections of Princeton Theological Seminary, where the manuscript is housed.

the original pages) and also inserted some published materials.
Much of the first half of this lecture reappeared, some of it verbatim,
in the last half of his 1895 article, "The Present-Day Conception of
Evolution" (pp. 157–69). Other segments of the lecture parallel comments made in reviews over the next few years. By the early twentieth century, Warfield, while maintaining many of the perspectives of
this lecture, moved on in an effort to discriminate among providential understandings of evolution, mediate creation, and creation *ex
nihilo*. That effort set the stage for the more positive attitude toward
evolution found in his last writings on the subject.

Although Warfield's handwriting is not always entirely clear, the
wording of almost all of the lecture can be deciphered. The uncer-
tainties that remain are set in [brackets]. The material that Warfield
added after the initial composition of the lecture is set in {braces}.
Warfield's contractions and the ampersand have been silently expanded; capitalization, punctuation, and italicization have been
modified to modern standards.

There are three general positions which may be taken up with
reference to the various development or evolutionary hypotheses
now so common:

1. We may look upon them as furnishing an adequate philosophy of being and use them in the mass—including the nebular hypothesis, spontaneous generation, and transmutation of forms—
as supplying a complete account of the origin and present state of
the universe. From a religious point of view, this position is tantamount to atheism and is but a new form for the expression of
an atheistic philosophy. When Mr. Darwin put forth his *Origin of
Species,* he was confining his survey to the origin of the various divergent forms of animated existence, and consequently he postulated the existence of life and living forms. Moreover, ever shifting his opinion as to divine things, he wrote that book at a stage
when he was feeling theistically; and therefore he spoke throughout it in a theistic sense and used theistic language. But that the
theory as held by him was essentially atheist, as Dr. Charles
Hodge asserted, is illustrated by the history of his own drift away
from theism as recorded in the recently published *Life and Letters
of Charles Darwin* by his son.

2. We may consider the evolutionary hypothesis as a discovery
by science of the order and conditions under which the various
living forms have as a matter of fact come into existence, and thus
we may use it simply as an account of the way or manner in

which forms have been produced. In this interpretation the theory is not made to account for anything more than other second causes account for; it is made a second cause and implies a first cause. In this interpretation, therefore, the theory is certainly not inconsistent with theism but implies and presupposes theism. This is the interpretation held by Dr. McCosh.[1]

3. We may look upon the hypothesis as a more or less probable, or a more or less improbable, conjecture of scientific workers as to the method of creation; others use it merely as a working hypothesis which is at present on its probation and seeking to try itself by the facts. This is the position which I should [like] to commend to you as a reasonable one to occupy.

The first position looks upon evolution as a fact and as itself the sufficient account of phenomena, that is, both as demonstrated fact and as the all-sufficient force and cause. The second also looks upon evolution as a fact, but not as the sufficient account of any phenomenon, that is, as demonstrated fact but as supplying only the method through which the force and cause works. The third looks upon evolution as a suggested account of the method of the working of the creative force; that is, it is yet on its trial as to whether it be fact or not.

We need, then, to investigate these two subjects, to wit: (1) Whether, if the evolutionary hypothesis be allowed to be accordant to fact, it will sufficiently in itself account for the origin of being and the differentiation of forms; and (2) Whether it is as yet shown to be accordant to fact. The first of these questions is only another form for the presentation of the old problem of the materialistic philosophy, and this does not deserve a separate discussion now for no other reason than that a new form is given it. Our one important query is, then, whether the hypothesis of evolution may now be designated demonstrated fact or only a more or less probable or a more or less improbable conjecture.

It is to be observed that this is not equivalent to asking whether it be true or false. We may hold it to be probably true and yet agree that it is yet on trial and not yet shown to be true. What we ask is whether it has yet been shown to be true, or is

---

1. [See pp. 66–67 for Warfield's review of McCosh's *Religious Aspect of Evolution*.]

still to be considered only a more or less probable or a more or less improbable hypothesis. The religious bearing of this question is that if we answer that evolution has been proved to be true, then we must adjust our theological thinking to it; but if we answer that it is as yet a hypothesis on trial, we are at liberty to wait a while and see whether it be true before we adjust our thinking to it. Nay, while we may point out tentatively its relation to our theology and the changes it may possibly involve, we shall not *adjust* our theology to what is as yet a more or less doubtful conjecture.

{Evolution not yet proven

Now, of course, it must be borne in mind that it is illegitimate to ask anything like demonstration or even anything like direct proof for a theory of this sort. We are not moving in a sphere of demonstrable facts, and direct proof of all sorts is in such matters out of the question. That species grew out of species by insensible stages and in the course only of incalculable ages is a hypothesis; no *direct* proof that this process has taken place could be obtained except by an intelligence which itself had lasted through these ages, and had watched over the process with scientific exactitude and caution. Proof of a hypothesis of this sort can be of only a probable kind, and can arise only out of inferences from the observed effects to the cause and process. As such, however, it is quite conceivable that it might become of stringent validity and command our assent. But its force would depend on its ability to explain with ease and completeness all the observed facts. And by this we must mean something more than merely that it *can be made* to explain the facts.

The Ptolemaic theory could be twisted into an explanation of most of the phenomena of the universe: a false theory may often be shown to be capable, on supposition of its truth, of explaining in one way or another all the facts. A theory thus becomes more and more probable in proportion (1) to the number of the facts it can explain—up to all, (2) to the clearness with which it explains them, and (3) to the ability with which it illuminates the connection between the facts and then furnishes a basis for *deduction* by which (a) we may deduce from the terms of the theory all the facts known to exist, and [indecipherable word] prove its truth, and (b) may deduce even new facts, not hitherto known, by which it becomes *predictive,* and the instrument of the discovery of new facts.

It is quite possible, by a combination of these results, for a theory of this sort to be so fully proved that the mind cannot resist the evidence. It may so perfectly explain the facts—with such power of illumination discern and reveal new and unsuspected elements of facts—and with such certainty determine the facts subsumed under it, and lead us on to the discovery of others, that we cannot avoid the conviction that in it we have exactly the key that belongs to this lock. And of course it follows that the more complicated the lock, the greater the certainty that we have its true key when we have a key that fits every ward. The simplest bent wire will often serve as a pick to open a lock, but nobody dreams we have found in it the proper key to the lock. The probability that we have the true key grows in proportion to the complications of the wards of the lock and the perfection with which the key fits them.

Not every theory, then, that will open a problem is its true key. But on the one hand we are fully persuaded that no theory that will not open the problem can be the true key, and on the other that the probability that we have the true key will grow with its ability to open the lock of a problem smoothly, and by fitting at every point, and by revealing and working well with its most subtle mechanism. Let us remember, however, that there is such a thing as picking the lock of a problem, as well as of a safe, and that science needs protection from burglars just as much as do banks.}

The subject may be still further clarified by our observing that any hypothesis has to run two gauntlets. A hypothesis is proposed in order to account for the observed facts. It must be shown of it (1) that it is capable of accounting for all the facts. Some people appear to suppose that this is all, and that when this is shown, the hypothesis is proved. By no means. This done, all that is done is that it has been shown that should there be reason to believe that this hypothesis is the true one, it may be accepted as the true one. No factors in the case oppose it. We must then show of it (2) that among the various theories that will account for the facts, this is the right one to assume in order to account for them. In other words, when we have shown that a hypothesis will, on supposition of its truth, account for the facts, we then have to challenge the clause "on supposition of its truth," and to ask for the evidence for that supposition. We must fit the various theories that will account for the facts together, and ask *which* of them is the right theory. Everything is not true that might possibly be true; often the theories are equally able to account for the facts. The race is run between the various theories that have been shown to be able to account for the facts. The preliminary showing that a theory can account for the facts is only a conforming to the conditions of entry for the race. It is amazing that anyone should claim the prize before the race is run, and, much more, even before the entry is approved.

Now from this point of view what is the status of the evolutionary hypothesis? I believe that no one will assert that it has yet been shown that it can account for all the facts. This is just what is being now investigated: whether the facts as known can be accounted for on this theory. And this is just what has not yet been successfully done. When Dr. McCosh says that we have the same proof for it that we have for Newton's theory of gravitation, he has allowed his enthusiasm to run away with his judgment. (For Flint: *Encyclopaedia Britannica,* s.v. "Theology.")[2] As yet evolution is on its trial as to this very point: Can it account for the observed facts? You will observe that I do not assert that it cannot account for them, but anyone who asserts that it can has certainly overstepped the boundary line of determined fact and made overdue use of his scientific imagination. But if this is true, evolution is as yet not even entered for the race of theories. What folly for anyone to claim for it already the prize! Now all this is true, I repeat, whether we believe it to be likely or unlikely that it will be hereafter shown to be able to account for the facts. The plain fact be-

2. [See p. 67 for Warfield's reference to Flint at the end of his review of McCosh's *Religious Aspect of Evolution.* Flint had delivered the Baird Lectures in 1876 (on "Theism") and in 1877 (on "Antitheistic Theories"), claiming that all atheism is irrational. He objected to Darwinism because of its tendency to blur the distinction between man and animals. Thoroughly convinced of the validity of the theistic proofs for God's existence, he applauded Hodge's *What Is Darwinism?* and believed that evolution could serve only to vindicate Paley's argument that natural order provides strong evidence for the existence of a Creator-God.]

ing only that it has not yet been made plain that it can account for
them, and therefore that it does not come into competition as yet
with any theory which can be shown to be able to account for
them. That still remains for the future, if ever.

There is the other confusion that we should rid ourselves of. If
it doesn't follow that, because evolution can be shown to be capable of accounting for the facts, it is therefore the true account
of the facts, much less does it follow that, because it can be
shown to be able to account for *some facts,* it is therefore to be assumed to be capable of accounting for *all* the facts. Suppose we
can make out a possible genealogy of the Equidae which might
be accounted for by evolution.[3] We haven't yet "demonstrated"
(Dr. McCosh's word quoted from Prof. Scott)[4] that this is the actual genealogy of the Equidae or that evolution is the right account of it if it were; and much more I say, we have not yet
proved that because evolution may possibly account for Equidae,
it must also be the true account of the origin of the species and
genera, say, of the Trilobites, for which we could make out any
genealogy which is at all consistent with evolution!

Yet this is just the present attitude of evolutionists. They construct a genealogy of the horse as [i.e., from] the tapir, which
might be consistent with evolution; they then show that the testimony of the rocks will allow such a genealogy; then they assume that evolution is the true account of it since the rocks here
allow the possibility of it; and then they tell us that since evolution is "demonstrated" thus to be the true account of the genealogy of the horse, it must also be assumed as the true account of
the origin of all other animals, even for those for which the testimony of the rocks forbids such a genealogy! {And all this is defended by the application of the law of the continuity and uniformity of nature—as if this were not a sword which would cut both
ways.} This may be science, but it is not sense. {And it would be

3. [Equidae are a family of mammals which includes horses, asses, and ze-
bras. Trilobites are extinct Paleozoic marine arthropods whose bodies were divided into three parts.]

4. [This reference could be to William Berryman Scott, Charles Hodge's
grandson, who, after various junior appointments, had been since 1883 professor
of geology at the College of New Jersey.]

too easy to be worthwhile to do it, to show the illegitimacy of the appeal to the uniformitarianism of nature in such a connection.}

On the other hand, let us remember that we do not need to believe that, because evolution cannot be shown to be the true account of the origin of all forms, it therefore may not be (or may not be accepted as) probably the true account of some differentiations. There may be such a thing as descent with variations forming new species, and yet *not* such a thing as descent with variations forming new genera—or new classes—or new kingdoms. We might believe that the horse is a modification of the Eohippus and is descended from him, and yet deny that the whole body of animated life came in like manner from the Eozoon.[5] We see what artificial selection can do in modifying the type in domesticated animals; we do not need to multiply original forms because we cannot see that all existent forms came from one original form. The question of "how many" may be left for future investigation, and we may welcome evolution as accounting for much while yet seeing that it is not proven to account for all or, if we see clearly, that it cannot account for all.

But here we may take another step

Let us admit that evolution is *not yet* proven, and we are still asked how much the "not yet" involves. Is it not at least *probable?* Has it not been made so probable that prescient minds can anticipate the proof? Many think so; many more would like to think so; but for myself, I am bound to confess that I have not such prescience. Evolution has not yet made the first step toward explaining, e.g., the origin of the Trilobites in the Silurian rocks, or of the fishes in the Devonian (despite Prof. Le Conte's very remarkable attempt!).[6] And, in an unprejudiced way, looking over the proofs

5. [The eohippus ("dawn horse") was an early member of the horse family from the Lower Eocene epoch. It was about the size of a fox and had toed feet. *Eozoon* are a banded arrangement of ophicalcites—crystalline limestone or marble spotted with greenish serpentine—found in Canada and once thought to be the remains of an animal.]

6. [Joseph Le Conte (1823–1901) was a geologist at the University of California. Like his teacher, Louis Agassiz, he came to see much design in nature, and his work attempted to reconcile evolution and Christianity for the public. Silurian rocks are a series of geological strata lying below the Devonian sandstone; they

evolution has offered, I am bound to say that none of them is at all, to my mind, stringent. Take the great outstanding argument from the paleontological succession of forms and from the embryological development. I do not fear to assert that both arguments are really against, not for, the theory in at least its usual form of descent with gradual increments of variation accumulating through numerous generations—i.e., to use recent nomenclature, in the Neo-Darwinian form[7]—the form in which it is presented by Wallace and Weismann.[8]

1. While the geological record preserves forms in its upper strata which with much manipulating care may be arranged, in the cases of a very few types, in an ascending order that would either suggest or at least leave room for a theory of descent with gradual modification, and while the record in its general scope clearly reveals a plan of gradual and ever rising creation, the geological record when taken in its whole scope and in its mass of details is confessed as yet irreconcilable with the theory of development by descent. Darwin *defends* himself against the geological record rather than appeals to it. Subsequent discovery, while hav-

---

are of marine origin and contain the remains of an abundant variety of marine organisms, including trilobites. "Fishes in the Devonian" refers to a series of stratified fossiliferous and igneous rocks formed during the Devonian period, which features so many different kinds of fish that it was sometimes called the "age of fishes."]

7. [At this stage, prior to the "New Darwinian Synthesis" of the 1930s, "Neo-Darwinism" referred to those evolutionary theories entirely rejecting even the remnants of Lamarckism that Darwin himself retained, allowing no role to environment for inducing hereditary variations.]

8. [On Wallace see p. 97 n. 97 (Warfield's 1888 essay on Darwin's religious life). It is pertinent to note here that Wallace differed from Darwin's later views in that he affirmed man's mental powers as not being governed by the law of natural selection. Wallace eventually became a spiritualist and argued that biological evolution is compatible with a religious view of humankind. August Weismann (1834–1914) was a German zoologist who denied any role in species development to the inheritance of acquired characteristics (the Neo-Lamarckian view) in favor of the all-sufficiency of the principle of natural selection. Yet Weismann also rejected Darwin's theory of pangenesis (a theory of inheritance postulating the existence of gemmules) and instead proposed a theory of heredity that, based on the continuity of germ plasm, became the precursor of modern genetics. Despite such differences, Weismann was known as one of the most influential voices of Darwinism in the late nineteenth century.]

ing done something for a few later forms, has not altered this general situation.

2. It is impossible, without great confusion of thought, to conceive that the individuals of the higher races preserve in the stages of their embryological development a transcript of the previous race development of the species. And yet this is the essence of the appeal to embryology. Let us look this matter in the face. If the theory of gradual differentiation by successive births with variations constantly accumulating generation by generation be sound, the embryonic development of the individual ought to retain no trace of it. For, according to that theory, each new birth is born slightly different from its parent, not because it had been first exactly like the parent and then altered from it, but because of some slight aboriginal difference. In the point in which the new birth varies, the likeness to the parent is not in it, but is gone. The offspring of the new birth would in turn not be, then, first like the parent, then like the new birth, and then different, but in the points where it differs it would be unlike both. From the beginning, it would preserve in its growth no record of the types from which it diverged. On the other hand, the embryonic development is the history of the individual life and suggests a descent from an individual that had gone through these changes in its individual life. The embryonic development then is inconsistent with the theory of evolution as commonly held, and suggests instead a series of changes in an ancestor's span of individual life.

Take an example. I can conceive of a newt which, crawling out of the water and under the necessity of breathing air, exchanged his gills into lungs, bearing offspring with gills which in course of time became lungs. I can conceive of this process of changing being pushed back into embryonic development, so that the newt, now become a lizard, bears lizards with lungs, while any it fosters has traces of gills. I can conceive of this lizard now shaking off its tail, and bearing an offspring that inherited first gills and a tail, then exchanged gills for lungs, and then shook off his tail; and I can conceive of all these processes being squeezed back into embryonic time, so that now a tailless lizard is born, while the embryo goes through these developments. This is thinkable. But here we have a series of changes which have taken place, each in the midst of an individual life, and which each individual goes through and which are all transmitted. Such an assumption will account for the embryonic development now observed. But a theory of descent with gradual modifications, not in the individual's life, but from birth to birth, is absolutely and logically inconsistent with observed embryonic changes. If a five-toed horselike animal produced a four-toed horselike animal, it would be a monster; this one now would have four toes and except by reversion could not produce a five-toed animal. And the series thus produced could not reproduce itself all in the span of an individual's development. In a word, by postulating gradual *race* development, this theory estops itself from pleading the fact of an observed *individual* development as a proof of its disparate condition.

3. In like manner it is argued that the demands which the Darwinian form of evolution makes on time, which are again felt by Mr. Darwin to be a great difficulty, have become, as investigation has gone on, an even more serious obstacle in its way. All new estimates of the period of the life of our globe agree in lessening its length. And now when it is a question as to the length of time during which life has existed on the globe, we have no longer eternity at our disposal and may be even confined to some hundreds of thousands of years. Moreover, the earliest human remains differ in type in no respect from the men of our day—shortening the time for the evolution of man on this side also. The matter of time that was a menace to Darwinism at the beginning thus bids fair to become its Waterloo.

4. We may add that, so far as observation can evidence, there appear to be limits to the amount of variation to which any organism is liable, and these limits are within the *type* characteristics. We may say, if we choose, that the varieties of pigeons are so divergent that a naturalist would class them as species if found in nature. But so also would he class them as pigeons. No one oversteps the line which the type "pigeon" sets. All cows—however divergent—remain cows; all men, men; all types in a kind retain their type characteristics. So it is in the highest degree improbable that the line that separates them is passable.

{5. Phylogenesis where most carefully investigated tends to parallel this (Hubrecht). [At this point Warfield pasted on the back of his lecture the review of Hubrecht's *Descent of Primates* that he published in October 1898.]}[9] On these and similar grounds, I should therefore venture to say that any form of evolution which rests ultimately on the Darwinian idea is very improbable as an account of how God has wrought in producing species. I would not have this understood as equivalent to denying either that species have come by descent, or that natural selection as held by deists and in varying degrees may be held to bear the impress of the divine intelligence in its working and results. We may even hold to practically the same theory of the working of the evolutionary process and yet be theists, believing in an everywhere present and active God who nevertheless acts only according to law. So far as theism is concerned, therefore, there is no necessary conflict with evolution in any of its forms.

But to be a theist and a Christian are different things. And a thoroughgoing evolutionism cannot be held in entire consistency with some other Christian doctrines. {The frank supernaturalism of Christianity cannot comport with a thoroughgoing system of evolutionary philosophy, which insists on accounting for everything by the action of forces inherent in matter. Christianity has no difficulty in acknowledging the reality and activity of second causes or in submitting to their rule a vast sphere of being; but it cannot attribute to them—even under the direction of God—all the effects that come to pass, all the products that have come into being. The most that any thoroughgoing system of evolution can allow in the way of the supernatural is the indirect supernatural of a leading and directing intelligence, but Christianity demands and must demand also the direct supernatural interference and immediate production by which something new is introduced which the existing matter and forces are incompetent to produce. At this point there is absolute conflict which cannot be compromised. One or the other must be overcome, and in being overcome must be so far discredited.}

9. [Ambrosius Arnold Willem Hubrecht (1853–1915), a Dutch zoologist, focused on the development of vertebrates and suggested that mammals were derived directly from amphibians. For Warfield's 1898 review of Hubrecht's *Descent of the Primates* see pp. 183–87.]

The Christian doctrine of the substantiality and immateriality of the soul and its consequent persistence in life after the dissolution of the body cannot be held consistently by those who embrace all mental phenomena in the evolutionary process and make this process wholly by natural law. Mr. J. J. Murphy therefore understands resurrection and immortality to be convertible terms.[10] To hold the common doctrine of the soul, we must then believe that the evolutionary process has been broken *at least* at the point where an immaterial principle of life as distinguished from what we may call physical life came in. It may not matter when we place this point of interference—whether at the apparition of man, or at the influx of animal life, or at the beginning of life itself. If the soul be immaterial substance, it was not the product of material substances and forces.

{Prof. Le Conte seems to believe in an immortality of the soul even though the soul has "grown out of something already existing in animals." His idea is "that as the *organic embryo* at birth reaches independent natural and temporal life, even so the *spiritual embryo* at birth (i.e., at *its* birth) attains independent spiritual life." Hence "man alone is a *child* of God, capable of separate spiritual life, separate but not yet wholly independent of nature. Nature is no longer gestative [indecipherable word] of spirit—we are weaned out by death" (see his *Evolution and Its Relation to Religious Thought* [1890]).

A somewhat similar notion seems to underlie Mr. Romanes' view of the origin of self-conscious life.[11] He describes it as gradual: "I say 'gradual' because the process is throughout of the nature of a growth. Nevertheless there is some reason to think that when this growth has attained a certain point, it makes, so to

10. [Joseph John Murphy (1827–94), an amateur naturalist from Belfast whose work attracted the attention of Darwin himself, contributed an article entitled "Evolution and Man's Faculty of Knowledge" to *Christianity and Evolution: Modern Problems of the Faith,* which Warfield reviewed in April 1888; see pp. 61–62. Murphy also authored *Habit and Intelligence* and *The Scientific Basis of Faith.*]
    11. [George John Romanes (1848–1894) was an English biologist and physiologist. He applied Darwinian evolution to the development of the mind. Allowing for more evolutionary factors besides natural selection, he affirmed the role of "physiological selection" and varietal isolation in the process of evolution. He returned to theism a year before his death. For Warfield's 1896 review of Romanes' *Darwin and After Darwin* see p. 172.]

speak, a sudden leap of progress which may be taken to bear the same relation to the development of the mind as the act of birth does to that of the body (*Mental Evolution in Man* [1889]). Mr. Romanes is here speaking of the evolution of self-consciousness in the child, not in the race. Would he say the same of the origination of self-consciousness in the race? If so, we should need to ask (1) What was the cause of the sudden leap? and (2) Was it the communication of a new essence or out of new forces?

The very able reviewer of Romanes in *The Guardian* (Feb. 6, 1889) does not fear the effect of the proof of a gradual process of soul-making: "On the *a priori* question Christianity has no particular view. The creation of the soul by God is neither more nor less true than the creation of the body by him, and therefore if science can by a patient application of its own methods tell us something here of the *modus creandi* [the means of creation], we may hope that Christians have learned enough from the past to be ready to meet the attempt with something more than a glum disapproval." All that the reviewer cares to assert is that "Christianity knows of only one origin for all things, however widely they differ in kind. If of man it is said that God 'breathed into his nostrils the breath of life and man became a living soul,' it is also said of beasts and fishes, 'When Thou lettest Thy breath go forth, they shall be made; and Thou shalt cover the face of the earth.'" Hence if Mr. Romanes thinks "he has triumphed over somebody who believed that the soul came from God, and the body from somewhere else, we congratulate him on his victory over a revived Manicheanism.[12] If difference in kind means what Mr. Romanes wants it to mean, namely, difference in origin, there is no such thing as difference of kind, either for idealist or realist, for pantheist, materialist, or Christian, and Mr. Romanes has only given the *coup de grace* to a moribund deism." This is good writing and valid reasoning up to the point to which it extends. But it omits to note that it has given up the Christian and biblical idea of the nature of the soul as an immaterial [somewhat(?)], not of the earth earthy, but

12. [Manicheanism, which originated as a dualistic, gnostic religion in Persia during the third century, emphasized a radical dualism between good and evil and taught that the spirit, which is good, comes from the true God, while matter, or the body, was created by the demiurge, a lesser god. Manicheans usually sought the release of the spirit from matter through asceticism.]

from God. An immaterial soul cannot be made through the instrumentality of simply material forces and materials. To make a soul there is required a new creation of a new order of material and force.}

Science may itself support other breaks: we may need to assume a break at the origin of motion, at the origin of life, at the origin of sensation, at the origin of consciousness. And these breaks may support the view of evolution which allows not only the directing hand but also the *interfering* hand of God. But however this may be, if we believe in the substantiality of the soul and in its immateriality, we require a supernatural origin for it. Hence this doctrine is inconsistent with so thoroughgoing an evolutionism as allows no place for God's action except to direct physical forces and thus allows no product for which, in esse, physical forces are incompetent.

Again, it may be found that a thoroughgoing evolutionism which embraces moral sense in its sphere is inconsistent with the biblical doctrine of man's first probation and fall. The term "moral sense" is a misnomer in any materialistic theory of evolution (as anyone can satisfy himself by reading the chapter on the moral sense in Darwin's *Descent of Man*). In a deistic scheme we can see that it might be truly moral and bear the impress of the divine. In a theistic scheme we can see how true morality might be arrived at even by development from the brutish mind—the culminating product being what God always intended to be the outcome and the outcome to which he has actively brought things. But unless we assume a supernatural interference, there seems to be no place in this scheme for the race probation depicted in the Bible. In a slowly and gradually developing moral sense, there is no place where such tremendous issues could be justly suspended on the developed morality of the agent. In the biblical doctrine of probation, in other words, a fully developed moral sense is assumed in the first man, and the verdict of history bears this out. We do not seem today to have any better a conscience (its education is another matter) than David, Abraham, or Adam had.

{Accordingly, evolutionists are constrained to reverse the whole biblical teaching in this matter. What the Bible represents as a descent from morality, they necessarily represent as an ascent into morality. The preceding state, which the Bible represents as a state of moral perfection, they represent as a state of immoral imperfection; and the crisis called the fall, so far from being a crisis of morality, was the condition of morality. This view may be illustrated from a recent book by Francis Howe Johnson (Boston 1891) called *What Is Reality?*[13] Mr. Johnson teaches that man was first physically formed from a brutish original and only afterwards became what we call a moral being.

[Here Warfield inserted two paragraphs from E. J. Hamilton's review of Johnson's book in the *Presbyterian and Reformed Review* 4 (April 1893): 342–43.][14]

Ages pass after this primal evolution of man from the brute before that change in man's moral condition which we commonly call The Fall took place. This fall, however, was by no means a lapse from an original condition of high moral excellence; it was simply a great illumination and elevation of the human mind when it became so far developed as to see the heinousness of sin. Man really fell upwards, not downwards. Hence this philosophy also designates "the entrance of Christianity into the world as a fall. Like the first great ethical event of the race it was preeminently and distinctively a great moral illumination. Like that, also, it was a moral condemnation of the profoundest significance. . . . The revealer is the same in both. Conscience, the light that lightens every man that cometh into the world, is also the eternal Logos that in the form of man preached the Sermon on the Mount."

The atonement of our Saviour is the culminating point of this second illumination of mankind, and has its whole value in the fact that it brings out fully the antagonism between sin and righteousness, appealing to all to range themselves on the side of right. "As in the first fall, so in the second, the deep, abiding impression of the nature of sin was to be developed and stamped upon the consciousness of the race by its own act. . . . The holiness of God, that at first had feebly declared itself in conscience, is now declared fully and clearly in the form of a perfect humanity, and the

13. [The full title of this volume by Johnson (1835–1910) was *What Is Reality? An Inquiry as to the Reasonableness of Natural Religion, and the Naturalness of Revealed Religion.*]

14. [Edward John Hamilton (1834–1918), an ordained Presbyterian minister, graduated from Princeton Theological Seminary in 1858. He was a professor of philosophy, specializing in ethics, logic, and epistemology, at Princeton, Hamilton College, and the State University of Washington.]

Warfield on Evolution and Science

result is an outbreak of bitter hostility. . . . Perfect righteousness
coming into a world of sin demonstrated the nature of sin; and by
so doing, it provided, at the same time, the most powerful organ
of conviction and the most expressive medium of confession."

I do not see that the evolutionary theory can do better than this
with this fundamental Christian doctrine of a primary probation
if it is to be made inclusive of mental as well as bodily phenomena. But this is to *reverse* Bible teaching and to stand the whole
system of Christian theology on its head.}

And this brings us naturally to the test point with us as Christians. If evolution is consistent with theism, we must still as
Christians ask, Is it also consistent with the Bible? And that question encompasses (1) the biblical doctrine that we have already
been discussing and also (2) biblical statements. And therefore we
now need to ask, Is evolution consistent with the biblical account
of the origin of things in general and of man in particular? I am
free to say, for myself, that I do not think that there is any general
statement in the Bible or any part of the account of creation, either as given in Genesis 1 and 2 or elsewhere alluded to, that need
be opposed to evolution. The sole passage which appears to bar
the way is the very detailed account of the creation of Eve. It is
possible that this may be held to be a miracle (as Dr. Woodrow
holds),[15] or else that the narrative may be held to be partial and
taken like the very partial descriptions of the formation of the individual in Job and the Psalms; that is, it teaches only the general
fact that Eve came of Adam's flesh and bone. Neither view seems
natural. And we may as well admit that the account of the creation of Eve is a very serious bar in the way of a doctrine of creation by evolution.

The upshot of the whole matter is that there is no *necessary* antagonism of Christianity to evolution, *provided that* we do not
hold to too extreme a form of evolution. To adopt any form that
does not permit God freely to work apart from law and that does

15. [James Woodrow (1828–1907) served as professor of natural science in
connection with revelation at Presbyterian Theological Seminary in Columbia,
South Carolina. In 1886 Woodrow was dismissed from his teaching position because of his views on evolution, though he was never convicted of heresy nor lost
his standing as a minister in the Southern Presbyterian church.]

not allow *miraculous* intervention (in the giving of the soul, in creating Eve, etc.) will entail a great reconstruction of Christian doctrine, and a very great lowering of the detailed authority of the Bible. But if we condition the theory by allowing the constant oversight of God in the whole process, and his occasional supernatural interference for the production of *new* beginnings by an actual output of creative force, producing something *new,* i.e., something not included even *in posse* [potentially] in preceding conditions, we may hold to the modified theory of evolution and be Christians in the ordinary orthodox sense.

I say we may do this. Whether we ought to accept evolution, even in this modified sense, is another matter, and I leave it purposely an open question.

December 12, 1888

"With faith enough to bridge the chasm
'Twixt Genesis and Protoplasm."
J. R. Lowell[16]

---

16. [James Russell Lowell (1819–91) was editor of the *Atlantic Monthly* and a prominent member of the renowned group of nineteenth-century American writers which included Emerson, Hawthorne, Whittier, and Longfellow.]

January 1889
Homiletic Review 17:9–16
(reprinted from *SSWW* 2:132–41)

Darwin's Arguments against Christianity and against Religion

This article is a simplified abridgment of Warfield's 1888 article on Darwin's biography. Even more clearly than that lengthy monograph, this shorter essay highlights Warfield's understanding of Darwin's rejection of God and also of the role that Darwin's theories played in it. As in the earlier article, Warfield asserts here that Darwin's loss of faith was not necessarily "an inevitable result" of his scientific conclusions.

The burden of this essay, however, is Warfield's effort to explain simply, and without as much quotation as in the earlier article, why Darwin felt he had to give up his faith. Warfield is not impressed with any of Darwin's intellectual moves, especially his unwillingness to trust his own immediate convictions that the world in all its diversity and complexity was designed. According to Warfield, Darwin was self-referentially incoherent at this point. If human convictions about the orderly intelligence of nature are not to be trusted (because, according to Darwin, the human mind is only the evolutionary descendant of the minds of brute beasts), then why, asks Warfield, should Darwin trust his own thoughts about a complex matter like evolution by natural selection (since those thoughts too are descended from the same source)? In the end, Warfield attributes Darwin's loss of faith to the allegiance he displayed to the rigidly naturalistic (if also questionable) conclusions he drew from his formulation of a theory of evolution.

Science has not broken with religion. But a large number of the scientific thinkers of our generation have. When we ask why, the reason returned is apt to be colored by the personal feelings of the answerer. One attributes the present situation to the bondage into which what he speaks of as "so-called modern science" has fallen, to materialistic philosophy, or even to satanic evil-heartedness. Another finds its explanation in the absorption of scientific workers, in this busy age, in a kind of investigation which deadens spiritual life and spiritual aspirations within them, and totally unfits them for estimating the value of any forms of evidence other than that obtained in the crucible or under the microscope. Others suppose that it is the crude mode in which religion is presented to men's minds, in these days of infallible popes[1] and Salvation Armies,[2] which insults the intelligence of thoughtful men and prevents their giving to the real essence of faith the attention which would result in its acceptance. Others, still, conceive that it is advancing knowledge itself which in science has come to blows with religion and the outworn superstitions of a past age.

In such a Babel of discordant voices it is a boon to be able to bend our ear and listen to one scientific worker, honored by all, as he tells us what it was that led him to yield up his Christian faith, and even, in large measure, that common faith in a God which he shared not with Christians only but with all men of thought and feeling. A rare opportunity of this sort has been afforded us by the publication of the *Life and Letters of Charles Darwin* by his son, in which is incorporated a very remarkable passage extracted from some autobiographical notes written by this great student of nature, as late as 1876, with the special purpose of tracing the history of his religious views. Certainly no one will hesitate to accord to him a calm hearing; and we cannot but be instructed by learning by what processes and under the pressure of what arguments so eminently thoughtful a mind was led to desert the faith in which he was bred, and gradually to assume a position toward the problem of the origin of the world which he can call by no more luminous name than that of agnosticism.

The history of the drift by which Mr. Darwin was separated from faith in a divine order in the world divides itself into two well-marked periods. The first of these, which was completed at

1. [In 1870 the First Vatican Council declared that under certain restricted conditions the pope was infallible in doctrinal matters. This decree appalled Protestants for religious reasons and Western progressives for social and political reasons.]

2. [The Salvation Army was founded by William Booth in 1865. Although evangelical in most of its teaching, the Salvation Army rejected the sacraments, stressed the moral aspects of Christianity, and in general promoted too much heedless joyfulness ever to be approved by a sober conservative like Warfield.]

about the time when he reached his fortieth year, ends with the
loss of his Christianity. During the second, which extended over
the remainder of his life, he struggled, with varying fortunes, but
ever more and more hopelessly, to retain his standing at least as a
theist. At the end of the first he no longer believed that God had
ever spoken to men in his Word; at the end of the second he more
than doubted whether the faintest whisper of his voice could be
distinguished in his works. Darwin was never prepared dogmatically to deny God's existence; but search as he might he could
not find him, and he could say only that if he exists he is, verily,
a God that hides himself.

Let us take up the matter in the orderly form which Mr. Darwin has himself given it, and inform ourselves seriously what
were the objections to Christianity and the difficulties in reasoned theism which led him to such sad conclusions.

Darwin's account of his loss of Christianity takes the shape of
a personal history. He gives us not so much an argument against
Christianity as a record of the arguments which led him to dis-
card it. These fall into two classes: in the first stands the single decisive argument that really determined his anti-Christian attitude,
while in the second are gathered together the various supporting
considerations which came flocking to buttress the conclusion
when once it was attained. The palmary [i.e., best, deserving the
palm] argument depends for its weight on a twofold peculiarity
of his personal convictions. He had persuaded himself not only
that species originated by a process of evolution, but also that this
process was slow, long continued, and by a purely natural development. And he held, with dogmatic tenacity, the opinion that
the Book of Genesis teaches that God created each species by a
separate, sudden, and immediate fiat. If both these positions were
sound, it followed necessarily that either his theory or Genesis
was in error; and to him, in his naturally enthusiastic advocacy of
his theory, this meant that Genesis must go.

Now he was ready for another step. Genesis is an integral part
of the Old Testament, and the Old Testament is not only bound
up with the New Testament in a single volume, but is in such a
sense a part of Christianity—as its groundwork and basis—that
Christianity cannot be true if the Old Testament record is untrustworthy. To give up Genesis is, therefore, to give up Christianity.

Thus Darwin's chief argument against Christianity reduces itself to a conflict between his theory of evolution and his interpretation of Genesis, about the accuracy of both of which there are the gravest of doubts. Here is the form in which he himself describes his reasoning: "I had gradually come by this time, that is, 1836 to 1839, to see that the Old Testament was no more to be trusted than the sacred books of the Hindus. The question then continually rose before my mind, and would not be banished: Is it credible that if God were now to make a revelation to the Hindus he would permit it to be connected with the belief in [the gods] Vishnu, Siva, etc., as Christianity is connected with the Old Testament? This appeared to me as utterly incredible."

It was impossible, however, to deal with Christianity as if it came claiming our acceptance uncommended by evidence of its own. The assumed conflict with Genesis would be fatal to the theory of evolution if the Christianity in vital connection with Genesis were confessed to be truth demonstrated by its own appropriate historical evidence. Mr. Darwin could not, therefore, rest in his short refutation without calling to its aid other more direct arguments such as would suffice to place Christianity at least on the defensive and thus allow the palmary argument free scope to work its ruin. Thus we read further:

> By further reflecting that the clearest evidence would be requisite to make any sane man believe in the miracles by which Christianity is supported, and that the more we know of the fixed laws of nature the more incredible do miracles become; that the men at that time were ignorant and credulous to a degree almost incomprehensible by us; that the Gospels cannot be proved to have been written simultaneously with the events; that they differ in many important details, far too important, as it seemed to me, to be admitted as the usual inaccuracies of eyewitnesses—by such reflections as these . . . I gradually came to disbelieve in Christianity as a divine revelation. The fact that many false religions have spread over large portions of the earth like wildfire had some weight with me.

This is Mr. Darwin's arraignment of the Christian evidences. A close scrutiny will reveal the important place which miracles occupy in it. It may almost be said that Mr. Darwin concerns himself with no other of the evidences of Christianity except miracles. It looks as if in his objection to Christianity, arising from the conflict that existed in his opinion between Genesis and his theory of evolution, he felt himself faced down by the force of the miracles by which, as he says, "Christianity is supported," and felt bound to throw doubt on this evidence or yield up his theory. In one word, he felt the force of the evidence from miracles. It is instructive to observe how he proceeds in the effort to break the weight of their evidence.

He does not shortly assert, as some lesser scientific lights are accustomed to assert, that miracles are impossible. He says merely that they need clear evidence of their real occurrence to make us believe in them, and that this is increasingly true as the reign of law is becoming better recognized. And then he tries to throw doubt on the evidence of their occurrence: the age in which they are declared to have been wrought was credulous; the documents in which they are recorded cannot be proved to be contemporaneous with their asserted occurrence, and are marred by internal contradictions in detail which lessen their trustworthiness; and it is not necessary to assume the miraculous origin of Christianity in order to account for its rapid spread. In a word, Mr. Darwin deserts the metaphysical and what may be called the "scientific" objections to miracles, in order to rest his case on the historical objections. He does not say miracles cannot have occurred; he says merely that the evidence on which they are asserted to have occurred falls something short of demonstration.

Were our object here criticism rather than exposition, it would be easy to show the untenableness of this position: it was not in the field of the historical criticism of the first Christian centuries that Mr. Darwin won his spurs. There are also many more sources of evidence for Christianity than its miracles. It is enough for our present purpose, however, to take note of the form which the reasoning assumed in his own mind. It has a somewhat odd appearance, and was about as follows: The miracles by which Christianity is supported are not demonstrably proved to have really occurred; therefore the conflict of my theory with Genesis, and through Genesis with Christianity, is not a conflict with miraculous evidence; therefore my theory may as well be true as Christianity. The validity of the inference seems to rest on the suppressed premise that none but miraculous evidence would suffice to set aside his theory. And there is a droll suggestion that his state of mind on the subject was not very far from this: "I was very unwilling to give up my belief," he writes; "I feel sure of this, for I can well remember often and often inventing day-dreams of old letters between distinguished Romans, and manuscripts being found at Pompeii or elsewhere, which confirmed in the most striking manner all that was written in the Gospels. But I found it more and more difficult, with free scope given to my imagination, to invent evidence which would suffice to convince me. Thus unbelief crept on me at a very slow rate, but was at last complete. The rate was so slow that I felt no distress."

Nothing short of a miracle would, then, have convinced him; and nothing short of a miracle could have convinced him of a miracle. Surely a man in such a state of mind would be refused as a juror in any case. In lesser causes we should speak of him as under bondage to an invincible prejudice; in this great one we are certainly justified in saying that his predilection for his theory of the origin of species, and that in the exact form in which he had conceived it, lay at the root of his rejection of Christianity. If both Christianity and it could not be true, why then Christianity certainly could not be true, and a full examination of the evidence was unnecessary.

It was some years after his giving up of Christianity before his belief in the existence of a personal God was shaken. But as time went on this also came. The account given in his autobiography of this new step in unbelief is not thrown into the form of a history so much as of ordered reasoning. So that we have, strangely enough, as part of a brief body of autobiographical notes, a formal antitheistic argument. The heads of theistic proof which Mr. Darwin treats in this remarkable passage are the following: (1) "The old argument from design in nature as given by Paley"; (2) "the general beneficent arrangement of the world"; (3) "the most usual argument for the existence of an intelligent God at the present day, the argument drawn from the deep inward conviction and feelings which are experienced by most persons"; and (4) the argument "from the extreme difficulty or rather impossibility of conceiving this immense and wonderful universe, including man with his capacity of looking far backwards and far into futurity, as the result of blind chance or necessity." The full development of these propositions, while it would be far, no doubt, from exhausting the argument for the existence of God, would afford quite a respectable body of theistic proof. In offering a refutation of them, one by one, Mr. Darwin evidently feels that he is sufficiently treating the whole fabric of theistic argumentation, and he draws an agnostic conclusion accordingly. It will be very instructive to note, in as much detail as space will allow, his answers to the theistic proofs.

To the first—the argument from design as developed, say, by Paley—he replies that it "fails, now that the law of natural selection has been discovered." "We can no longer argue," he adds, "that, for instance, the beautiful hinge of a bivalve must have been made by an intelligent being, like the hinge of a door by man. There seems to be no more design in the variability of organic beings and in the action of natural selection than in the course in which the wind blows." By this he means that the adaptations of means to ends, as observed in nature, are the necessary result of the interaction of the purely mechanical forces of nature, and would result from them whether there is a God or not; and that therefore they cannot be pleaded as a proof that there is a God. This conception of the working of nature is the result of the stringency with which he held to his theory of evolution by natural selection in the exact naturalistic form in which he first conceived it.

The second argument, that drawn "from the general beneficent arrangement of the world," he meets by a reference to the great amount of suffering in the world. As a sound evolutionist he believes that happiness decidedly prevails over misery; but he urges that the existence of so much suffering is an argument against the existence of an intelligent first cause, "whereas the presence of much suffering agrees well with the view that all organic beings have been developed through variation and natural selection," which he appears to assume to be a necessarily antitheistic conception.

In treating the third argument, derived from man's "deep inward conviction and feelings" that there is a God to whom his aspirations go out, on whom he is dependent, and to whom he is responsible, Mr. Darwin confuses the "conviction" with the "feelings," and sets the whole aside as no more valid an argument for the existence of God than are "the powerful, though vague, and similar feelings excited by music." He sorrowfully recalls the time when he too had such feelings rise within him in the presence of grand scenery, for instance—times when he could not adequately describe the "higher feelings of wonder and admiration and devotion which filled and elevated his mind." But he confesses that they no more visit him, and that he might truly be said to be like a man who has become color-blind and whose loss of perception is therefore of no value as evidence against the universal belief of men. But then he denies that the "conviction of the existence of one God" (why *one* God?) is universal among men, and hints that he believes that all these feelings can be reduced to the "sense of the sublime," which, could it only be analyzed, might be shown to involve the existence of God no more than do the similar emotions raised by music. The confusion here is immense—confusion of a conviction that accompanies, or rather begets and governs, feelings with the feelings themselves—confusion of the analysis of an emotion into its elements with the discovery of its cause, and the like. This confusion and Mr. Darwin's method of seeking relief from his puzzlement are characteristic traits which may teach us somewhat of the value of his testimony as to the scientific aspects of faith.

The fourth argument, that which rests upon our causal judgment, is the only one to which he ascribes much value. He does not hesitate to speak of the "impossibility of conceiving this immense and wonderful universe as the result of blind chance or necessity." But the question arises, Impossibility to whom? And here again Mr. Darwin's theory of the origin of man, by a purely natural process of development from brute ancestors, entered in to void the unavoidable conclusion. "But then," he adds, "arises the doubt, Can the mind of man, which has, as I fully believe, been developed from a mind as low as that possessed by the lowest animals, be trusted when it draws such grand conclusions?" Or, as he writes later, after having again confessed to "an inward conviction that the universe is not the result of chance": "But then with me the horrid doubt always arises whether the convictions of man's mind, which has been developed from the mind of the lower animals, are of any value or at all trustworthy. Would anyone trust in the convictions of a monkey's mind, if there are any convictions in such a mind?" Thus the last and strongest theistic proof fails, not because of any lack in its stringent validity to the human mind, but because so brute-bred a mind as man's is no judge of the validity of proof.

We are tempted to turn aside and ask, Why, then, are the theistic proofs so carefully examined by Mr. Darwin? Why is so much validity assigned to the judgment of his human mind as to the value of the argument from design, for instance? Why does he trust that brute-bred mind through all the devious reasonings by which the theory of development by natural selection, on the basis of which the value of the mind's conclusions are now challenged, was arrived at? In a word, is it not certain, if man's mind is so brutish that its causal judgment is not trustworthy when it demands a sufficient cause for this universe, that it is equally untrustworthy in all its demands for a sufficient cause, and that thus all the fabric of our knowledge tumbles about our ears, all our fine theories, all our common judgments by which we live? When Mr. Darwin chokes down this "inward conviction" and refuses to believe what he confesses to be "impossible" to him not to believe, he puts the knife at the throat of all his convictions, even of his conviction that he exists and his conviction that a world lies about him such as he sees with his eyes and theorizes about with his "bestial" mind; and there necessarily go out into the blackness of nescience [i.e., ignorance] all thought, all belief, all truth.

But we remember that we are not now criticizing, but only trying to understand Mr. Darwin's reasons for refusing to believe in "what is called a personal God." This much is plain, that the root of his agnosticism, as of his rejection of Christianity, was his enthusiastic acceptance of his own theory of evolution in the mechanical naturalistic sense in which he conceived it. We raise no question whether this was an inevitable result; there have been many evolutionists who have been and have remained theists and Christians. But this was the actual course of reasoning with him. It was because he conceived of each organic form as liable to indefinite variation in every direction, and to development into other forms by the natural reaction of the environment on these variations through the struggle for existence, that he denied that the hand of God could be traced either in the line of variation or in the selection of the types to live. It was because he included all organic phenomena, mental and moral as well as physical, in this

natural process, that he found himself unable to trust the convictions of the mind of man, which was after all nothing but the
brute's mind beaten and squeezed into something of a new form
by an unmoral struggle for existence stretching through immemorial ages. In a word, Mr. Darwin's rejection of Christianity and
loss of faith in a personal God were simply the result of his enthusiastic adoption of a special theory of the origin of organic differentiation, and of ruthless subjection of all his thought to its terms.

And now, returning to our original query, we are prepared to
answer why one scientific man broke with faith. Mr. Darwin was
honest in deserting the faith of his childhood and the theistic convictions of his manhood. But was he logically driven to it? He
himself, despite himself, confesses that he was not. To the end his
"conviction" remained irreconcilable with his "conclusion." Yet
he was logical, if the evidence in favor of the extremely naturalistic form of the evolutionary hypothesis is more convincing than
that for God and the Bible—but logical with a logic which strips
of all its validity the very logic on which we are depending for our
conclusion, and leaves us shiveringly naked of all belief and of all
trustworthy faculty of thought. If we are to retain belief in our
own existence, Mr. Darwin himself being witness, we must believe also in that God who gave us life and being. We can account
for Mr. Darwin's failure to accept the guidance of his inextinguishable conviction here only if we recognize that his absorption in a single line of investigation and inference had so atro-
phied his mind in other directions that he had ceased to be a
trustworthy judge of evidence. Whatever may be true in other
cases, in this case the defection of a scientific man from religion
was distinctly due to an atrophy of mental qualities by which he
was unfitted for the estimation of any kind of evidence other than
that derived from the scalpel and the laboratory, and no longer
could feel the force of the ineradicable convictions which are as
"much a part of man as his stomach or his heart."[3]

3. [Warfield is paraphrasing an excerpt from a letter that Darwin's teacher at
Cambridge, the geologist Adam Sedgwick, sent to his former student. A longer
portion of this letter appears in the October 1888 essay on "Darwin's Religious
Life"; see p. 107 in the present volume.]

June 1891
Presbyterian and Reformed Review 2:163

Review of John William Dawson,
Modern Ideas of Evolution: As Related to Revelation and Science
(London: Religious Tract Society; New York
and Chicago: Fleming H. Revell, 1890)

The Canadian geologist and specialist in fossil plants, Sir John William Dawson (1820–99), whom Charles Hodge and James McCosh had earlier attempted to recruit for Princeton Seminary and the College of New Jersey, receives a glowing commendation for his conservative approach to Scripture, design, and evolution. Warfield suggests that Dawson would be an excellent candidate to provide a "new Paley," that is, to write an updated natural theology that could answer the pressures of late-nineteenth-century mechanistic Darwinism. Some of Warfield's own later essays may be considered as efforts on his part to incorporate evolutionary science into traditional theism in the way that Paley's *Natural Theology, or Evidences of the Existence and Attributes of the Deity* (1802) did for Newton's mechanistic philosophy.

Quite the best statement in brief compass and popular form of the real state of the question concerning evolution which has come to our notice. Dr. Dawson perceives that the Bible is not committed to any theory of the mode of creation (p. 17), and does not exclude evolutionary hypotheses up to a certain point (pp. 18–19, 49). But he also perceives the grave difficulties in the way of the current theories (e.g., pp. 76, 136, etc.), which are mostly kept out of sight by their enthusiastic advocates; and the inconsequent logic which may even be called the characteristic of their methods of reasoning (e.g., pp. 81, 125). In his view, evolution "up to this time remains an hypothesis, ingenious and captivating, but not fortified by the evidence of facts" (p. 145). A layman like ourself has no right to such an opinion, though it is within our province to say that the hypothesis is far from justified by the reasoning with which it has been supported, so that the evolutionists, if the facts are with them, have themselves to thank for the impression of unreality and fancifulness which they make on the earnest inquirer. Certainly every exact thinker will sympathize with Dr. Dawson in his rebuke of the now rather common mode of speech which refers to evolution as a "demonstrated" fact, or even as so certain as to be "axiomatic." Evolutionists would do well to adopt Prof. Huxley's creed: "In matters of the intellect do not pretend that conclusions are certain which are not demonstrated or demonstrable." Dr. Dawson's eminence as a paleontologist renders valuable his opinion that the grand procession of living beings in geological time does not make an impression on the mind of the trained observer favorable to the ordinary evolutionary hypotheses (p. 93), but that the testimony of paleontology is, on the whole, adverse to them (p. 135). Much of the volume is occupied with theistic problems, and especially with the design argument. We need a new Paley, of about the length of the old one, and adapted, like it, to classroom work. Will not Dr. Dawson prepare it?

October 1892
Presbyterian and Reformed Review 3:761–62

Review of Charles B. Warring,
Genesis I and Modern Science
(New York: Hunt & Eaton, 1892)

Warring (1825–1907) was a specialist in Hebrew and contemporary cosmogony at the Collegiate School in Poughkeepsie, New York. While Warfield approves of Warring's understanding that the Bible is not meant to teach science, he questions the author's ways of treating the "days" of Genesis 1 as the end points of geological ages and of fitting the biblical order of creation into geological eras. Warring's book is an early example of "concordism," or the effort to align what is known about nature with a particular interpretation of early Genesis.

D r. Warring has written on the scientific accuracy of the narrative of the first chapter of Genesis before; indeed, the substance of the present book appeared first a few years ago in *The Living Church*. In the book just mentioned his method is similar to that of Dr. Faunce—it is a dialogue with a rather complaisant and most unusually fair-minded "professor."[1] The object he sets before himself is expressed in "these two questions: Are the physical statements in the first twenty-seven verses true? and, Is their order correct?" (p. 17). He remarks: "It is important to remember that the Bible was not given to man to teach him science. Inciden-

---

1. [Warfield is referring to his review of Daniel Worcester Faunce's *Hours with a Skeptic,* which immediately precedes the Warring review. Faunce (1829–1911) was a Baptist minister from New England whose book Warfield describes as "an admirable body of primary apologetics" in the form of a series of interviews with "a dying man of skeptical turn."]

144

tally, as it were, it contains a vast amount of physical truth, but that is a very different matter" (p. 25). "The Hebrews could not have understood had Moses undertaken to tell how God created the heaven and the earth, and I very much suspect he would have no better success now, though he had Royal Societies and National Academies for his audience. But the simple fact that God did create the heaven and the earth the Hebrews could and, I may add, did understand as well as the wisest moderns" (p. 24).

These are very sensible remarks, and they adumbrate the true position regarding the relation of the Bible to science. Accordantly the author says that while God did not intend the Bible to teach science, neither "did He make the stars to teach astronomy; nor light to teach optics, but for all that, in them, potentially at least, are those sciences. I do not believe that science can be learned from the Bible any more than history can be learned from the prophecies; but as in the case of the latter we learn their true meaning from the history which records their fulfillment, so the science which gives us so many facts about creation enables us to know what is the true meaning of those brief descriptions which make up the narratives" (p. 175). This may be extremely stated, but it points out the truth in this much disputed matter.

In expounding the first chapter of Genesis thus in the light of science, Dr. Warring does not always carry us with him. He seems to be too minute in seeking correspondences, and sometimes to press the narrative under the thumbscrew of too severe an exegetical method. Nor do all of his harmonistic expedients commend themselves to us. The peculiarities of his exposition are chiefly the following: His view that the "days" of the narrative are ordinary days of twenty-four hours each, serving to mark the end of each successive period of varying length (pp. 190ff.)—a view which seems to be exegetically untenable; and his contention that the account in Genesis concerns the origin only of those things which man sees and with which he deals, only therefore of things contemporary with man, and "has nothing to do with the long succession of geological horizons, with plants and animals preceding and unlike those contemporaneous with man" (p. 26; see also 16–17, 191f.)—a suggestion which probably embodies an exegetical fact of importance, but which needs to be worked out more sympathetically than is done here. Dr. Warring's synchronizing of geological periods with the periods marked out by the days is also peculiar: the first day is made to cover pregeological time; the second the Azoic and Archaean times; the third, the whole stretch from the Lower Silurian to the Tertiary inclusive; while the Quaternary period is divided between the fourth, fifth and sixth days. The book is written with good temper and sufficient knowledge, but will probably be more valuable as an *argumentum ad hominem* to silence the gainsayer than as a constructive piece of work.

October 1893
Presbyterian and Reformed Review 4:714

Review of Nathaniel Southgate Shaler,
The Interpretation of Nature
(Boston and New York:
Houghton, Mifflin, 1893)

Nathaniel Shaler (1841–1906) taught paleontology and geology at
Harvard for nearly forty years. He had studied under Louis Agassiz,
but departed from his teacher's anti-Darwinianism to support a prov-
identialist view of evolution along the lines of the American Neo-
Lamarckian school.

This is a second edition of the Winckley Lectures delivered in
1891 at Andover Theological Seminary. Prof. Shaler's attitude is
one of kindly though outside friendliness towards a religious interpretation of nature. This attitude seems due to the failure of
the purely mechanical explanation of nature, which has borne itself in upon him as upon so many of the higher scientific minds.
But his standpoint is still phenomenal and naturalistic. In his per-
ceptions of nature, the mystery and the mysticism of nature have
broken in upon the hard, old mechanical theories for which alone
he once had an eye; but the tardy perception of mystery and mysticism leaves him rather in expectancy than with any true convictions as to the meaning of that "one increasing purpose" which
runs through all nature. To him, still, the present estate of man is
"the result of the physical and organic influences to which he has
been subjected during all his course from the lowest life to the
present time"; and religions are "the products of human history."
It is therefore the naturalistic evolutionary conception of life and
history which is kept prominent through all the discussion. And

147

148   **Warfield on Evolution and Science**

though there is a dim perception apparent of a primal endowment and impulse which the evolving process works out, yet the
conception of psychic capacities inherent in matter as matter—
unorganized and reduced to its mere chemical elements—suggests itself more strongly to him than does the conception of an
originating and directing Mind whose instruments physical and
psychic causes alike are. Prof. Shaler writes always in an excellent
tone and spirit and is on the upward trend; may it prove with him
a continuous trend.

October 1893
Presbyterian and Reformed Review 4:714–15

Review of Henry Calderwood,
Evolution and Man's Place in Nature
(London and New York: Macmillan, 1893)

Professor Henry Calderwood (1830–97), Scottish philosopher and ordained United Presbyterian minister, is here commended for his efforts to demonstrate that human intellectual and spiritual life, instead of stemming from natural evolution, actually provides evidence of a Creator. The review shows that, even during a period when Warfield was relatively skeptical about evidence for evolution, he nonetheless reacted favorably to efforts at incorporating evolutionary schemes within a teleological conception of the world.

It would be difficult to imagine a better corrective of Prof. Shaler's general attitude [as noted in the review immediately preceding] than this strong and lucid book of Prof. Calderwood's. Dr. Calderwood, too, stands frankly on the standpoint of evolution of organic life as maintained by Mr. Darwin and Mr. [Alfred Russel] Wallace. But his thought ranges more widely; and he presents with equal force the two sets of phenomena and the two spheres of knowledge which drive us to assert, as to man, a duality of life, physical and rational, harmonized in the individual; and as to nature, a divine background and cause. "Of Nature, as interpreted by Science, there is no key other than is found in recognition of an Immanent and Intelligent Cause that, in the midst of all and concerned with all, belongs to the history of Being. This is the first Cause—the eternal Personality—related to the spiritual life of rational souls as He can be related to no other type of existence within the wide sphere of creation." We owe Dr. Calderwood a new debt of gratitude for this timely book.

April 1895
Presbyterian and Reformed Review 6:366

Review of James Iverach,
Christianity and Evolution
(London: Hodder & Stoughton; New York:
Thomas Whittaker, 1894)

James Iverach (1839–1921) was another Scottish scholar and theologian, a professor of apologetics and exegesis at the Free Church College of Aberdeen, who became engaged in the debates over evolution. Like Warfield, he did not reject the "great idea of evolution," but viewed it as a process that takes place under God's guidance and according to his purpose and plan. Warfield's only reservation about Iverach's argument is the almost universal scope he assigns to evolution. Warfield has no difficulty with evolution under God, but he worries about a structure where God is thought to be under evolution.

D r. Iverach, in this ably and interestingly written booklet, sets himself to rescue the idea of evolution from its defamation by charlatanry and soiling by ignoble use. He argues unanswerably that this great form of thought can never come to its rights save as it is filled with the Christian conception of God as the living God who works immanently in all things, producing by means which from the point of view of efficiency we call causes the ends of his own choice. The issue which he has before his mind is not, therefore, one "between 'evolution' and what our friends are pleased to call 'special creation'; it is between evolution under the guidance of intelligence and purpose, and evolution as a fortuitous result." He shows solidly that evolution is meaningless save as a formula for an immanent God working according to plan; that the progressive discovery of laws under which the process

151

proceeds, so far from ever more and more weakening the theistic argument, strengthens it; and that the grandeur, intelligibility and manifest purposiveness of the process proclaim its divine author. "Our position is," he says, "that each new discovery is a fresh testimony to theism, and each new law found in phenomena is only a fresh argument for God—for intelligence as the source of order and the only ground of law." This is an important issue, and Dr. Iverach has met it admirably. Whether it is the only important issue in the case—"the issue of today" (p. 104), as he calls it—is perhaps worth further consideration.

The great idea of evolution can never come to its rights save under the conception of the Christian doctrine of God. But does the Christian doctrine of God come fully to its rights in the conception of evolution? Some of Dr. Iverach's readers may understand him so to suggest. He is very cordial in his recognition of evolution both as a fact and as an apparently all-pervasive fact. "To me," he says, "creation is continuous. To me everything is as it is through the continuous power of God; every law, every being, every relation of being are determined by Him, and He is the Power by which all things exist. I believe in the immanence of God in the world, and I do not believe that He comes forth merely at a crisis" (p. 175). Elsewhere Iverach excepts Christ from the process of creation by law, but adds: "But evolution will hold for all others" (p. 207).

We do not for a moment believe that Dr. Iverach intends to exclude the transcendent action of God; rather, his zeal is obviously to vindicate the reality of the Divine in his immanent action. But he appears to have spoken less guardedly than we could wish here. Christ is no doubt the great exception, but he is not the sole exception. "Evolution" can in no case be accepted as the formula of all that is; we must in any case rise above it to the higher formula of "God"—who is more than evolution, who indeed works in evolution, but also out of it. We say this is true "in any case"; we intend to leave the impression that we are by no means as sure as is Dr. Iverach of the reality of evolution in the wide range which he gives it. We would not willingly drag behind the evidence, indeed—nor would we willingly run ahead of it.

April 1895
Presbyterian and Reformed Review 6:366–67

Review of George Clark Hutton,
"The Ascent of Man":
Its Note of Theology
(Paisley and London:
Alexander Gardner, 1894)

Warfield approves of this Scottish Presbyterian minister's criticism of
the effort by Henry Drummond, another Scottish cleric, to subordinate all reality to science—a notion that Warfield identifies as re-
cycled eighteenth-century rationalism. George Clark Hutton (1825–
1908) argues against this subordination of Scripture and Christianity,
which are supernatural and authoritative in origin and content, to
the lesser rule of nature.

Principal Hutton devoted the opening lecture of the United Presbyterian College, Edinburgh, last autumn, to this keen and yet genial, thorough and yet eloquent criticism of the theological standpoint of Prof. Drummond's Lowell Lectures.[1] He finds ground to
complain, first of all, about the assumption that runs through the
lectures—and not through these lectures alone, but alas, in mod-

---

1. [Henry Drummond (1851–97), minister in the Free Church of Scotland, became professor of natural science at the Free Church College in Glasgow. He attempted to articulate evolutionary theory in a spiritual and devotional tone by
suggesting that natural law applies as equally to the realm of grace as it does to
the realm of nature. Drummond was a friend and firm supporter of the American
evangelist D. L. Moody. On the complexity of his opinions and relationships, see
James R. Moore, "Evangelicals and Evolution: Henry Drummond, Herbert Spencer, and the Naturalisation of the Spiritual World," *Scottish Journal of Theology* 38
(1985): 383–417.]

ern thinking—that it is to science that we must go for the final test of truth. Dr. Hutton says:

> The unsatisfactory features in their theological implications seem due to a latent but dominating theory of the place of science, reducing Scripture to mere subordination. Scripture is interpreted according to the exigency of a Theory of Nature rather than recognized as an independent authority and witness to God, a product and living expression of His Spirit, not of secondary consideration. . . . God means what He says in Nature, and it is sure, if we can find it out; but it is not surer when we have found it out than what He says in the words which the Holy Ghost teacheth.

Dr. Drummond's attitude here is, of course, simply the reiteration of the *fundamentum* of the old rationalism—and its effect is, of course, now as then, to reduce Christianity to the level of a natural religion. That this is what Prof. Drummond's theories come to, Dr. Hutton shows in detail, and then sums up, sorrowfully:

> We rank unwillingly this respected thinker among those of various schools who exalt Christianity only to a supremacy in the order of Nature. . . . The sum of the author's demand may be expressed: Christianity must be based in Nature, if it is to be received by Science—by Man. This implies that Man must be excused if he rejects all of Christianity which Nature does not teach. . . . We are asked to hope for a common *credo,* resting on Nature, "where all the faiths and all the creeds may meet; the Universal Religion which Science could accept." And this, it is said, we have already in Christianity as defined, rather as undefined, only by all means Evolutionary but not Supernatural.

Thus faithfully Dr. Hutton. When will the church at large awake to the fact that the problem which the newer religious thinking is putting before her is simply the old eighteenth-century problem in a fresh form? Though Christianity may be the crown and capstone of natural religion, is it only a natural religion for all that? Or is Christianity a supernatural religion—supernatural in origin, in sanctions, in power and in issue? When a man answers that question honestly with himself, he will know what to do with the newer religious thinking.

April 1895
Presbyterian and Reformed Review 6:367

Review of Robert Watts,
Professor Drummond's "Ascent of Man" and Principal Fairbairn's "Place of Christ in Modern Theology" Examined in the Light of Science and Revelation
(Edinburgh: R. W. Hunter, 1894)

As noted with Warfield's 1888 review of Watts's *Reign of Causality*, Robert Watts (1820–95) was an Irish Presbyterian who, like Warfield, had studied at Princeton under Charles Hodge. A theological conservative, Watts held the chair of systematic theology in the Presbyterian College, Belfast. Warfield clearly agrees with Watts's critique of the logic and presuppositions of two contemporary, more liberal theologians who had written popular works about science and religion.

D r. Watts, who keeps his eye on the progress of thought, here subjects two of the most sensational publications in recent theological literature to a calm but trenchant criticism. He shows that the principles enunciated by each of the popular teachers whom he criticizes are logically subversive of true religion, and that neither is free from confusion of thought in working out his ideas. Given Dr. Watts's exposures, Prof. Drummond will be puzzled as to where to find a place for a true supernaturalism in his theories of the "ascent of man." And Dr. Watts as clearly shows that an appeal to the "consciousness of Christ" as the source of theology will carry Dr. Fairbairn,[1] if he will apply it with thoroughness, whither he would not.

1. [Andrew Martin Fairbairn (1838–1912), a Congregational minister, theologian, and principal of the Congregational Theological College in England, had studied at Berlin under Ernst Hengstenberg and became an advocate of a freer and broader theology.]

August 22 and December 5, 1895
Presbyterian Messenger, August 22, 1895,
pp. 7–8; and December 5, 1895, pp. 7–8 (reprinted here from a twelve-page pamphlet containing both parts of this article and published by
the College Printing Office, Emporia, Kansas; there
are only minor differences of capitalization and
punctuation between the two printings)

The Present-Day Conception of Evolution

This essay expands on themes from Warfield's 1888 lecture at Princeton Seminary, from which most of the second part here derives.
Again, Warfield's main thesis is that evolution is a working hypothesis or conjecture that remains to be proved. He allows for the possibility that a limited version of evolution may have explanatory power,
while he criticizes those who would universalize this theory beyond
its demonstrated scope. Significantly, in an era of increasing academic professionalization, he repeatedly refers to "scientific workers" rather than "scientists," perhaps to remove some of the authoritative aura from the most enthusiastic advocates of evolution.

I

There seems to be an impression abroad that the adherents of
the doctrine of evolution have hopelessly fallen out among themselves, and threaten to destroy by internecine conflict the hold
which this doctrine has obtained upon scientific thought. This
impression is an erroneous one. Evolutionists do differ gravely
from one another on such subordinate matters as the causes of
variation, the classes of variation which may be preserved by heredity, and the selective factors at work in the gradual molding of
organic forms. In particular two strongly marked parties have
emerged among evolutionists, differing radically upon these subordinate matters. One of these, led by Prof. Weismann, holds that

157

all hereditable variations are congenital and purely fortuitous, and that natural selection, acting upon these fortuitous congenital differences, gradually molds the successive organisms into better and better harmony with their environment [i.e., Darwin's view]. The other party, to which probably the majority of evolutionists give their adhesion, holds that variation is strongly stimulated by use and disuse of organs, that such acquired qualities are hereditary, and that thus natural selection has not merely a body of purely fortuitous variations, but a series of definitely adaptive changes to work upon [i.e., Neo-Lamarckianism]. The difference between these two forms of the theory of evolution is not a small one. But it is obviously not a difference fundamental to the conception of evolution itself, but one which has reference only to the modes of its working. Evolutionists appear to be entirely and even increasingly at one in their fundamental conception of the doctrine.

We have lately been led to observe this, in an interesting way, by the circumstance of the appearance, in a single issue of a quarterly journal, of two general papers on evolutionary philosophy by such representative evolutionists as Prof. Joseph Le Conte of the University of California and Prof. E. D. Cope of Philadelphia.[1] Possibly no two American workers could be brought together who would more fairly represent the conceptions which rule among evolutionary thinkers. Both have been decidedly committed to this scheme of thought from the beginning, and have shown themselves leaders among their fellows. Yet they stand very far apart in many respects. Prof. Le Conte has devoted much consideration to the religious bearings of the new philosophy, while Prof. Cope has spent his strength in purely scientific investigations. Where these two meet, so-called Christian evolution meets with so-called

1. [Warfield is probably referring to two articles in *The Monist* 5 (1894): Le Conte, "Evolution and Social Progress," and Cope, "Present Problems of Organic Evolution." On Le Conte see p. 121 n. 6 in the present volume (Warfield's 1888 lecture). Edward Drinker Cope (1840–97), American paleontologist, rejected Darwin's natural selection as the fundamental mechanism of evolutionary change on the grounds that it could not explain nonfortuitous variations or retardations. He relied heavily on Spencer's biology and argued for the inheritance of acquired characteristics, suggesting that if a creature adapted before reproduction, this adaptation could be passed along to its offspring.]

purely scientific evolution, so that their agreements will register for us what may be fairly looked upon as the common ground upon which evolutionary thinkers meet today.

The first thing that is apt to strike the reader of the two papers is the absolute unity of the two writers in their conception of what evolution is. Each gives a formal definition of evolution, and the two definitions read like the product of a single pen. Prof. Cope says: "The doctrine of evolution may be defined as the teaching which holds that creation has been and is accomplished by the agency of the energies which are intrinsic in the evolving matter, and without the interference of agencies which are external to it." Prof. Le Conte says: "Evolution may be defined as continuous progressive change according to certain laws and by means of resident forces, i.e., by natural forces residing in the thing evolving." In brief, each alike conceives evolution as a doctrine of *self-creation*. As over against all conceptions of creation by powers, forces or agents intruding into nature from without, evolution is conceived by them as a doctrine of creation by the energies and forces of nature itself. The emphasis in both cases is placed on the contention that the forces operative in the process are "intrinsic," or "resident," in the thing evolving. Prof. Le Conte still further accentuates this by the added definition, "i.e., by *natural* forces *residing* in the thing evolving." Prof. Cope does the same by adding to the positive statement the negative clause, "and without the interference of agencies which are external to it." It is quite clear that with both the fundamental point is that evolution is a doctrine of *self-creation*. If, and so far as, there is intrusion of force or interference of agency from without, evolution ceases.

The next thing that is apt to strike the reader is the thoroughgoing radicalism of both writers as to the sphere which they hand over to this process of self-creation. To both alike the universe and all it contains is the sphere of this all-inclusive self-production. All that is, with the exclusion of nothing, is the product of the interaction of the forces or energies intrinsic or resident in the primal substance. Prof. Cope says simply that the energy by which all is accomplished "is a property of the physical basis of tridimensional matter, and is not outside of it." Prof. Le Conte is equally thoroughgoing. He enumerates several grades of evolution. He tells us that "matter by combination, recombination, and therefore by purely *chemical* forces, rose to higher and more complex forms until it reached protoplasm," and "in achieving protoplasm" it achieved "with it mobility and sensibility, i.e., life." Under the guidance of this "higher form of resident force," matter went on until it achieved man and, with man, self-conscious reason; under the guidance of this new resident force again matter is to go on until it achieves society and finally the divine man. Throughout the whole process nothing comes in from the outside, either in the way of energy or in the way of direction. "Matter" stands at the bottom with its resident forces, or, as Prof. Cope phrases it, "the physical basis of tridimensional matter" with its "intrinsic energies." And all that comes to be comes into being only through the movements of this matter by means of its resident forces. So it is not only a theory of *self-creation,* but it is a theory of the self-creation of *all that is.*

And this means, it will not fail to strike the reader further, that evolution is, in the hands of both these writers alike, *a philosophy of the universe.* It will not suffice to say that they, or either of them, look upon it merely as a theory of the method of creation, of the mode in which differentiations of form have come into being. It is presented by both of them alike as a theory of creation itself, accounting for all things that are. It is not merely that they omit to mention the higher directive power that may yet preside over the process of change and lead it to a preconceived goal; it is not even merely that they render the assumption of such a power superfluous; they directly and emphatically exclude it. Prof. Cope tells us plainly that, in his mind, there is an active exclusion of interfering agencies from without. And Prof. Le Conte, with scarcely less emphasis, gives us to understand that it is "nature" which is through this process "struggling upwards" towards "the divine plane from which it originated," and not God who is molding nature through the ages to his will. To both writers alike, evolution is a philosophy—a philosophy which accounts for the universe as it is, and for all that is in it, without calling in any interference from without.

Naturally, both must have something to start with in this process of self-creation. And for both alike this "something to start with" is phenomenally *nothing other than matter* with its primary qualities. Prof. Cope calls it, indeed, "the physical basis of tridimensional matter." But by this he means only that he conceives that, behind matter as we know it, there lies yet a simpler form of substance, so that matter as we have it—"tridimensional matter"—is itself a product of evolutionary process. This simplest primordial substance is still physical; and it is by its intrinsic energies alone that it has lifted itself first into tridimensional matter, then into organized matter, and then into reasoning matter. Prof. Le Conte's ontology is no less materialistic. He gives us to understand, to be sure, that "the plane from which all evolution sprang" was "divine," even as the goal to which it tends is "divine," so that "nature by evolution through infinite time has struggled upward to reach again the divine plane from which it originated." But "the thing evolving" in its primordial stage he identifies with what we know as matter in its simplest form, endowed with or at least active in only "its purely chemical properties." The emergence of further and higher qualities comes later on, in the process of evolution itself. Thus to identify God with matter, or to call matter God, does not appear to us to improve things. The difference between a pantheistic and a materialistic ontology is insignificant in a connection of this kind; in both alike, it is from what we know as matter in its simplest form that all that is has come. Whence this primordial matter comes neither writer tells us. Probably both would speak of it as eternal. The one might possibly take this in the materialistic sense and, projecting his imagination backwards, expect to find nothing but "the physical basis of tridimensional matter" behind. The other may take it in a pantheistic sense and conceive behind all changes what he calls "God"— but God in the form of simple undifferentiated matter. To both alike, simple matter, with its own intrinsic or resident forces, is all that is; and all that has come to be is its evolution, i.e., its changes of form under the action of its own intrinsic energies.

It assuredly will not escape the reader that this philosophical theory has no claim to be called science. It is purely *a priori* construction. Who has shown Prof. Cope his physical basis of tridimensional matter? What scientific discovery has revealed to Prof. Le Conte that God is identical with primal matter and can be attained by primal matter rising, through the operation of its resident forces, back to the plane from which it started? What discovery has shown him that protoplasm is a simple chemical compound? that life is a product of chemical reaction? that reason is modified life? that God is advanced reason? Observed fact cuts no figure in these theories. Indeed, the reader will nowhere find himself more emancipated from the trammels of fact than when reading such an imaginative construction as Prof. Le Conte's. In skimming the opulent pages the reader may feel himself in the hands of a poet whose feet scorn the earth. But he cannot discover the foundations of fact on which these great dreams are built.

Nor can it possibly escape the reader that evolution conceived thus as an all-inclusive philosophy leaves little room in the universe for what the Christian calls God. Even a materialistic scheme of evolution may, to be sure, comport with a deistic conception of God. After all, Professor Cope is not entitled simply to assume "a physical basis of tridimensional matter" so endowed that by virtue of its intrinsic energies alone it may unfold itself into a universe of order and of mind. We need still to ask whence this physical basis of matter and whence its wonderful powers, enfolding within themselves the promise and potency of every form of life. At the least, we need a power outside and beyond the evolving stuff to make the stuff, to give its forces to it, and to set it going—a *primum movens* [prime mover] in this sense.

Furthermore, the most entire system of self-creation equally may comport with a pantheistic conception of God. Prof. Le Conte may teach that all that exists was once involuted in simple matter and gradually evolves from it up to God himself—if he understands by God only the All whose varying manifestations the changing world is, who is not only entangled in but indistinguishable from matter, and who is only as matter is and what matter may at any moment chance to be.

But it seems perfectly obvious that this evolutionary philosophy leaves no place for the Christian's God, who is not the God afar off of the deist, and not the simple world-ground of the pantheist, but the living God of the Bible—at once above the world and in the world, the author of the world and its strong governor who is not far from any one of us but yet is a being outside and above us, who is to the world and to man at least an external power making for righteousness.

Theism has, of course, no quarrel with second causes. It would not substitute the direct divine action for the operation of the natural forces which God has made and which are real forces, really operative just because "he who can" has made them such. But neither can it permit second causes to be substituted for the living God, who doeth his pleasure amid the armies of heaven and among the inhabitants of the earth. The universe was not self-created. It was God that made it, and without him was not any thing made that has been made. No philosophy that as its basic principle leaves God out of its account of all that is can possibly take a really theistic view of the world. In this sense, evolution as conceived by both of our present writers is, therefore, tantamount to atheism. It has no room in all its thought for a living God—for a God who not only is, but who can and who does.

II

There are three general positions which may be taken up with reference to the doctrine of evolution, which has so deeply affected modern thought as to the origin of the universe and all that it contains.

1. We may look upon this doctrine as supplying an obviously true and adequate philosophy of being, and treat it as furnishing a complete account of the origin and present state of the universe. It is so looked upon by a large number of writers of light and leading. Thus Prof. Huxley affirms "that the whole world, living and not living, is the result of the natural interaction, according to definite laws, of the powers possessed by the molecules of which the primitive nebulosity of the universe was composed." This position is, of course, tantamount to atheism; and it is a matter of indifference to the theist whether it takes a materialistic or a pantheistic shape. When Mr. Darwin put forth his *Origin of Species,* he was confining his survey to the origin of the divergent forms of animated existence. He consequently postulated the existence of life and living forms. Moreover, in his ever shifting opinion as to divine things, he wrote that book at a stage when he was feeling theistically; he therefore spoke throughout it in a theistic sense and theistic language. But that the theory, as held by him, was essentially atheistic, as Dr. Charles Hodge pointed out in a vigorous little volume, was fully exhibited by his drift away from theism, as recorded in his *Life and Letters.*

2. We may consider the doctrine of evolution as a discovery by science of the process through which this ordered world in which we live has, as a matter of fact, come into existence; we may treat evolution merely as an account of the manner in which the universe, considered as a cosmos, has been produced, and all the forms of being which constitute it have been brought into being. In this form, evolution is not conceived as the ultimate account of any thing; it is made a second cause and implies a first cause working by and through it. In this form, accordingly, it is not only not atheistic, but implies and presupposes theism. This is the form in which it is conceived by theistic thinkers. A notable example of its presentation from this point of view may be found in the writings of the late Dr. James McCosh. Dr. McCosh speaks of evolution as "demonstrated" fact and yet harnesses it to his own theistic conceptions, making it subservient to and indeed give way before his Christian supernaturalism. When so dealt with, the doctrine of evolution supplies the Christian thinker only with an account of the mode and method of creation.

3. We may look upon the doctrine of evolution as a more or less probable, or a more or less improbable, conjecture of scientific workers as to the method of creation; and thus we may treat it as only a working hypothesis suggested to account for the manner in which the universe has come into being, and seeking now to try itself by the facts. This has always been the attitude of the more cautious thinkers, and in the progress of scientific investigation it is becoming now somewhat more common to find it adopted even by scientific workers themselves. An increasing caution is observable in assertion, perhaps, we may even say, an increasing doubt as to the universality and sufficiency of evolution. In the new edition of his admirably restrained and sensible lectures on *The Bible Doctrine of Man,* Dr. John Laidlaw points out how much less frequently now than a few years ago the claim is made for the evolutionary hypothesis "as a universal solvent of the question of origins."[2] And he points out how this change of attitude affects the duty of the Christian thinker. "In face of these

2. [John Laidlaw (1832–1906), Scottish Presbyterian pastor, theologian in the Free Church of Scotland, and a professor of systematic theology at New College, Edinburgh, was a strict adherent to the Westminster standards and was cautiously critical of higher criticism.]

recent confessions of the merely tentative character of the hypothesis," he remarks, "the lesson for the interpreter of Scripture is plain. For him to hasten to propound schemes of conciliation between the Mosaic account of creation and the Darwinian pedigree of the lower animals and man would be to repeat an old and, now, an unpardonable blunder."

In a word, the really pressing question with regard to the doctrine of evolution is not, on the one hand, whether it supplies in itself an adequate account of the origin of being and the differentiation of forms, nor, on the other, whether the old faith can live with this new doctrine. The first of these questions only raises in a new form the old problem of the atheistic philosophy; it does not deserve a new discussion merely because it has put on a new dress. The second question opens only a purely idle speculation which is careless whether it deals with realities or shadows. We may be sure that the old faith will be able not merely to live with, but to assimilate to itself all facts. "The gold of fact," says Dr. Laidlaw finely, "will form at length the perfect ring of truth when the crust of suppositions which have helped in its formation shall be dissipated into dust and ashes." Meanwhile, having "a revealed account of the origin of the world and man, which coincides with the instinctive beliefs of the human mind, with the plan of human history, with the faith and hope that are in God," we need not be overanxious whether or not it can be shown to coincide also with every tentative supposition. The only living question with regard to the doctrine of evolution is whether it is true. And the only reasonable reply which can be given to this question today is that it is *sub judice.* This is not equivalent, of course, to saying that it is not true. We may hold it to be probably true, and yet agree that it is still upon its trial and has not yet been shown to be true. But we think it must be admitted that it has not yet been shown to be true, and must still be ranked not as "demonstrated" fact, but only as a more or less probable or a more or less improbable working hypothesis.

To be sure, it is to be borne in mind that it is scarcely legitimate to ask anything of the nature of a strict demonstration, or even anything like direct proof, for a theory of this sort. Proof of a hypothesis of this kind can be only of a probable order, and can arise only out of inferences from observed effects to causes and processes. It is quite conceivable, however, that such proof might reach stringent validity and command assent. Its power to do so would depend on the ability of the suggested hypothesis to explain with ease and completeness all the observed facts. And by this we must mean something more than merely the possibility of wrenching some kind of explanation of the facts out of the hypothesis.

Consider, for example, that most of the phenomena of the universe could find some sort of explanation in the Ptolemaic theory. But the probability of a theory increases not only in proportion to the number of the facts of which it supplies an explanation, but also in proportion to the cleanness, so to speak, with which it explains them, and its power to illuminate the connection between the facts and thus supply a basis for deduction by which we may (1) deduce from the terms of the theory all the known facts, and thus, as it were, prove its truth; and (2) deduce also new facts, not hitherto known, by which it becomes predictive and the instrument of the discovery of new facts which are sought for and observed only on the expectation roused by the theory. It is quite possible, by a combination of such results, so fully and powerfully to commend a suggested hypothesis that the mind cannot resist the evidence in its favor. It may with such cleanness and perfection explain all the observed facts, with such power of illumination uncover obscure points and reveal new and unexpected elements of fact, and with such certainty determine the facts subsumed under it and lead on to the discovery of others, that we cannot escape the conviction that in it we have exactly the key that belongs to this lock. And, of course, it follows that the more complicated the lock is, the greater is the certainty that we have found its true key when we have a key which smoothly and cleanly fits every ward. But it must fit the wards. The simplest bent wire will often serve as a pick to open a lock. And as not every key that will open a lock is the proper key, so not every theory that will open a problem is the proper explanation. There is such a thing as picking the lock of a problem as well as of a safe, and science needs protection against burglary just as truly as do banks.

But if it is true that not every theory which will provide some sort of explanation for the facts is the true theory, it is, of course, *a fortiori* true that no theory which will not explain the facts can possibly be the true theory. Every theory proposed to account for a body of facts must run two gauntlets. It must first of all be shown to be capable of accounting for the facts. It is sometimes assumed that this is all that can be asked of it. But all that has been so far shown is that, should there be reason to believe that this hypothesis is the true one, it may be accepted as such—no facts stand in the way. We must now ask what reason exists for supposing it to be the true account of the facts. In other words, we must now range it alongside of whatever other theories exist also capable of accounting for the facts, and seek grounds for choice between them. Everything is not true that is shown to be possibly true. The race is to be run between the various theories which have been shown to be able to account for the facts. The preliminary exhibition of ability to account for the facts is only a conforming to the condition of entry for the race. Assuredly the prize cannot be claimed merely on presentation of clean entry papers before the race is run. Much more assuredly, the prize cannot be claimed before the entry is itself approved.

If now it be asked what is the exact status of the doctrine of evolution, it will scarcely be possible to affirm that it has as yet been shown that it is capable of accounting for all the facts. Precisely what is now under investigation is whether the facts as known can be accounted for on this hypothesis. There is a widespread feeling abroad that, if it can be shown that it is capable of accounting for all the facts, this is the proper theory to assume in order to account for them. And there is a widespread expectation that sooner or later, in one form or another, the evolutionary hypothesis will be shown to be able to account for all the facts. But it is surely premature to say of it that it has already been shown to be able to account for all the facts. And we cannot but think that enthusiasm has run away with good judgment when we hear it said, as we sometimes do hear it said, that we have the same proof for the doctrine of evolution that we have for Newton's theory of gravitation. There is an essential difference in kind between these two cases, as readers of Dr. Flint's paper on "Theology" in the ninth edition of the *Encyclopaedia Britannica* will have lucidly expounded to them. But apart from this, it would seem to be too evident that the proof that evolution will account for all

168   **Warfield on Evolution and Science**

the facts observed in the sphere for which it has to account as yet
lags. It may be far from plain that it cannot account for all these
facts. It is as yet equally far from plain that it can account for them
all. A thousand scientific investigators are now engaged in the effort to show that it can account for them.

The overenthusiastic assertion that evolution has been shown
to be able to account for all observed facts in the sphere of its assumed operation may possibly find its explanation, in part, in a
perhaps not unnatural extension of a happy experience in a nar-
rower to an unwarrantedly broadened field. The doctrine of evolution has served us, we will say, in our endeavors to unravel
some exceptionally hard problem. In the enthusiasm of this experience we declare it able to unravel all similar problems. This is
the natural history of all panaceas. It is scarcely stringent logic,
however, to infer from the fact that a theory can account for some
facts, that it therefore can account for all facts. Yet this is a logic
from which advocates of evolution have not kept their skirts free.

A possible genealogy is made out, for example, for the Equidae
which might possibly be accounted for by the doctrine of evolution. It is then assumed that this is the actual genealogy of the
Equidae and that evolution is the right account to give of it. And
then it is forthwith assumed that because evolution may thus
possibly account for the Equidae, it is also the true account to assume for the origin of species and genera for which we cannot, as
yet at least, make out any genealogy which is at all consistent
with the doctrine of evolution—of the Trilobites, say, or of the
Devonian fishes. Students of logic might obtain some very entertaining examples of fallacy by following the processes of reasoning by which evolutionists sometimes commend their findings to
a docile world. The treatment of the apparition of the fishes in the
Devonian age in Prof. Le Conte's *Manual of Geology* is a shining instance which, unfortunately, does not stand alone. But we
scarcely need a better example than that in hand. Because a possible genealogy can be constructed for a number of forms, chiefly
in the upper strata, for which evolution might possibly supply an
account, it does not follow that evolution is shown to be the true
account of the whole series of forms presented to us in the crust
of the earth. And it will hardly do to clench this somewhat violent
inference by an appeal to the law of continuity and uniformity in

nature, which is rather too sharp a two-edged sword for evolutionists safely to wield at this stage of the investigation.

It ought not to be necessary to add that none of this is said with a view to giving the impression that the doctrine of evolution has been disproved. It is not even intended to suggest that it is improbable. We wish to point out as clearly as we can only that it is as yet unproved, that its present status is that of a suggested explanation of the facts of nature which is as yet on its trial as to whether it can supply an account of these facts or not. We may deem it probable or we may deem it improbable that it will ever be shown to be able to account for these facts. It will certainly conduce to a clearer conception of the state of the case if we will recognize it according to our different judgments as, as yet, only a more or less probable or a more or less improbable conjecture of scientific workers as to the method and course of creation.

April 1896
Presbyterian and Reformed Review 7:382–83

Review of John M. Tyler,
The Whence and Whither of Man: A Brief History of His Origin and Development through Conformity to Environment
(New York: Scribner, 1896)

John M. Tyler (1851–1929) was a professor of biology at Amherst College in Massachusetts. Although Warfield commends Tyler's presentation of human origins and is sympathetic to his theistic outlook, he finds the book wanting in fulfilling its stated goal of examining the effect of evolutionary theory on religious beliefs. Warfield expresses a strong desire to see the proofs of this theory—and its moral and religious consequences—more fully treated.

As the title already advises us, Prof. Tyler undertakes in these lectures to trace the origin of man according to the development hypothesis. While thoroughgoing and inclusive of all that is in man, his evolutionism is held in harmony with a theistic worldview and is therefore conceived as process and not as cause. Tyler does not undertake in these lectures to show that this conception of man's origin is the true one: "the limits of this course of lectures have required us to choose between alternatives, either to attempt to prove the truth of the theory of evolution, or, taking this for granted, to attempt to find its bearings on our moral and religious beliefs" (p. 115). The truth of the evolutionary account of man's origin is therefore assumed. Nevertheless, the lectures fail in their attempt to "find the bearings of this doctrine on our moral and religious beliefs." Rather, they are devoted simply to a lucid exposition of the elements of the evolutionary account of man's origin. The first lecture outlines the problem; the second, third and fourth present a hypothetical genealogy of man's physical structure; the fifth does the same for mental functions; the sixth and seventh expound the effects of environment; the eighth presents man himself as an evolved and evolving being; the ninth is a not very helpful presentation of the teachings of the Bible relevant to the exposition; and the tenth (the most interesting chapter in the volume) describes the "present aspects of the theory of evolution," i.e., the various theories which are now held by the several parties of evolutionists. At the end we have a phylogenetic chart after the manner of Haeckel, tracing man hypothetically from protoplasm up.[1]

The book is brightly but somewhat loosely written. Its whole tone is reverential and even devout. It would have been more helpful, however, to discuss thoroughly one or the other of the questions which are passed by—whether there is any sufficing proof of the evolutionary theory of man's origin, and what effect, if it is true, it will have on our moral and religious beliefs. Most men today know the evolutionary construction of the origin of man; there are many of us who would like to be better instructed as to its proofs and effects.

---

1. [The German zoologist Ernst Haeckel (1834–1919) was such an enthusiastic supporter of Darwin that he was called "the apostle of Darwinism" in Germany. He systematically placed Darwin's ideas into a philosophical system he called monism. This monism was to facilitate the unity of mind and matter through a mechanical-causal approach to life instead of the dualist position which differentiated between mind and matter. Haeckel coined the term "ecology" in 1866 and developed a phylogenetic chart that traced the descent of the human race in twenty-six stages from protoplasm and single-celled organisms through chimpanzees.]

April 1896
Presbyterian and Reformed Review 7:383

Review of George John Romanes,
Darwin and After Darwin: An Exposition of the Darwinian Theory and a Discussion of Post-Darwinian Questions
(Chicago: Open Court, 1895)

The British biologist George John Romanes (1848–94) formed an early friendship with Darwin and supported and popularized his theories. Based on lectures Romanes delivered at the Royal Institution from 1881 to 1891, *Darwin and After Darwin* dealt with the development of the theory of organic evolution. While Romanes moved away from orthodox Christian faith in the 1870s and 1880s, he appeared to be returning to orthodoxy shortly before his death.

There is certainly no loose writing here, and no padding. Mr. Romanes' discussions go to the roots of the matters treated and constitute one of the best aids yet to the understanding both of the problems that have arisen as it has been sought to apply the evolutionary hypothesis to the origin of forms, and of the various schools of thought which have sprung up in consequence. The introduction (which we had already read as a paper in *The Monist*) is the most lucid possible statement of these divergent views, while the following chapters discuss with great thoroughness the nature of characters hereditary and acquired, adaptive and specific. No one who wishes to be informed as to the present aspects of thought in this department of investigation can afford to neglect this strongly reasoned book.

July 1896
Presbyterian and Reformed Review 7:561–62

Review of Randolph S. Foster,
Creation: God in Time and Space
(New York: Hunt & Eaton; Cincinnati:
Cranston & Curts, 1895)

Randolph S. Foster (1820–1903) was a bishop in the Methodist Episcopal Church and served as president of Northwestern University in
the 1850s. He became professor of theology at Drew Theological
Seminary in 1868 and then president from 1870 to 1872. Warfield
summons up only faint praise for this "voluminous volume" on the
universe, the fourth of a six-part Studies in Theology series that Foster published between 1889 and 1899. The review closes with Warfield's assertion of the priority of the written Word of God over scientific facts, since the latter are mediated and interpreted by humans
and therefore fallible. Such an assertion illustrates Warfield's commitment to Princeton Seminary's historic effort to deal fully with
both Scripture as divine revelation and nature as the arena of God's
creating activity.

This voluminous volume forms the fourth part of Bishop Foster's extended series of Studies in Theology. The present instal-
ment attempts a survey of the universe, with a view to showing
the vastness of the work of God's hands in both space and time.
Its primary object, therefore, is not to discuss the doctrine of creation or the method of the origination of the universe, but to
place before the reader some conception of its immensity. Little
space is given, accordingly, to questions of origin, though they are
not wholly omitted, and the author pronounces against the evolutionary hypothesis in the course of their discussion.

173

The strength of the book is in its descriptive side, and here the facts established by the several sciences are freely drawn upon. It must be acknowledged that the discussion is written somewhat diffusely, and that a great deal of matter is transferred to these pages from not very inaccessible sources. But the selections are made with good judgment, and the whole is compacted skillfully into a treatise which supplies useful as well as agreeable reading for the popular audience for which it is intended.

The fundamental principle which the author lays down with reference to the theologian's attitude towards the facts of the universe does not appear to be stated with exact accuracy. It must indeed be admitted that an ascertained fact will and ought to prevail against any word-statement. But is it so obvious that our ascertainment of a fact is more trustworthy than any word-statement? All statements will find their test in facts, but it does not thence follow that revelation will find its test in science. Science is not fact, but human reading of fact; and any human reading of fact may well bow humbly before the reading given by God. In the conflict between the infallible Word and "infallible science," it is the part of reason to prefer the word-statement sufficiently authenticated as divine to the word-statement which is obviously very human indeed.

January 1897
Presbyterian and Reformed Review 8:120

Review of Sir John William Dawson,
Eden Lost and Won: Studies of the Early History and Final Destiny of Man as Taught in Nature and Revelation
(New York, Chicago and Toronto:
F. H. Revell, 1896)

As in his 1891 review of Dawson's *Modern Ideas of Evolution,*
Warfield appreciates the way in which the geologist integrates his
substantial scientific knowledge with an orthodox reading of Scripture, in particular the Old Testament narratives. Contrary to many in
his era, Dawson finds that Scripture and the physical evidence shed
positive light on each other, a view which Warfield clearly finds
encouraging.

These ten interesting papers by one of our oldest and best-furnished students of the borderland between science and revelation originally appeared in the pages of *The Expositor,* and "are now collected, with some additions and amendments." They are arranged here under two captions: the first seven papers present "physical and historical probabilities respecting the authorship and authority of the Mosaic books," and the last three contain remarks on "man and nature, fallen and restored."

Those who are familiar with Dr. Dawson's former works will find much here reminiscent of them and something repeated from them. There are the same calm mastery of the scientific material, the same sober judgment of the biblical statements, the same mental independence and clear presentation which characterize all his writings. It will go without saying that in this volume, too, Dr. Dawson comes forward as the defender of the essential truthfulness of the scriptural narrative, a sphere in which he has ever done good service to the cause of truth. He even ventures to represent that there is a physical as well as an archaeological commendation of the earlier narratives of the Bible, which appeals especially to a student of nature, and which he, therefore, is specially called upon to present. The student of nature alone, he tells us in his preface, "can fully appreciate the internal evidence [the early narratives] afford of antiquity and accordance with the earlier remains and monuments of our species. He alone can measure their accordance with physical facts open to observation in relation to the past, present and future of humanity." As an illustration, he thinks that the writer of the second chapter of Genesis infallibly fixes his geographical point of view on the banks of the Euphrates and his chronological standpoint between the deluge and Abraham. In matters of this kind, Dr. Dawson's judgment is peculiarly valuable, and it is the physical side of the book which should receive very special attention.

January 1897
Presbyterian and Reformed Review 8:157

Review of Luther Tracy Townsend,
Evolution or Creation: A Critical Review of the Scientific and Scriptural Theories of Creation and Certain Related Subjects
(New York, Chicago and Toronto:
Fleming H. Revell, 1896)

Luther Tracy Townsend (1838–1922) was both an accomplished academic and a popular apologist for traditional evangelical theology. An ordained Methodist minister, he became professor of church history and then practical theology at Boston Theological Seminary (later Boston University School of Theology). This monograph was intended for the general reader and, according to Warfield, stands firmly within the classical Christian tradition of affirming God as the origin of all things and Scripture as the ultimate authority.

Prof. Townsend in this volume seeks to answer for Christian people, perplexed by the trend of much recent discussion, the fundamental question, How came the human race on this earth? Unterrified by any strength of assertion to the contrary, he replies emphatically, Not without God. He does more. Rejecting not merely the naturalistic but also the timidly supernaturalistic answers, he insists that man came into the world just as the Bible says he did. Prof. Townsend has his feet planted here on the rock. When it is a question of scriptural declaration versus human conjecture dignified by any name, whether that of philosophy or that

177

of science, the Christian man will know where his belief is due. Prof. Townsend has his individual opinions, of course, which we may or may not share. He writes also for a popular audience, and with more or less looseness of thought and expression. But his trust in the affirmations of the Word of God as the end of all strife will commend itself to every Christian heart.

July 1898
Presbyterian and Reformed Review 9:510–12

Review of Andrew Dickson White,
A History of the Warfare of Science with Theology in Christendom, 2 vols.
(New York: D. Appleton, 1896)

Along with John William Draper, author of *History of the Conflict between Religion and Science,* first published in 1874, Andrew Dickson White, president of Cornell University, played a major role in promulgating the thesis that the history of science was largely the story of a struggle between two forces—human rationality and traditional faith. In this review of White's two-volume work, Warfield challenges that thesis on several fronts. In particular, because Warfield conceived of theology as one of the sciences, he felt that White's postulation of a conflict between Science (with a capital S) and theology was as incoherent as speaking of a conflict between Science and botany. Warfield's final judgment that the work constituted a piece of "special pleading" anticipated the judgment of modern historians who have concluded that White was engaged in projecting then-current controversies back into the past.[1]

1. See, for example, David C. Lindberg and Ronald L. Numbers, introduction to *God and Nature: Historical Essays on the Encounter between Christianity and Science,* ed. Lindberg and Numbers (Berkeley: University of California Press, 1986), 3: "White read the past through battle-scarred glasses." The entirety of *God and Nature* is an effort to show the immense complexity in what White pictured as a simple antagonism. Much the same purpose informs James R. Moore, *The Post-Darwinian Controversies: A Study of the Protestant Struggle to Come to Terms with Darwin in Great Britain and America, 1870–1900* (New York: Cambridge University Press, 1979), ch. 1, "Draper, White, and the Military Metaphor," 19–49.

Few books have come to us recently which do more credit to the bookmaker's art than do these two handsome volumes: it is a pleasure to handle them, and the eye delights in their well-printed pages and large, clear type. The work which they embody is an evolution and approaches its readers with all the comfortable assurance of an old friend. In its babyhood it was introduced to the public as a lecture on "The Battlefields of Science," published in the columns of the *New York Tribune.* Soon it had grown into "a little book called *The Warfare of Science* (1876). That waxed into "New Chapters in the Warfare of Science," a long series of articles in *Popular Science Monthly.* Finally, the full-grown work appears, swelled to nearly a thousand octavo pages, in the volumes now before us.

At its first appearance in book form Dr. James McCosh felt constrained thus to comment upon it: "President White has in his *Warfare of Science* brought forward an agglomeration (very indiscriminate and uncritical) of facts to show that religious men have opposed science, and been defeated. As no doubt he wishes to be impartial, I suggest that he gather a like body of facts to show that savants have used their science to put down religion, which stands as firm as ever" (*The Development Hypothesis: Is It Sufficient?* [1876], 75).

After all its growth in size, the same judgment must be passed upon the completed work: it is still an "indiscriminate and uncritical agglomeration of fact," brought together for the support of a thoroughly one-sided and fatally misleading proposition. Dr. McCosh indeed did more than justice to the work when he said that its intention is "to show that religious men have opposed science." That is its effect, and we may readily infer from the exposure in these erudite and well-packed pages that not all religious men of all ages have been perfectly informed or entirely wise or invariably right. But Dr. White does not so read his thesis. He is eager to put into conflict not some religious men and the advancing conceptions of scientific thought, but distinctly what he calls "Dogmatic Theology" and "Science"; and he defines Dogmatic

Theology as the theology "based on biblical texts"—to which he adds, no doubt, "and ancient modes of thought," but only as an unimportant indication of what he thinks Dogmatic Theology really is. The thesis which he is actually striving to make good is that the doctrinal teachings of the Bible, so far as they concern matters with which science has to do, are simply a mass of mythological conceptions; the attempt to hold to them as truth has thrown up a dam across the advance of the stream of knowledge—a dam which this irresistible stream has repeatedly been at necessity to break through and bear away.

White considers himself a Christian man and reverences "the blessed Founder of Christianity." He labors—even in the publication of this volume—for the spread of "pure and undefiled religion," but the sphere of religion is to be sharply limited and the whole sphere of science left undisturbed by its influence. The sphere of science, moreover, is made as broad as possible. In the twenty chapters gathered in this book announcing so many instances of the rout of Theology before advancing Science, the latter term is made to cover with its aegis every department of human research from pure Metaphysics to the Higher Criticism. It is amazing what a wealth of detail Mr. White has brought together in support of his thesis. Of course, it has not been possible for him to collect all these details and record them without falling into errors of fact. A considerable list of such errors might easily be drawn up, a good number of which would impinge upon the thesis they are adduced to support.

But the trouble with the book does not lie in these inevitable and insignificant errors of detail. It lies in its fundamental conception and in the whole disposition of its material. Here there is such fatal one-sidedness that the entire treatise—valuable as it is and will remain as a magazine of facts—is hopelessly vitiated. As Dr. McCosh pointed out twenty years ago, all that it proves is that some religious men have been slow to follow the advance of science. The same could easily be shown of some scientific men. It was not because they were men of religion, but because they held too tenaciously to the current ideas of men of science, that these men lagged behind the vanguard of advance.

Least of all does Dr. White's argumentation, in any case, prove that there is warfare between Science and Theology, and he has done grave injustice to his own cause and his own book by writing this thesis down on its title page and making the validation of it the object of his labors. What after all, in strictness of thought, can be meant by affirming a warfare between Science and Theology? There is no such thing as Science with a big S: sciences there are, but the *scientia scientiarum* [knowledge of the fields of knowledge], which alone can be meant by Science, is a philosophy, and can be interpreted only as a general worldview supposed to be involved in the results of the various sciences.

But how can Science, with a big S, in this sense come into conflict with Theology? Theology is itself a science, one of the *scientiae* [fields of knowledge]. Because Science is the abstract expression of the results of the *scientiae,* to speak of a conflict between the two is to say that the whole we have erected in our minds will not comport with one of its component parts. The absurdity of it all will be at once perceived when we shift the assumed conflict to another department of science. How would it do to speak of the warfare between Science and Botany, say, or between Science and Geology? The self-contradiction can be voided only by a preliminary arbitrary exclusion of Theology from the domain of Science, and it is just this narrow point of view which characterizes Dr. White's attitude and vitiates his conclusions *ab initio* [at their base]. If this assumption is not made to start with, it is very clear what happens to Science if it is in conflict with Theology. When Science gets into conflict with one of the sciences, which it assumes to represent, it is, of course, Science that goes to the wall.

Our complaint against Dr. White's book, then, is that in its fundamental viewpoint it is the outgrowth of pure prejudice, and that in its elaboration it is one-sided and thoroughly misleading. A "history" is just what it is not: it is a polemic treatise and a polemic treatise which in its whole spirit and effort is painfully like a partisan attorney's plea. A history of the adjustments of theological thought and general culture through the ages was well worth writing. A piece of special pleading like this was not worth writing, and the undeniable ability of the performance and the richness of the material assembled will not save it from this condemnation. All that the book as a whole really proves is the narrowness of Dr. White's *Weltanschauung* [worldview].

October 1898
Presbyterian and Reformed Review 9:780–82

Review of A. A. W. Hubrecht,
The Descent of the Primates:
Lectures Delivered on the Occasion of the Sesquicentennial Celebration of Princeton University
(New York: Scribner, 1897)

With considerable irony, Warfield dissects the assumptions and logic of Ambrosius Arnold Willem Hubrecht's published lectures on primate evolution given at the 150th anniversary of the founding of Princeton University (originally the College of New Jersey). Hubrecht (1853–1915) was a professor of zoology and comparative embryology at the University of Utrecht. A convinced Darwinian, he devoted his research to seeking evidence for phylogenetic relationships, especially in the early embryonic stages. Warfield points out that the results of Hubrecht's work lead more to the conclusion of separate, parallel development amongst primates than the phylogenetic tree with a single common origin preferred by Darwinians. Warfield also suggests that the case for the existence of the phylogenetic tree rests on the prior assumption of evolution and speculative imagination rather than on the basis of factual evidence (which he views as increasingly counter to Darwinian evolutionary hypotheses).

Prof. Hubrecht's lectures supply another notable example of the fascinations of speculative science. As a result of his studies in the embryology of Tarsius and the lemurs, he has been led to separate the Lemuridae widely from the primates while still including Tarsius among the primates.[1] This necessitates a new construction of the phylogeny of the primates, with its involved new genealogy of man.

In these lectures Hubrecht gives a clear and interesting popular account of his conclusions. There are two things which most strongly impress the lay reader of his presentation: first, what must appear to him the serious overworking of the principle, reasonable in itself, but certainly capable of being unduly pressed, that similarities of structure imply genealogical connection; and, secondly, the facility with which speculatively constructed facts are made to take their place along with facts of observation as the basis of argumentation. The whole theory presented here, for example, is based not more on the observed embryology of Tarsius than on the assumed embryology of Anaptomorphus (p. 19).[2] In the face of the extensive complications of the resemblances and differences which are traceable between forms as observed, and which are often most unexpected until observed, both of these procedures [inferring genealogical connection on the basis of similar structure and making observation and speculation of equal weight] must seem to the lay reader somewhat hazardous. For himself he is inclined to insist on confining inference to strict induction from the really ascertained facts of observation, and allowing due play to the principle, equally valid in itself with that of genealogy, that like conditions tend independently to produce like effects. And he is very apt to rise from the perusal of books like the present one *[Descent of the Primates]* with a strong suspicion that, if their writers did not put evolution into their premises, they would hardly find so much of it in their conclusions.

They all start out with the assumption of evolution as a thing "as universally acknowledged as is gravitation" (p. 2), and supplied long since with "demonstrative evidence" (p. 4); but they oddly enough appear to be still on the outlook for evidence for it,

1. [*Tarsius* is a type of primate between the lemurs and the apes. Lemurs *(Lemuridae)* are primates differentiated from both monkeys and apes; according to the 1910 *Encyclopaedia Britannica,* lemurs were generally believed to be the stock from which monkeys originated.]

2. [*Anaptomorphus* is a genus of extinct short-skulled, large-eyed lemurs from the Eocene epoch in North America; they are sometimes regarded as near the ancestral line of the anthropoids.]

and cannot avoid speaking now and again of valuable material for its establishment (p. 4). This varied attitude toward their fundamental assumption seems to the lay reader not altogether unaccountable. He gets an impression that as greater and greater masses of fact are accumulated, the load is becoming a little too heavy for the original assumption of evolution to carry.

What, for example, is the result of the new facts which Prof. Hubrecht has brought forward? A new and better construction of the phylogeny of the primates, he tells us. Well and good. What is the direction in which this new construction moves? This is his generalization: "The genera known to us very rarely converge toward known predecessors as we go backward in geological time; their respective genealogies run much more parallel to each other, the point of meeting being thus continually transported further backward toward yet older geological strata" (pp. 39–40). But to say that the accumulation of facts gives the lines of descent more and more the aspect of parallel lines is certainly not to say that the progress of research is in the direction of establishing the original evolutionary assumption.

The appearance of the genealogical tree remained no doubt intact when, only the other day, Mr. Topinard told us that the common origin of man and the anthropoid apes is to be found in an animal of the type of the Old World monkeys, while all the monkeys in turn find a common root in a type like that of the lemurs.[3] It became somewhat different when Prof. Cope suggested that advancing knowledge led to the belief that the Anthropomorpha (including man and the anthropoids) are not derived from the monkeys, but the two stirpes run back independently to find their first connection in the lemurs, the common source of both; but not, he added, in any existing type of lemur, but in extinct forms of the Eocene period. The treelike appearance is still further destroyed now that Hubrecht tells us that still advancing knowledge sets the lemurs also to one side, and suggests that it may be not unwise to assume as the ancestor of man and the anthropoids an early Eocene primate "differing from the Simiae, Catarrhinae,

3. [Paul Topinard (1830–1911) published *L'Homme dans la nature* (Man in nature) in 1891, which examined the relation between man, especially the "negroid races," and the anthropoid apes.]

Platyrrhinae and Tauridae," while these tribes unite only in a
"Mesozoic insectivorous ancestor," and back of that we are not to
assume descent through Marsupials, Monotremes and Sauropsids, but must go back independently to the amphibian father
of all.[4]

Here are more parallel lines with a vengeance; and a layman
may be pardoned for beginning to suspect that they converge at
all, away back there in the world's young prime, only because
evolution was in the assumption. Certainly if every new obtru-
sion of facts should still further separate the lines at their back
ends, the genealogical tree will soon begin to look amazingly like
a plantation of canes, each growing independently from a common soil; and the lines may become so nearly parallel that they
will meet only in infinity. Possibly this result may not disturb evolutionists: they seem to be more concerned to lay down new hypothetical lines of phylogeny here, there, and everywhere, than
to ask seriously whether any such really exist in nature; and they
appear to have nothing less than eternity to dispose of (p. 26). But
laymen, who are more concerned to learn what is true than to adjust an old theory to fit the new facts which may from time to
time be brought forward, will not fail to observe that every eon
in the infinite past back into which the origin of man is pushed,
and every step toward making the lines of descent of the various
animal forms more parallel, raises a new difficulty in the path of
the prevalent assumptions of evolution.

The steps which are made in this direction by Prof. Hubrecht,
and which are so interestingly outlined in these lectures, will suffice to rouse in the lay mind (or what he is prone to call his mind)
a reflection of that scientific imagination by the aid of which Prof.
Huxley was enabled to look back into the infinite past and see
"the evolution of living protoplasm from not living matter"; and
to tempt it to contemplate as possible the coming of the time

4. [*Simiae* denotes monkeys and apes; *Catarrhinae* form a division of primates
comprising Old World monkeys, higher apes, and hominids; *Platyrrhinae* are a division of New World monkeys; Warfield writes *Tauridae* (which refers to cattle)
but probably meant *Tarsiidae,* a genus of prosimians from southeast Asia;
Monotremes are the lowest class of mammals, represented by the platypus and
echidnas. The term *Sauropsids* was introduced by T. H. Huxley in 1869 to designate a group of the *Vertebrata,* comprising the classes of reptiles and birds.]

when the accumulation of facts will press out all the main lines of phylogeny into real parallels, and push back the origin of man to "the Beginning." Possibly this time may never come, just as the time seen by Prof. Huxley never was; but the time has already fully come when the adherents of evolution should do something to make it clear to the lay mind that a full accumulation of facts to prove their case can never come—or else abate a little of the confidence of their primary assumption.

July 1899
Presbyterian and Reformed Review 10:546–47

Review of William Elder,
Ideas from Nature:
Talks with Students
(Philadelphia: American Baptist
Publication Society [1898])

Although this publication by William Elder (1840–1903), a professor of chemistry at Colby College, is based on the Christian premise of a Creator-God, Warfield finds fault with the author's dependence on process for the development of created matter. This Warfield terms "the cloven hoof of evolutionary philosophy"—that is, an absenting of God from the formation of the universe after the initial moment of creation—the belief that all further development comes from forces inherent within created matter itself. Warfield argues strongly for a vigorous conception of God that allows for his continuing supernatural role in the world, whether in the governance of forces that he has put into motion or in direct ("miraculous") intervention that creates something new—Warfield will later stress the incarnation of Christ and the creation of souls as examples of such intervention. He is thus moving toward his later efforts to distinguish among providentially guided evolution, mediate creation, and creation *ex nihilo*. The concept of miracles is important for these later proposals as well as for his response to Elder.

Five calm, well-informed, thoughtful causeries on "Design," "Objections to Design," "Energy," "Natural Law and Miracle," and "Nature a Manifestation of Law." In style and contents alike these talks are peculiarly attractive; there is no exaggeration either on the one side of scientific claim or on the other side of religious dogma, but an unusual precision and balance is preserved throughout. "It is indeed true of religion and science as is often said," Prof. Elder says with fine discrimination of their relations, "that each has its own province and methods, and we must not try to apply methods where they are not applicable. They are separate lines of mental activity, but they are not parallels whose only requirement of each other is that they be kept forever apart. They are ordinates springing from a common origin in the divine. All truth is one and harmonious; whatever is found to be true in one department must supplement truth in every other department. God has not called us to confusion in the intellectual sphere of our being any more than in the emotional" (p. 133).

Prof. Elder's doctrine of physical causation is, to our thinking, insufficient, and will ultimate [i.e., result] in denying any real causality outside of Will and therefore in identifying all the energy in the universe with the Will of God: "that continuity of cause and effect which science declares to be the rule of nature," he says, "is simply the continuity of divine activity." It is important, on the contrary, that we allow the reality of created energy as well as of created stuff.

Elder's doctrine of miracles is defective in an opposite way, as he conceives them as wrought by God by means of energy resident in the created universe—by means of the *potentia ordinata* in a word—and so reduces them to the category of "Providential acts," in the strict theological sense of that term. Accordingly, when speaking of the origin of the universe, he supposes that an intelligent observer of the process "could trace changes, more manifold truly, but not *in kind* [Warfield's italics] different from those we see when we study the evolution of a bird from an egg" (p. 175). From a sentence like this we see that the cloven hoof of evolutionary philosophy is not wholly eradicated from the thought of even such graceful and gracious Christian scientists as Prof. Elder.

The quarrel of the Christian with evolutionism turns on the precise point that, not content with providing a schema for the method of creation, evolution substitutes itself for the fact of creation. Men of the quality of Prof. Elder cannot indeed follow the crudity of thought characteristic of men like Haeckel and assume a process without a beginning, and they therefore postulate a primal creation. But after that primal act of creation it is apt to be all

process with them—divinely led, if the Christian or even speculatively theistic conception is operative with them, but not in
kind different in any step from what we see about us in the providential government of the world.

One would like to know the basis of this point of view. Did
God *create* the primal stuff by means of precedently present
forces? Why then must he *mold* the stuff, thus created by immediate act, only by mediate activities? Through what mediate
forces could, for example, the immortal soul be produced? Or, to
come to the supreme point, the God-man? The Christian man
need not hesitate to allow that to an external observer the origin
and development of the universe might seem to proceed without
break of continuity; but he is bound to insist that there have been
operative in it not merely the divinely led forces inherent in it
from the beginning, but here and there the divine energy itself
acting immediately and producing something which was not
even potentially included in its precedent conditions, and which
is therefore new, not merely in the sense that the undirected
forces of the universe could never have brought it into being, but
in the sense that it was beyond their power to produce even under the infinitely wise and powerful guidance of God and required for its production a truly creative act.

This directly supernatural activity must needs be confessed for
the production of the created stuff in the first instance; it must
needs be confessed also in the subsequent molding of that stuff
into the forms we see about us, whenever a new stage of development is attained; and it must needs be confessed also in the
production of what we call with the highest right a miracle. Prof.
Elder does not seem to confess it, though otherwise his exposition of the whole doctrine of miracle is singularly well balanced
and satisfactory.

April 1901
Presbyterian and Reformed Review 12:296

Review of Abraham Kuyper,
Evolutie: Rede bij de overdracht van het Rectoraat aan de Vrije Universiteit of 20 October, 1899
(Evolution: Address at the transfer of the rectorship at the Free University) (Amsterdam and Pretoria: Hoveker en Wormser, 1899)

Abraham Kuyper (1837–1920) was the foremost leader of the Neo-Calvinist movement in the Netherlands. He served in the academy, in the church, and in government and sought systematically to apply Calvinistic thought to a broad range of contemporary social and political issues. This brief notice illuminates one of the fundamentals on which both Kuyper and Warfield based not only their analyses of evolution, but their view of life in general. Both men centered on the opening statement of the Apostles' Creed, which avows belief in an almighty God, the Creator of all things.

The whole question of evolution is treated by Dr. Kuyper in this striking address with his wonted fullness of knowledge and wideness of view. He lifts the discussion out of the ruts in which it usually runs and contemplates it in a higher atmosphere and amid its broader relations. As over against the grinding selection of natural forces, he places the election of the good God, and counsels us strenuously to maintain in preference to a mechanical evolution the first of all articles of faith: "I believe in God the Father almighty, maker of heaven and earth." It is a most instructive and inspiring address.

April 1901
Presbyterian and Reformed Review 12:296

Review of David MacDill,
Common Sense and Logic Applied to Darwinism and Teleology
(Xenia, Ohio: Marshall & Beveridge;
Philadelphia: Presbyterian Board of
Publication, 1899)

This review highlights the difference—crucial in Warfield's thought concerning evolution—between *theism,* that is, the belief in an active creating deity, but not necessarily as revealed in Scripture, and *biblicism,* which looks to the Old and New Testaments for ultimate explanations of all things. David MacDill (1826–1903) was professor of apologetics at the Presbyterian Xenia Theological Seminary in Ohio.

Careful inquisition and comprehensiveness of treatment characterize this fresh examination of Darwinism. After a short introduction (pp. 5–18) on the general subject, in which the distinction (too often neglected) is made between theism and biblicism, the main body of the treatise is given to a thorough investigation specifically of Darwinism. Only a single chapter (pp. 130–67) is devoted to the special question of teleology. The book is plainly written and solidly argued.

July 1901
Presbyterian and Reformed Review 12:506

Review of Otto Pfleiderer,
Evolution and Theology,
and Other Essays
(London: Adam & Charles Black;
New York: Macmillan, 1900)

Coming off his bruising battles in the Presbyterian church with those
who wanted to modify traditional Calvinism for modern Christian
purposes, Warfield was probably glad to read someone who was not
claiming that efforts to modernize Christianity were really identical
with the historic faith. A professor of theology at the University of
Berlin, Otto Pfleiderer (1839–1908) had studied in Tübingen under
F. C. Baur, who applied Hegelian principles to New Testament criticism and theology. Warfield opposed the modern theology of the
Tübingen school—which had a moderate influence in America—as
well as its accommodation to enthusiastic claims for modern science.

This volume contains ten essays by Prof. Pfleiderer on a great
variety of subjects, but the most characteristic of them belong in
the category of "Prolegomena to Systematic Theology." Here, for
example, may be placed the title essay of the volume, which is an
instructive account of how modern theologians first assume that
there is nothing in existence which is not entirely the product of
the precedent conditions existent in the world complex, and
thence draw out an antisupernaturalistic theology. By its side
range also the papers on "Theology and Historical Science," "The
Essence of Christianity," "The Notion and Problem of the Philosophy of Religion," "The Task of Scientific Theology for the
Church of the Present"—all of which are developments of the

same theme. Of the remaining essays the most interesting are those on "Luther as the Founder of Protestant Civilization," "Jesus' Foreknowledge of His Sufferings and Death," and "The National Traits of the Germans as Seen in Their Religion." Prof. Pfleiderer's frank naturalism is refreshing.

July 1901
Presbyterian and Reformed Review 12:507

Review of Herman Bavinck,
Schepping of Ontwikkeling
(Creation or development)
(Kampen: J. H. Kok, 1901)

The key element for Warfield in this lecture is its assessment of twentieth-century scientific method as an atheism excluding the possibility of a Creator in its assumptions, methodology, and conclusions. Accordingly, Warfield describes evolutionism as an essentially atheistic philosophy of being, since its intent is to prove a world without God. Herman Bavinck (1854–1921) was a major Reformed theologian who, along with Abraham Kuyper, stimulated a revival of Calvinist theology in the Netherlands. Except for his lack of interest in evidential apologetics, he was close to Hodge and Warfield dogmatically; in 1908 he delivered the Stone Lectures at Princeton Seminary.

In this eloquent lecture Prof. Bavinck outlines the great conflict facing the church of the twentieth century—the conflict with the so-called scientific method, which is determined to explain the whole world and all that is within it without God, without any unseen, supernatural, spiritual element; it holds, instead, that everything in our universe has come out of the simple data of stuff and force. Bavinck uncovers with great skill the inconsistencies of the evolutionary philosophy and exposes its vast assumptions, and sets over against it the creationism or supernaturalism of the biblical world-conception. The address divides itself into three parts, in which are contrasted successively the two views of the world with reference to the questions of

the origin, nature, and end of things, the result being to show
that the evolutionary scheme stands helplessly before each of
these three problems. It is a very thorough and very telling exposure of the essential atheism of evolutionism considered as a
philosophy of being.

July 1901
The Bible Student, n.s. 4.1:1–8

Creation, Evolution, and Mediate Creation

Warfield's two essays in *The Bible Student* (1901 and 1903) offer his fullest positive account of how best to harmonize Christian trust in an active biblical God and responsible scientific research. The essay from 1901 does this through an extensive effort at defining three methods of divine interaction with the world: evolution (which Warfield considers a way for God to control certain material developments providentially), creation *ex nihilo* (the divine origination of something out of nothing), and mediate creation (the divine origination of something new out of a preexisting something that does not possess the intrinsic force to produce the new object). In this threefold scheme, evolution and creation are opposites; evolution means development based on preexisting potential while creation means the active origination of something new.

As he summarizes his main ideas toward the end of this essay, Warfield holds that evolution cannot take the place of creation: it cannot explain the origination of matter in the first place, it cannot account for miracles and the incarnation of Christ, and it is inadequate for explaining the origin of human self-consciousness and of individual souls. What then is left for evolution? Warfield has no quarrel with evolution when, "confined to its own sphere" of developments in the natural world, it is viewed as "a suggested account of the method of divine providence."

The essay from 1903 in *The Bible Student* expands upon Warfield's view of how evolution and creation interacted in the production of humankind. In that later essay, Warfield no longer uses the phrase "mediate creation," but he explains the origin of humanity in terms conforming to his 1901 definition of "mediate creation."

Throughout both these essays it is apparent that Warfield is as concerned about the best way to describe miracles as he is con-

cerned about the origin of the earth and of humanity.[1] It is also clear
that he remained steadfastly vigilant against evolution when taken
as a total philosophy of life excluding the activity of God. At the
same time he was moving toward incorporating evolution, properly
defined and limited, into the Calvinist interpretation of Scripture that
he outlined in reviews and articles appearing over the next dozen
years.

Creation versus Evolution. "I believe in God the Father almighty, maker of heaven and earth." That is the first article of the
baptismal creed of Western Christendom. "In the beginning God
created the heaven and the earth." That is the first sentence in the
Christian revelation. That God alone is the first and the last, who
changes not; that all that exists is the work of his hands and depends on his power for both its existence and its continuance in existence—this is the unvarying teaching of the whole Bible. It is part
of the very essence of Christianity, therefore, that the explanation
of the universe is found in God; and its fundamental word is, accordingly, "creation." Over against the Christian conception there
has arisen in our day, however, a movement which has undertaken
to explain the world and all that it contains without God, without
any reference to any unseen, supernatural, spiritual element. The
watchword of this movement is "evolution." And its confession of
faith runs: "I believe in an eternal flux and the production of all
things out of their precedent conditions through the natural interworking of the forces intrinsic to the changing material."

Pfleiderer's Evolutionary Scheme.[2] Perhaps as good a presentation of this evolutional program as can easily be turned up is
Otto Pfleiderer's discussion of "Evolution and Theology," which
holds the first place in the volume of essays lately published by
him under that title. The era of "scientific theology" is at last
come, he tells us. And he explains scientific theology to mean a
theology that has adopted the scientific method. "This method,"
he proceeds, "is simply that of causal thinking according to which
every event is the necessary effect of causes whose operation is

1. For Warfield's use of the phrase "mediate creation" in an article on miracles
that was written about the same time, see "The Question of Miracles," in *The Bible Student*, n.s. 7.3–6 (March–June 1903), as reprinted in *SSWW* 2:167–204.
2. [See pp. 193–94 for Warfield's 1901 review of Pfleiderer's *Evolution and Theology.*]

again determined by their connection with other causes, or by their place in a reciprocal action of forces according to law." Thus everything that comes into being "is to be regarded as the effect of the causes lying in the preceding condition, these causes again serving as means for the purpose of the following condition."

On the universality of the application of this principle Pfleiderer insists with the utmost emphasis. "There is only the one choice: either the evolutionary mode of thought is right, in which case it must be uniform in all fields of investigation, in history, then, as well as in nature; or it is wrong, in which case the views of nature acquired by means of it are not justified, and we have no right to prefer them to the traditions of faith." Accordingly the supernatural is excluded from every sphere of action—"not merely the nature miracle, . . . but also just as much the spiritual miracle, i.e., the intervention of a foreign power in the human soul whereby conditions are produced in it which do not result from the causal connection with antecedent conditions." The "cardinal proposition of the science of today" is "that we have to explain every condition as the causally determined development out of a preceding one," and "this excludes on principle the appearance of any condition, event, action, or possibility which is not explicable out of the factors of the preceding conditions and according to the laws of genesis in general." The intrusion of "causes which are outside the causal connection of finite forces" is to be sternly denied.

A God Not Necessarily Denied. The evolutional program, when taken in its entirety, obviously involves the substitution of an eternal series for the eternal God. Its account of the universe is that it is self-formed by the interaction of its intrinsic forces. Evolution, however, is not always, perhaps not even generally, taken in its entirety. It is not always pressed, for example, to the denial of the existence of God, or even of a transcendent God, or even of a God who directs the course of evolution in a truly providential government. Pfleiderer himself speaks of the divine as "always everywhere . . . lying at the basis of the total historical development." He makes, indeed, this fact the ground of his denial of the supernatural. Because God lies at the basis of everything, he remarks, "*no single* historical event is to be isolated as a supernatural effect or phenomenon and taken out of the connection of finite causes and effects."

A God may be admitted; even a governing God may be acknowledged, provided only that he governs in, with and through natural causes only, so that all that comes to pass finds its entire account in the second causes operative in its production. It is "causal thinking" that is contended for. That is, what is asserted is that all that is is the product of the natural causes operative in the conditions out of which it emerges. God, if there be a God, produces nothing directly and immediately. He is not a productive cause. At the best he is but a directive cause. There may possibly be "providence"; there cannot possibly be "creation."

But Evolution and Creation Are Mutually Exclusive. Evolution, it thus appears, is the precise contradictory of creation. This it is, indeed, *ex vi termini* [by the force of its limits, i.e., by definition]. Evolution is an *unrolling,* and the process of unrolling—say of a ball of twine—produces nothing; the unrolled twine is just what the rolled-up twine was, that and nothing more. The only difference is a difference of *state:* what was rolled up before is now unrolled. Creation, on the contrary, is definitely *origination;* creation produces something that did not exist before. When we say "evolution," we say thereby that there has been no origination; we say that there has been only *modification*—and modification in itself implies preexistence in unmodified form. When we say "creation," we say, on the other hand, that there has been no modification. We say there has been *origination*—and origination in itself implies previous nonexistence and hence excludes modification. When we say "evolution," we definitely deny creation; and when we say "creation," we definitely deny evolution. Whatever comes by the one process by that very fact does not come by the other. Whatever comes by evolution is not created; whatever is created is not evolved.

Antisupernaturalism of Evolutionists. This mutually exclusive relation of evolution and creation is of course recognized by all consistently thoughtful adherents of evolution, and indeed constitutes often the very reason of their adherence to evolution. "It is clear," says Prof. James Sully,[3] for example, "that the doctrine of evolution is directly antagonistic to that of creation. Just as the

3. [James Sully (1842–1923), English psychologist and philosopher, wrote primarily on education, social progress, and art.]

biological doctrine of the transmutation of species is opposed to that of special creations, so the idea of evolution, as applied to the formation of the world as a whole, is opposed to that of a direct creative volition. *It substitutes within the ground which it covers the idea of a natural and necessary process for that of an arbitrary volitional process.*" Again: "The theory of evolution, by assuming an intelligible and adequate principle of change, *simply eliminates the notion of creation from those regions of existence to which it is applied.*" The attraction of evolution for its adherents often seems indeed to reside just in its assumed capacity to explain the origin of things without the assumption of creation.

It will be remembered that Charles Darwin asserted that he would cease to care for evolution if it did not supersede the necessity for assuming even a directing activity of God. And the same zeal for the exclusion of all supernaturalism is apparent in such a remark as the following from Wiedersheim's *Structure of Man* (p. 2):[4] "Blood relationship and not some unknown plan of creation unites organisms in various degrees of similarity, and in this great family man must find his place; he forms but a link in the chain and has no right to consider himself an exception." Why is the negative clause "and not some unknown plan of creation" inserted into this sentence? It is not a true disjunctive to the positive proposition—for it may be true that blood relationship does unite organisms, and yet this may be in accordance with the plan of creation. It is gratuitously inserted for no other purpose than to reject the idea of a plan of creation, and so betrays Wiedersheim's primary interest in the doctrine of evolution; namely, it enables him to do without a plan of creation. He is, in a word, as an evolutionist polemically antisupernaturalistic.

Can the Evolutionist Get Along without Creation? We are not saying that the evolutionist can get along without a doctrine of creation. We are saying only these two things. First, that evolution and creation are contradictory processes, and that whatever comes by the one process does not come by the other, so that in so far as the one is affirmed the other is denied. And sec-

4. [Professor Robert Wiedersheim (1848–1929) specialized in comparative anatomy and embryology at the University of Freiburg. His *Comparative Vertebrate Anatomy* appeared in English in 1886.]

ondly, that the idea of evolution is frequently utilized nowadays just in order to exclude creation, and that men, when they affirm evolution, commonly mean nothing more than to deny creation. It is easy to point out, to be sure, that evolution does not provide a satisfactory substitute for creation. At the best, it offers, of course, only an infinite series as its account of the origin of things. Break up this series into a series of cycles if you will—it is still but an infinite series of cycles, and an infinite series of cycles is not less unthinkable than an infinite series of events in a straight line. There is obviously a *present.* We have attained at this present moment a particular stage of evolution. Whether this particular stage of evolution is given a place in a cycle or in a straight line of development, the very fact that it is a particular stage of evolution implies that the series in which it finds a place had a beginning. And the question presses, In the beginning—what? We cannot hang the chain upon *nothing,* and the further we project it into the past the less can we hang it on nothing. Let the links be particular events or cycles of events—it is all one. We must have something to hang it on—"in the beginning."

Account for all you see, then, as mere modifications of what has gone before, if you choose. You cannot push this series of modifications into eternity; you must posit a beginning and with it a Beginner. To obtain the evolutionary stuff with all its potentialities as exhibited in the process of its evolution, you must therefore posit a creation. But the positing of this creation, it is obvious, is the denial of evolution. It is posited just because a need is found for which evolution will not provide, and it is called in to do what evolution cannot do. So far as creation is operative, evolution is inoperative; only when creation is complete does evolution begin. The one furnishes the stuff; the other can be called in only to account at most for the various forms this created stuff has taken in its successive subsequent modifications.

Theistic Evolution. It has become quite common, accordingly, to distribute the account of the universe between the two processes in this manner: creation, it is said, supplies the original material; evolution accounts for all its subsequent modifications. And this is called theistic evolution. It may well be that. It is another question whether it may be fitly called also Christian evolution. For observe: it confines the creative operations of God to the origination of the primal world-stuff. Everything subsequent to that is withdrawn from the sphere of creation, i.e., is explained as a mere modification of the primal world-stuff by means of its intrinsic forces. The providential guidance of God need not be excluded, to be sure; the theist will readily allow that God directs the evolution. But all origination, all production of what is really new, is necessarily excluded throughout the whole process of evolution. And this is the definite exclusion of all creation.

This result is, indeed, not always explicitly recognized. On the contrary, it is quite common to speak of evolution as God's method of creation. It is quite common, indeed, to put it forward as the process of a mediate creation. We find even Prof. Cope defining the doctrine of evolution as "the teaching that holds that *creation has been and is accomplished by the agency of the energies which are intrinsic in the evolving matter.*"

Little wonder that the unscientific drop into the same self-contradictory mode of speech. "What is the doctrine of evolution?" asks Dr. Hillis.[5] And he replies: "Fundamentally it is the doctrine of creation by gradualism rather than by instantaneous fiat." "Almost no one," remarks Dr. R. S. MacArthur,[6] "doubts that 'creation has a history.' It is certain that, as it has been pursued in time, so also it has been pursued by method. As Hartshorne has shown, Prof. Asa Gray, Doctor McCosh, Baden Powell, the Duke of Argyll, and others all teach the view of orderly creation by law under the immediate action of divine power working by natural causes or forces.[7] This power, as he says, has been rightly described as a theory, not of supernatural or miraculous interference, but rather of *creative evolution.*" If evolution and creation are mutually exclusive, however, to talk of creation as ac-

5. [Newell Dwight Hillis (1858–1929) was a prominent clergyman known for his brilliant preaching. He was involved in many contemporary social and political issues and held the pastorate at Henry Ward Beecher's former church, the Plymouth Congregational Church in Brooklyn.]

6. [Robert Stuart MacArthur (1841–1923) served at the Calvary Baptist Church in New York City for forty-one years. He was a well-known speaker and prolific author who expounded his conservative theology in books and various Baptist periodicals.]

7. [Henry Hartshorne (1823–1897) was a physician and professor of physiology in Philadelphia. Gray, McCosh, Baden Powell, and the Duke of Argyll all incorporated theories of evolution into an overarching Christian theism.]

complished by evolution, of evolution as "creation by gradualism," of "creative evolution," is certainly misleading. You cannot modify by originating; you cannot originate by modifying.

What Is "Mediate Creation"? Are we forgetting, then, the old doctrine of mediate creation? Certainly not. The name may not be exact, but the thing is very real. Indeed, it is in order to assert its reality and to defend the importance of its being recognized that we are resisting the current effort to confuse it with evolution. All the old writers recognize the distinction between absolute or immediate creation and the so-called mediate creation; they so define creation as to leave room for both varieties. But they also so define it as to preserve mediate creation from confusion with evolution.

The matter may be found fully discussed, for example, in Turretine (*Locus* 4, Q. I, § 6).[8] We will quote here in preference, however, the brief definitions which Wollebius gives in his remarkable little compend.[9] "Creation," he says, "is that act by which God, for the manifestation of the glory of his power, wisdom, and goodness, has produced the world and all that is in it"—we relapse now into his Latin—*"partim ex nihilo, partim ex materia naturaliter inhabili"*—that is to say, in part out of nothing, and in part out of preexisting material indeed, but material not itself capable of producing this effect. Again: "to create is not only to make something out of nothing but also *ex materia inhabili supra naturae vires aliquid producere"*—to produce out of this inapt material something above what the powers intrinsic in it are capable of producing. Thus the mark of creation, namely, the production of something new for the production of which nothing in the precedent conditions can account, which transcends all that is present

8. [Francis Turretini (sometimes Turretin or Turretine) (1623–87), last of the giants of Genevan Reformed orthodoxy, was a leading figure in the formation of the Formula Consensus Helvetica (1675). He authored the influential *Institutio Theologiae Elencticae,* which was used in its Latin original as the theology text at Princeton Seminary (as well as other Presbyterian schools) until the appearance of Charles Hodge's *Systematic Theology* in 1872.]

9. [Johannes Wollebius (1586–1629) was a Swiss Reformed pastor and theologian in Basel and author of *Compendium Theologiae Christianae* (1626), a widely acclaimed textbook of Reformed dogmatics.]

in the antecedent conditions, is preserved in this definition. And it is only because this is preserved that the process described can be called creative at all.

Now it is to be observed that evolution by its very definition, and by its inherent nature, is the antipode of this. The primary fact concerning anything that is evolved is that it was already present in the precedent conditions and needed only to be educed from them, that its evolution is accomplished by the resident forces, that there is no production of anything truly new—no real origination, but only a modification. By this very fact it is, then, no creation at all, whether immediate or mediate, but merely an unrolling, a development.

Dr. Zahm's Definition of Evolution. Examples are thick about us, however, of the care which the evolutionists take not to distinguish evolution from mediate creation, but rather to confuse it with mediate creation. We select an instructive instance from the Roman Catholic writer Dr. J. A. Zahm:[10]

> Another reason for the prevalent confusion of thought regarding the relation of theology to evolution arises from the erroneous notions entertained by so many respecting the true significance of creation and evolution. They fail to distinguish between absolute creation *ex nihilo* and derivative creation. Absolute creation embraces only spiritual intelligences and the material elements of which the universe is composed. Derivative creation on the contrary means only the formation of something from preexistent material, and includes all organic and inorganic compounds, all form of vegetable and animal life, for all these have been produced from those elementary bodies which constitute alike the earth and all the orbs of the firmament.
>
> Only absolute creation therefore is creation properly so-called. Derivative creation, however, is nothing more than development under the action of the laws of nature imposed by God on the elements in the beginning. It is evolution from lower to higher forms under the action of what St. Thomas calls the Divine Administra-

---

10. [John Augustine Zahm (1851–1921), American naturalist and explorer, was a leading Catholic scientist and president of the board of trustees of Notre Dame University. He articulated a theory of evolution consonant with the teachings of the Roman Catholic Church, for which he received an honorary Ph.D. from Pope Leo XIII in 1895.]

tion, and in consequence of the action of what St. Augustine terms seminal reasons—*rationes seminales.* Absolute creation is direct, immediate, supernatural; derivative creation is indirect, and is effected by the Almighty through the agency of secondary causes. In the beginning God created the elements once for all, but on these simple elements he conferred the power of evolving into all the countless forms of beauty which now characterize the organic and inorganic worlds. What, then, the older theologians called secondary or potential creation or formation—development under the guidance of God's providence—we may now call, and with the utmost precision of language, evolution. For God, as St. Augustine observes, did not create animals and plants directly, but potentially and causally *in fieri, in causa, potentialiter atque causaliter* [the Latin is translated loosely by "potentially and causally"].

This, however, is theistic evolution, not agnostic evolution, which relegates God to the region of the unknowable; nor atheistic evolution, which finds in the chance interaction of eternal force and eternal matter an adequate explanation of all the problems of the existing universe. For, let me insist, evolution does not and cannot account for the origin of things. The best it can do is to throw some light on their historic development, and this for the simple reason that it does not and cannot deal with the origin of things, but only with the *modus creandi* [means of creating], or rather with the *modus formandi* [means of forming], employed by Omnipotence after the universe had been called into existence by the Divine Fiat. "Evolution then," as I have elsewhere shown (*Evolution and Dogma* [1896], pp. 431–32), "postulates creation as an intellectual necessity," for if there had not been a creation there would have been nothing to evolve, and evolution would therefore have been an impossibility.

What Does Dr. Zahm Do with "Mediate Creation"? The confusions of this passage are typical. They are not only matched in the treatment of the subject by the whole mass of theistic evolutionists, but ordinarily much more than matched. For Dr. Zahm, after all, has some glimmering of the fact that his derivative creation is no creation at all, but just providential guidance. The passage is very fairly illustrative, nevertheless, of what we are seeking to illustrate. This to wit: that even the writers who frankly allow that evolution has no account to give of the origination of the stuff evolving, yet seek to make evolution take the place of creation in the sphere of mediate creation. Dr. Zahm tells us that the primal act of absolute creation brought into being only the chemical elements of the material universe and "spiritual intelligences." And he tells us that everything else that exists has been brought into existence "through the agency of secondary causes," which he himself explains as nothing more than "development under the guidance of God's providence." In the course of this development nothing absolutely new is produced. There is only the evolution into new forms of what was from the beginning included in the primally created stuff. What is meant by ascribing to the production by absolute creation not only "the material elements of which the universe is composed" but also "spiritual intelligences" is not, to be sure, perfectly clear—beyond Dr. Zahm's obvious intention to divide the universe into the two disparate substances of matter and spirit. If it is meant that at the formation of Adam there accompanied the derivative creation by virtue of which his body was formed (not created) from the lower animals an act of absolute creation producing the immortal spirit, or that at the birth of every human being there accompanies the act of derivative creation by which the body is derived from its parents an act of absolute creation of the soul, Dr. Zahm is really allowing here for the old divines' category of mediate creation without his being aware of it, a category standing between his absolute creation by which an origin is given to the world and his derivative creation by means of which God's providence leads second causes to the production of effects level to their power indeed, but wrought only in accord with his will.

The Real Meaning of "Mediate Creation." Perhaps, though, it is too much to suppose that this was Dr. Zahm's intention. The noting of it as possibly lying in his words, however, will enable us to point out more clearly and exactly what mediate creation is and precisely what the issue is that is raised by the attempt to substitute evolution for it. By mediate creation is really meant the truly creative acts of God occurring in the course of his providential government by virtue of which something absolutely new is inserted into the complex of nature—something for the production of which all that was previously

existent in nature is inadequate, however wisely and powerfully
the course taken may be led and governed—something for the
production of which there is requisite the immediate "flash of
the will that can."[11]

By the recognition of this mode of production, a third category is erected alongside of the products of creation pure and
simple and of providence pure and simple, namely, products of
creation and providence working together, and each contributing something to the effect—mixed products of the immediate
and of the mediate activity of God. As Wollebius expresses it, it
is creation not *ex nihilo*, but *ex materia inhabili supra naturae vires*.
Now the issue raised by the so-called theistic evolutionists in
their attempt to make evolution do all the work subsequent to
the primal act of creation is just whether such a category as mediate creation exists—whether there are any products of the divine power which are inserted into the course of providence by
an immediate operation of God, and emerge as something new,
for the production of which the second causes operative in the
case are inadequate.

The Question of the Direct Supernatural. It will be seen
at once that this issue is the issue of the direct supernatural. The
question raised is whether God has acted immediately only
once, namely, in the original production of the primal worldstuff, or whether he has also acted immediately subsequent to
this original act of creation—whenever, to wit, the purposes he
is executing require the production of something which the
powers operative in nature are inadequate to produce. Let it be
carefully observed that there is no tendency in the affirmation
of this mode of activity to deny or disregard or minimize God's
providential activity. This is affirmed with all the emphasis
which theistic evolution can possibly throw upon it. It is insisted only that God's providential activity—evolution, if you
choose to call it such—does not comprise in itself the totality of
God's activities since the primal act of creation, and that it can-

11. [In "Question of Miracles" Warfield provides the complete quotation from
Robert Browning: "Here is the finger of God, a flash of the will that can—/ Existent behind all laws, that made them, and lo! they are!"]

not fitly bear the name of creation because it is in its very nature diverse from the thing.

There is a mode of action of God midway between creation pure and simple and providence pure and simple—a mixed mode of action. It is to this mixed mode of action that, historically, the name of mediate creation has been attached. Within the limits of this mode of action fall miracles and everything else which, like miracles, occurs in the complex of natural causes and yet not by means of the forces operative in the natural causes. Whenever and wherever during the course of God's providential government anything comes into being for the production of which natural causes are inadequate, *that* is an act of mediate creation. But it is not an act of evolution, for it is not a product of the forces intrinsic in the evolving stuff nor a mere unrolling of what was present before in a rolled-up state.

The Christian's Attitude toward Evolution. What, then, is to be the attitude of the Christian man toward the modern doctrine of evolution? He is certainly to deny with all the energy given to him that the conception of evolution can take the place of creation as an account of the origin of the universe. Evolution offers no solution of the question of origins. For its operation it presupposes not only already existent material which can unroll into fresh forms, but material within which all that is subsequently evolved already potentially exists.

And he is to deny with equal strenuousness that the conception of evolution can take the place of mediate creation as an account of the origination of new things in the course of the divine government of the world. Since the first origin of the world there have come into being things which did not lie potentially within the primal world-stuff, needing only to be educed from it. If nothing else, the God-man has come into being, and that not as the product of precedent conditions in the world, but as an intrusion from without and above. And with him, the whole series of events that constitute the supernatural order of the kingdom of God. Nor is there any reason to doubt that the same intrusion of purely creative force, productive of something absolutely new, may have occurred also in the natural order of the first creation—

say, at the origination of self-conscious, immortal beings in the complex of nature.

On the other hand, the Christian man has as such no quarrel with evolution when confined to its own sphere as a suggested account of the method of the divine providence. What he needs to insist on is that providence cannot do the work of creation and is not to be permitted to intrude itself into the sphere of creation, much less to crowd creation out of the recognition of man, merely because it puts itself forward under the new name of evolution.

November 1903
The Bible Student, n.s. 8.5:241–52

The Manner and Time of Man's Origin

This essay is an exercise in mediation. It deals primarily with two questions: the manner of human creation and the time of that creation. On the first issue, Warfield proposes "a composite transaction" or "a double act" whereby humanity appears as a product of divinely superintended evolutionary processes (with evolution defined as in the 1901 article) and of a miraculous bestowal of the *imago dei* (creation *ex nihilo* or perhaps mediate creation as defined in the earlier essay). Without yet using the term *concursus* that he later employs in his 1915 essay on Calvin's view of creation, Warfield is moving toward a view of human origins defined by his Calvinistic understanding of *concursus.*

The second, longer section of the essay considers the age of the earth and the duration of human existence on earth. Warfield holds that these questions are not significant for theology. The mediation he works at this point is to convince Christians that the Bible does not demand an earth only six thousand years old and to show to the scientifically inclined that it is not necessary to postulate an immensely old earth. To accomplish his first purpose Warfield draws on the work of Princeton Seminary professor William Henry Green, who had argued that the genealogies of Genesis should not be read as providing a chronology for the cosmos. To accomplish his second purpose Warfield draws on a broad range of reading in geology, biology, and physics to show the wide differences among scientists on this issue. Along the way Warfield reflects the scientific consensus of the early twentieth century that the theory of evolution solely by natural selection was insufficient to account for organic diversity.

Warfield closes this essay, with its appeal for a truce between biblical belief and scientific research, by reasserting his conviction that the kind of evolution that denies all divine actions of any sort is much more a philosophical claim than a product of science. On that point he remained fixed exactly where Charles Hodge had been in 1874 with *What Is Darwinism?* even as Warfield was going beyond Hodge

to find ways of accommodating modest forms of evolution within
his Calvinistic theology.

**Pervasive Bible Witness to Man's Origin in God's Creative
Act.** It is not merely in the opening chapters of Genesis that the
Scriptures teach that man owes his being to a creative act of God.
This is, rather, the constant presupposition of every portion of
Scripture, and is expressly asserted in numerous passages. No
more striking indication of the fundamental place occupied by
this assumption in the consciousness of the biblical writers could
be afforded than that supplied by the way in which it underlies
the expression of the religious emotions of the people of God in
the Psalms. It lurks in the background of Psalm 8, that noble
hymn in praise of man's dignity as the lord of creation. And when
the voice of the psalmist sinks into a wail in view of the sad fate
of man, the fact that it is God that has created him is made the
very ground of the complaint: "Oh remember how short my time
is: For what vanity hast thou created all the children of men!" (Ps.
89:47). The implication is that it is incredible that God should
really intend only evil for the work of his hands. Another psalm
makes God's creation of humanity the ground of a claim on him
for blessing—because, as the psalmist phrases it (Ps. 119:73),
"Thy hands have made me and fashioned me."

It is especially in the opening chapters of Genesis, however,
that this constant teaching of Scripture is given in its most didactic form. It is thither therefore that we naturally go to find such
direct declarations as that "God created man in his own image, in
the image of God created he him; male and female created he
them" (Gen. 1:27); and "the Lord God formed man of the dust of
the ground, and breathed into his nostrils the breath of life; and
man became a living soul" (2:7).

Two Points of Conflict with Modern Speculation. No one
possessed of religious instincts is likely to boggle over the great
fundamental fact thus given expression. That we owe our being
to God is one of the most intimate convictions of our consciousness and can be discredited only when our general religious
nature is itself eradicated. But there are points in the biblical
teaching as to the origin of man which do not appear to be imme-

diately safeguarded by the native instincts of our religious nature, and about which a certain amount of hesitancy seems to have become widespread under the pressure of modern anthropological speculation. On one or two of these we may perhaps profitably touch. And we shall select for this purpose a couple of points upon which the conflict of modern speculation and the scriptural account seems to many acute. We refer to the questions as to the manner in which man has come into being, and the time at which he may be supposed to have come into being.

Man a Divine Creation or Self-Created? To bring the first of these matters to its sharpest expression, we may say that for the last half-century modern speculation has exhibited a strong tendency to represent man as having been *self-created,* while the Bible represents him as having been *created by God.* That is to say, there has been a widespread tendency among men of scientific proclivities to think of man as having come into being by an evolution from preceding forms, as having been wrought out solely by the interaction of forces intrinsic in the evolving material; while on the contrary those who are taught by the Scriptures have been wont to think of man as brought into being by an act of divine power operating immediately and from without. When so conceived, the conflict between the two views is complete; and the opposition, evolution or creation, is absolute. We have here in fact only a new form of the old conflict between naturalism and supernaturalism, between materialism and theism. There can never be any conciliation between these.

The Contradiction in Part Imaginary. It does not appear, however, why this conflict should be pressed to such an extreme. Why should the evolutionist insist that the ascent to man must have been accomplished by the blind action of natural forces to the exclusion of all oversight and direction of a higher power? Why should the biblicist assert that the creation of man by the divine fiat must have been immediate in such a sense as to exclude all process, all interaction of natural forces? It does not appear that either is, on the basis of his own data, justified in such an extremity of position.

Even though the evolutionist had before him the whole series of generations through which he supposes man to have risen to humanity, he would be as little justified in asserting that this series of steps was accomplished apart from the directing hand of God as would a lover of domestic animals be justified in excluding the breeder as a factor in producing a pen of, say, prime Berkshire pigs or of white leghorn chickens, because, forsooth, he could trace their descent through generations, given which the result could not fail to follow. The problem still remains, Why was just this series of changes followed? And Mr. Andrew Lang's question remains in the highest degree pertinent: "Evolution may explain everything; but what explains evolution?"[1] The dogmatic exclusion of the directing hand of God does not lie at all in the facts as observed, but is imported from an antitheistic prejudice.

On the other hand, the biblicist is scarcely justified in insisting upon an exclusive supernaturalism in the production of man such as will deny the possibility of the incorporation of natural factors into the process. In Psalm 89:47, for example, God is declared to have "created all the children of men," and in Psalm 119:73 to have fashioned the psalmist himself. But surely no individual since Adam has been fashioned by the mere fiat of God to the complete exclusion of the interaction of natural forces of reproduction. And in the case of the protoplasts themselves there is significant allusion to a preexistent stuff out of which they were formed (Gen. 2:7). It does not appear that the emphasis of the biblical assertion that man owes his existence to the creative act of God need therefore exclude the recognition of the interaction of other forces in the process of his formation. It looks therefore very much as if the difference between the parties to this debate might be in large measure due to each party's emphasis on a single side of a composite transaction.

Insoluble Remainder of Conflict. We say the difference looks as if it might be in large part due to a difference of emphasis. For after all [is] said, it remains clear that the Scriptures do not represent man as merely an evolution from preceding forms directed to that great end by the guiding hand of God. For after all [is] said, you cannot get out of preceding forms, by however wisely led an evolution, anything that was not already potentially at least in

1. [Andrew Lang (1844–1912), Scottish writer and philosopher, studied folklore and mythology and maintained an interest in psychic research.]

them; and the Scriptures clearly represent man as something specifically new.

The creation narrative itself in the first chapter of Genesis makes this sufficiently plain. The utmost care is taken in it not only to mark the creation of man as the culmination and climax of the whole creative work, but to separate off his creation as something involving a very special immediacy of the divine action and resulting in a specifically new product. In the preceding cases it was enough to announce a fiat—"Let there be." Here there are pause and counsel—"Let us make." In the preceding cases there is indicated what may be looked upon as a sort of secondary production—"Let there be"; "Let the waters, or the earth, bring forth." Here there is asserted a direct act of God—"Let us make." In the preceding cases each thing is presented as made after its own kind. Here man is set forth as created after the kind of God—"God created man after his own image." In the preceding cases all that entered into each new creation may have come up from below. In man's case a double act and a double result are signalized. He was formed, indeed, from the dust of the ground, but he was not so left; rather, God also breathed into his nostrils a breath of life, as if there were something to be signalized as belonging to his nature which did not take hold of what was beneath him, but reached up rather to what is above. The impression that is made by such features of the creation narrative is strengthened and reinforced by subsequent Scriptures, until it seems quite within the limits of what is required to affirm that the scriptural account of the origin of man cannot be satisfied by any evolution pure and simple, that is, by any providentially led process of development, but requires the assumption of a direct intervention of power from on high productive of something that is specifically new.

Properly Limited Evolution Not Excluded. This conclusion does not necessarily involve the denial of the interaction of an evolutionary process in the production of man. It involves only the affirmation that this evolutionary process, if actual in this case, is not adequate for the production of the effect, even though the evolutionary process be theistically conceived, i.e., as the instrument of the divine hand in producing man. It requires us to call in, at least at this point, an act of God analogous to what we know as a miracle, a "flash of the will that can," and to insist that in man God created something new, the elements of whose being were not all present even potentially in the precedent stuff.

The difference between the modern speculator and the biblicist cannot be conciliated at this point until and unless the speculator is willing to allow the intrusion into the course of evolution—if it be deemed actual in this case—of a purely supernatural act productive of something absolutely new which enters into the composite effect as a new feature. But there seems no reason why the speculator should not admit this, unless he occupies a position which is dogmatically antisupernaturalistic. The whole problem to him should turn on the simple question whether the created being which we call man includes nothing in his nature but what may be accounted for as a derivation from below. If there is anything at all in man's complex nature which cannot be accounted for as merely a more developed form of what is recognizable in lower creatures, then we must assume an intrusion from above. All that is not derived from nature must find its account in the entrance of the supernatural.

Man a Creature of Yesterday or of Inestimable Antiquity? Let us turn, however, to the second matter that has been brought into keen debate between modern speculation and the believer in the scriptural record of the origin of man. This concerns the time of the apparition of man on earth. Modern speculation has exhibited a tendency to represent man as having existed for a tremendously long period on earth, while readers of the Bible resting on a prima facie view of its record have been inclined to represent him as of comparatively recent origin. To be more specific, it has not been unusual for speculators to make immense drafts on time in their estimate of the duration that has been requisite for the attainment of the present condition of animate life on earth; they speak at times as if only hundreds or thousands of millions of years would suffice. On the other hand, students of the Bible text have been prone to compress the whole life of the world into very narrow limits indeed, often dating the creation of the globe only a few thousands of years back.

Professor Poulton in his address as president of the Zoological Section of the British Association for the Advancement of Science (Liverpool, September 1896), for example, treats as too short the longest time asked by geologists for the duration of the habitable earth, say, some 400 million years.[2] Dwelling on the number of distinct types of animate existence represented as far back as the Lower Cambrian period of geological time, and on (as he thinks) the necessarily slow process of evolution, he stretches out the time required for the process almost illimitably. On the other hand, the estimates of the life of the world current among Bible readers at large assign to it only something like a paltry six thousand years or so. Here then seems to be a conflict of the most acute kind.

No Biblical Data for a Precise Estimate of the Age of the World. On more careful scrutiny, however, the necessity for such a conflict appears far from stringent. It emerges that both sides lack solid grounds for the estimates of time presented. On the biblical side, for example, the material relied upon for constructing a chronology of the earlier periods of the world's life seems to be illusory. From Abraham down we have indeed the combined evidence of somewhat minute genealogical records, such so-called long dates as those of 1 Kings 6:1 and Galatians 3:17, and several precise statements concerning the duration of definite shorter periods, together with whatever aid can be derived from a certain amount of contemporary extrabiblical data. For the length of this period there can be no difficulty, therefore, in forming a solid general estimate. But for the pre-Abrahamic periods we are dependent entirely on inferences drawn from the genealogies recorded in the fifth and eleventh chapters of Genesis. And it has been repeatedly shown, most thoroughly of all perhaps, by the late Dr. William Henry Green in, for instance, a paper published in the *Bibliotheca Sacra* for April 1890, that it is precarious in the extreme to draw chronological inferences from these genealogies.[3] The genealogies of Scripture were not constructed for a chronological purpose, and any appearance they present of affording materials for chronological inferences is accidental and il-

2. [Sir Edward Bagnall Poulton (1856–1943), English zoologist, defended Darwin's theory of evolution, supported Weismann's theories, and wrote extensively on natural selection.]

3. [William Henry Green (1825–1900), Old Testament scholar at Princeton Seminary, was the last of the conservative Old Testament scholars there to command international attention. Warfield is referring to Green, "Primeval Chronology," *Bibliotheca Sacra* 47 (April 1890): 285–303.]

lusory. While they must be esteemed absolutely trustworthy for the purposes for which they were given, these genealogies are not to be pressed into use for other purposes for which they were not intended and for which they are not adapted. In particular, it is clear that the purposes for which the genealogies were given did not require a complete record of all the generations, but only an adequate indication of the line of descent. Accordingly, it is found that the genealogies of Scripture are freely compressed, and can seldom be confidently affirmed to contain a record of the whole series of generations.

A sufficient illustration of the biblical usage in this regard is provided by the two genealogies given of our Lord in the first chapter of Matthew. For there are, it is to be noted, two genealogies given of Jesus in this single chapter, differing in explication, no doubt, but in no respect in principle of record. The first is included in the first verse, and traces Jesus back to Abraham in two steps: "Jesus Christ, the son of David, the son of Abraham." The second is included in verses 2–17 and expands the same genealogy into forty-two generations, divided for purposes of symmetrical record and easy memory into a threefold scheme of fourteen generations each. The other genealogies in Scripture present the same feature of freedom of compression for all sorts of purposes. And as they are more and more studied, it becomes more and more apparent that it is illegitimate to use them as a basis for chronological calculations, except with the utmost caution and with our eyes clearly open to the fact that in so doing we are subjecting them to a use for which they were never intended. The genealogical tables from Adam to Abraham may be as compressed as, or more compressed than, the genealogy of Jesus given in the first verse of Matthew. Only we have in these cases no data derived from other quarters to correct our natural inferences from the prima facie appearance of the genealogies. In such circumstances it seems clear that we cannot safely found on a mere genealogical table a conclusion as to the lapse of time.

The Genealogies of Genesis 5 and 11 Not "Mere Genealogies." We have purposely used the phrase "a mere genealogical table" in order to prepare the way for taking note of the fact that the tables in the fifth and eleventh chapters of Genesis, which cover the periods between Adam and Noah, and between

Noah and Abraham, respectively, are not mere genealogical tables. On the contrary, they differ from all other genealogical tables included in Scripture in regularly giving for each generation the age of the father at the birth of the son. The effect of this is to provide what seems to be a continuous series of precisely measured generations, the numbers having only to be added together to supply an exact measure of the time that elapsed from Adam to Abraham. We do not read only that "Adam begat Seth, and Seth begat Enosh, and Enosh begat Kenan" and the like, as we do in mere genealogies. We read rather that "Adam lived an hundred and thirty years and begat Seth, and Seth lived an hundred and five years and begat Enosh, and Enosh lived ninety years and begat Kenan." Certainly it looks, at first sight, as if we needed only to add these 130, 105 and 90 years in order to obtain the length of time from Adam's creation to Kenan's birth; likewise, we would need only to add together the similar figures throughout the whole list to obtain the precise length of time that elapsed between Adam's creation and the birth of Abraham. Doing this we obtain a sum of only some 2,000 years according to the Hebrew text, or of only something like double that according to the Septuagint text, for this whole interval; and this admits of an estimate of only some 6,000 to 7,000 years for the whole duration of human life up to our own day.

Similar Features in Other Genealogies. Plausible as it seems, however, to find a concatenated series of numbers in these genealogies, this use of them appears on close scrutiny unjustified. It is not unusual to find interposed into the structure of the biblical genealogies a short note here and there telling some interesting fact about a person whose name occurs in the list. Several examples of this custom occur in the genealogy of Jesus recorded in the first chapter of Matthew, to which we have already referred for illustration. Thus in verse 2 we are told that Judah had brethren—a type of fact adverted to only in the case of two of the names that occur (vv. 2 and 11), and adverted to in this case doubtless because of the significance of the twelve sons of Jacob as fathers of the tribes of Israel.

In verse 3 we are told that Perez had a brother Zerah and was born of Tama[r]; in verse 5 that Boaz was born of Rahab, and Obed of Ruth; and in verse 6 that Solomon was born of "her of

Uriah"; while the genealogy closes with the information that the Joseph down to whom it leads was "the husband of Mary, of whom was born Jesus, who is called Christ" (v. 16). The introduction of the names of these notable women, the reasons for the insertion of which are very interesting to trace out—constitutes, it must be seen, a very remarkable feature of this particular genealogy.

Another feature of it is the information that David was "the king" (v. 6) and that Jechoniah's life span falls at the time of the carrying away to Babylon; the reason for these insertions is doubtlessly to be found in the artificial arrangement of this genealogy in three tables. The point illustrated by all these insertions of brief pieces of information is that a genealogy may be more than a mere genealogy and yet remain distinctly a genealogy, and that we need not be surprised to find similar insertions of interesting items of information into other genealogies. We should not be misled by them, when discovered, into fancying that the genealogies in question are framed for other than genealogical ends.

Peculiarity of Pre-Abrahamic Genealogies. The peculiarity of the genealogies of Genesis 5 and 11 will be seen to be a case precisely in point here. Into the fabric of these genealogies has been inserted a series of remarks designed to preserve the memory of certain notable facts concerning the individuals that constitute the links of the chain. These facts are all of one order. When each name is taken by itself, the facts operate to exhibit the vigor and longevity of the person named; when taken together, they exhibit in the clearest light the splendor of humanity in those old times. It is as if the narrative had set itself to manifest to us (in another sense from that which the words bear in Gen. 6:4) that "there were giants in those days." "And Adam lived an hundred and thirty years," we read, "and begat a son in his own likeness, after his image; and called his name Seth: and the days of Adam after he begat Seth were eight hundred years: and he begat sons and daughters; and all the years that Adam lived were nine hundred and thirty years: and he died." Truly, we involuntarily exclaim, this was indeed a *man!*

The narrative proceeds to tell us analogous facts about each link in the chain. The reader is impressed by the greatness of those grand men of old, towering, as they did, in strength and endurance above all that the world has since seen. This is just the impression the narrative was meant to make. The decisive proof that to produce such an impression and not to provide materials for a chronological calculation was the intention of the writer in attaching these interesting notes to the names, is supplied by the fact that all of the items in these notes reinforce this impression and are not utilizable for a chronological calculation except in a small part of their contents. For it is to be carefully observed that the writer does not confine himself to data which would serve a chronological end. He does not confine himself to saying: "And Adam lived an hundred and thirty years and begat Seth, and Seth lived an hundred and five years and begat Enosh." If chronology was in his mind, that is all he need have written. But what he says is: "And Adam lived an hundred and thirty years and begat Seth; and the days of Adam after he begat Seth were eight hundred years and he begat sons and daughters; and all the years that Adam lived were nine hundred and thirty years." We must find a reason that will account for all these additions to the mere genealogy. When a reason that will account for all of them is found, it will be illegitimate to seek a different reason for some of them.

Chronological Effect Illusory. That the genealogy assumes the appearance of a concatenated chain of chronological links when the names are placed side by side is due merely to the circumstance that the facts adduced in connection with each name are of the same order. Obviously, the appearance of chronological links is an accidental effect. So in order to understand the genealogy, we must resolutely read each note attached to a name in relation to that name alone. In other words we must read each note as in essence parenthetical—just like the notes in the genealogy in the first chapter of Matthew—and as meant to be read solely as referring to the name in hand.

If we wrote the list thus, we should perhaps see more clearly its essential meaning. For instance: "And Enosh (lived ninety years and) begat Kenan (and Enosh lived after he begat Kenan eight hundred and fifteen years, and begat sons and daughters; and all the days of Enosh were nine hundred and five years; and he died). And Kenan (lived 70 years and) begat Mahalalel," etc. If this be a just account of the state of the matter, we should read the genealogy proper without the parenthetical remarks, which serve their own purpose indeed, but cannot alter the essential nature of the genealogy into which they are inserted. And in that case the genealogy obviously falls under the laws that govern other genealogies and may be thought to be as compressed as many of them are—or possibly even more compressed than any of them are. Its apparent lending of itself to chronological calculations is illusory, and we are left by it in ignorance of everything except that it was through this line of notable men that Noah came down from Adam and Abraham came down from Noah, and that these men were notable men indeed. How many other men, possibly less notable than they, stood intermediately between the links, we have no means of discovering. For all that the genealogies tell us, there may have been many more passed over than were singled out for mention; and the sum of their years may immensely exceed the sum of the years here given. It does not appear extreme to say, therefore, as has been said by judicious men, that for all that appears from these genealogies, the period from the creation of Adam to Abraham may have been nearer two hundred thousand years than two thousand years. Genealogies as treated in Scripture are, in a word, so elastic that they may be commodiously stretched to fit any reasonable demand on time.

No Scientific Data to Justify a Long Estimate of the Age of the World. On the other hand, it cannot be allowed that modern speculation has solid ground beneath it in making the immense demands on time it has sometimes allowed itself. As a result of the manner of looking at things inculcated by the Huttonian geology, speculation during the first three-quarters of the nineteen centuries [i.e., of the nineteenth century] estimated the age of the habitable globe at hundreds of millions of years.[4] Under this influence Mr. Darwin in 1859 supposed that far more than 300 million years have elapsed since the latter part of the

4. [James Hutton (1726–97), Scottish geologist, was among the first to articulate a geological theory which posited a far older earth than previously accepted. He believed that the Mosaic account revealed the order of creation, but not a full natural history, and he maintained that the objectives of religion and natural philosophy, though compatible, were nonetheless separate. Commenting on creation, Hutton stated that "with respect to human observation, this world has no vestige of a beginning, no trace of an end."]

secondary period.[5] Prof. Jukes[6] in his *Student's Manual of Geology*
[1872], reviewing Mr.

Darwin's argument, and remarking on the
vagueness of the data on which it was founded, suggests that the
sum of years involved might be just as reasonably reduced or
multiplied a hundredfold, thus giving us as limits for the period
3 million and 30 billion years.

Professor Poulton, as we have seen,
even today considers 400 million years too few to assign for the
duration of life on earth, while Sir Archibald Geikie on the other
hand speaks as if 100 million years might possibly suffice, though
for his part he is prepared no doubt to allow as many more as may
be required by his fellow workers.[7]

These general estimates imply, of course, a generous allowance for the duration of human life on earth, although here too estimates vary extremely. French anthropologist Gabriel de Mortillet has lately reiterated his conviction that the appearance of man
on earth cannot be dated less than 230,000 years ago.[8] But almost
immediately afterwards we find Prof. George A. Dorsey of the
Field Columbian Museum bewailing the failure of speculators to
agree on "even the approximate time of man's appearance as man
on earth"—and noting that within the year estimates had been
published varying all the way from 200,000 to 15,000 years ago.[9]

5. *Origin of Species,* 1st ed., p. 287.
6. [Joseph Beete Jukes (1811–69), British geologist, established Hutton's theory that most of the earth's surface features were formed by precipitation and rivers. Darwin moved from his earlier view emphasizing maritime erosion to support Jukes's theory of river action as the principal agent in geomorphology.]
7. Address as president of the Geological Section of the British Association,
Dover, Sept. 1899. [Sir Archibald Geikie (1835–1924) was a Scottish geologist
who pioneered research in volcanic geology. He edited the third volume of Hutton's *Theory of the Earth* and was also involved in glacial research and geomorphology.]
8. *Revue Mensuelle* of the Paris School of Anthropology, for January 15, 1897.
[Gabriel de Mortillet (1821–98), French anthropologist, studied prehistoric man
and was the first to discover a Neolithic settlement in Italy. He expanded the system of cultural ages (Paleolithic, Neolithic, Bronze, and Iron) into fourteen epochs
and was at the forefront of French studies of archaeology and prehistoric art.]
9. *Science* for July 23, 1897. [George Amos Dorsey (1868–1931) was an anthropologist, curator at the Field Museum of Natural History in Chicago, and professor at the Northwestern Dental School and the University of Chicago. He wrote
numerous papers and books on anthropology, anatomy and human behavior and
authored *The Evolution of Charles Darwin* (1927).]

As a matter of fact there has been of late years a strong tendency to reduce the estimate of this period to very low terms indeed. The late Dr. Dawson supposed that from 6,000 to 8,000 years would be ample to allow [that is, provide enough time].[10] Prof. G. F. Wright suggests some 16,000 to 20,000 years.[11] And there is an obvious tendency abroad to acquiesce in an estimate approaching this low figure.

Why Later Speculators Reduce the Estimate. Numerous factors have produced this tendency to reduce the time assigned for the duration of human life on earth. These cannot be enumerated here. Some of those which have been most obviously at work may, however, be indicated in passing. First of all, we may adduce the revised estimates of the rate of denudation, erosion, and deposition of alluvial matter in deltas or of stalagmitic matter on the floor of caves.[12] From very exaggerated conceptions of these processes support was formerly sought for immensely long periods of time. More-careful study has invariably corrected these exaggerated conceptions, and has thus taken away from the long estimates of geological time their sole solid basis in computable fact. The determinations of the rate of stalagmitic deposit in British caverns by Boyd Dawkins and of the rate of recession in the Niagara gorge by Gilbert and Pohlman are but examples of prima facie evidence leading to immense reduction in the estimates of geological time.[13]

10. *Fossil Men* (1880), 246.

11. [George Frederick Wright (1838–1921), American geologist, was a Congregational minister for twenty years, after which he accepted a professorship in the harmony of science and revelation at Oberlin College, where he taught theology and geology from 1881 to 1907 and edited the theological journal *Bibliotheca Sacra* from 1883 to 1921. He helped lay the foundation for modern glacial theory, arguing for a recent end to the Ice Age and the presence of humanity in North America during the glacial period.]

12. [Denudation: a stripping away of covering or surface layers. Alluvial matter: clay, silt, sand, or gravel deposited by running water. Stalagmitic matter: deposits of calcium carbonate like an inverted stalactite formed on the floor of a cave by the drip of calcareous water.]

13. [William Boyd Dawkins (1837–1929), British geologist, did research on fossil mammals and early man and was the first to discover caveman art in Britain. Karl Gilbert (1843–1918) and Grove Pohlman (Gilbert's assistant) were American geologists who did significant work on erosion and glaciation and developed some of the principles which led to geomorphology. The findings of these three

The effect of these revised estimates has been greatly increased by growing uncertainty among biologists as to the factors
of evolution. As long as the Darwinian idea reigned unques-
tioned—that evolution had been accomplished by environmental
pressure selecting favorable variations that arose accidentally in
the midst of variations in every direction indifferently—an immense period of time seemed demanded for even the smallest advance in the structure of organisms. But when the sufficiency of
natural selection to account for the development of organic forms
came first to be questioned and then to be in wide circles denied,
the necessity for these large demands on time seemed to be more
and more removed. In proportion as evolution is conceived of as
advancing in determined directions, no matter the source of that
determination, and in proportion as evolution is conceived as advancing steadily onward by large increments, in that proportion
the demand on time is lessened and even the evolutionary speculator feels he can get along with less of it.

The relief given by this revised conception of the factors of
evolution was immensely increased by the fact that speculation
in other spheres of scientific research was showing itself more
and more unwilling to allow the biological speculator the time he
was proclaiming himself in need of. The physicists, for instance,
led by such men as Lord Kelvin, have become ever more and
more insistent that the time demanded by the old uniformitarian
and the new biological speculators is not at their disposal.[14] The
publication in the [eighteen-] sixties of Lord Kelvin's calculations
showing that the sun has not been shining 60 million years was
quite a bombshell in the camp of these speculators; and the situation already then acute has been made ever acuter by subsequent revisions of Lord Kelvin's work by which he has progres-

___

men corroborated evidence that the earth was younger than many evolutionists
had hypothesized.]

14. [Lord Kelvin, William Thomson (1824–1907), mathematician and geo-
physicist, is most famous for his absolute scale of temperature, but was involved
in dozens of significant theoretical and practical ventures. For example, he argued
that the sun has been cooling and hence could not have been shining for more
than 60 million years, and also that the earth could not have been solid for more
than 20 to 40 million years, both positions wreaking (temporary) havoc for the
theories of uniformitarian geologists and Darwinian biologists.]

sively diminished the time he, from the physicist's standpoint, is ready to allow for biological speculation to disport itself in. As Sir Archibald Geikie complains, "Lord Kelvin has cut off slice after slice from the allowance of time which he was at first prepared to grant for the evolution of geological history," until he has reduced it to not more than 40 and not less than 20 million of years, "and probably much nearer twenty than forty."

Sir Archibald Geikie, as we have seen, demands, for his part, at least 100 million years for the stratified rocks alone, and is well content to allow as much more as his biological friends "find to be needful for the evolution of organized existence on the globe." He warns them in "seeking to reconcile their requirements with the demands of the physicist" not to tie "themselves down within limits of time which on any theory of evolution would have been insufficient for the development of the animal and vegetable kingdoms." How poignant this warning must sound in the ears of the biological speculator is illustrated by a very pretty speculation in which Mr. T. J. J. See of the Naval Observatory at Washington determines the total longevity of the sun to be only 36 million of years, 32 of which belong to its past history.[15] For how much of these 32 millions the earth may be supposed to have been a habitable globe, and for how much of this latter period man may be supposed to have been one of its inhabitants, we must leave our readers to calculate for themselves.

The Battle Not the Theologian's. We are not seeking to give the impression that the speculations of the physicists must be given precedence over those of the biologists. Of course, there have been answers published to the physicists. *Nature* for April 18, 1895, contains Prof. Perry's very strong argument against Lord Kelvin's conclusions; and *Science* for June 25 and July 7, 1899, contains Prof. Chamberlin's very strenuous reply to Lord Kelvin's latest statement of his position, which appeared in the same journal for May 12 and 19 of the same year.[16] Notes of defiance have

15. [Thomas Jefferson Jackson See (1866–1962), American mathematician and astronomer, did significant research on double stars and stellar evolution. He held tenaciously to Newtonian physics.]

16. [John Perry (1850–1920), who was a former student of Lord Kelvin and noted for his ingenuity and heterodox scientific opinions, showed that while Kelvin's calculations were unassailable, his assumptions regarding the conditions

been and continue to be sounded, of course, by both geologists and biologists enough. It is no part of our purpose to interpose between the combatants in this warfare. Enough to point to the conflict and to found on it two remarks.

The first is that the conflict as to the age of man on earth is not between Theology and Science—any more than it is between Biology and Science, or between Physics and Science. It is not even between two sciences—whether these two sciences be Theology and Biology or Physics and Biology. It is between two sets of scientific speculators, the one basing their arguments on data supplied them in the course of their study of physics and the other on data supplied them in the course of their study of biology. Theology as such has no concern in this conflict and may stand calmly by and enjoy the fuss and fury of the battle.

The second remark is this: Science obviously has no doctrine concerning the age of man on earth. As long as speculators working in different branches of scientific investigation reach such diverse conclusions as to the possible age of man on earth, so long opinion is free as to the actual age of man on earth. The fact appears to be that there are as yet no reliable data in hand on the ground of which we may, from the side of scientific speculation, pronounce confidently how long man has lived on earth. Meanwhile the workers in every separate science owe it to the dignity of their own science, whether that science be Theology or Geology or Physics, to give primary validity in forming their conclusions to the data with which they have to deal as students of their own science; may none be in haste to desert the ground best known to himself and adopt at second hand the speculative opin-

---

of the earth's core were not necessarily the only possible assumptions. Thomas Chrowder Chamberlin (1843–1928), one of the foremost turn-of-the-century American geologists, pioneered work in glacial geology in Wisconsin, and was one of the first to doubt the Laplacian view of the early history of the earth. Laplace had postulated the atmospheric hypothesis regarding the birth of the solar system, suggesting that the original raw material of the universe consisted of extremely hot gaseous masses that surrounded the sun like atmosphere; the planets and their satellites were formed as the solar atmosphere cooled and contracted. Chamberlin formulated the planetesimal hypothesis, which suggested that planets grew by accretion of small celestial bodies and particles.]

ions of others that are based on data of which he has but secondary knowledge. **The Real Opponent a Veiled Atheism.** Let us pause in concluding only to observe that the debates which we have been led to review are very largely the creation of a special type of evolutionary speculation. This type is that which owes its origin to the brooding mind of Charles Darwin; up to recent times it has been the regnant type of evolutionary philosophy. Its characteristic contention is that chance plus time can accomplish everything. Naturally, therefore, heavy drafts have been made on time to account for whatever it seemed hard to attribute to brute chance. James Hutton had duly warned his followers against the temptation to appeal to time as if it were itself an efficient cause of results. "With regard to the effects of time," he said, "though the continuance of time may do much in those operations which are extremely slow [and in which] no change to our observation has appeared to take place; yet when it is not in the nature of things to produce the change in question, the unlimited course of time would be no more effectual than the moment by which we measure events in our observation."[17] The warning has not been heeded: men have seemed to imagine that if only time enough were given, effects could be counted on to come gradually of themselves without adequate cause. Aimless movement in time will produce an ordered world! You might as well suppose that if you stir up a mass of type with a stick long enough, the letters will be found to have arranged themselves in the order in which they stand on the printed pages of Dante's *Inferno*. It will never happen—though you stir for an eternity. And the reason is that such effects do not happen, but are produced only by a cause adequate to them and directed to the end in view.

Dr. Dawson puts his finger on the exact point of difficulty in the following criticism: "Seriously," he says, "the necessity for indefinitely protracted time does not arise from the facts, but from the attempt to explain the facts without any adequate cause, and to appeal to an infinite series of chance interactions apart from a designed plan, and without regard to the consideration that we know of no way in which, with any conceivable amount of time,

17. *Theory of the Earth,* 2:205.

the first living and organized being could be produced from dead matter. It is this last difficulty which really blocks the way and leads to the wish to protract indefinitely an imaginary process which must end at last in an insuperable difficulty."[18]

Assuredly, what chance cannot begin to produce in a moment, chance cannot complete the production of in an eternity. The analysis of the complete effect into an infinite series of parts, and the distribution of these parts over an infinite series of years, leave the total effect as unaccounted for as ever. What is needed is not time, but cause. Even an eternal process cannot rid us of the necessity of seeking an adequate cause behind every change. A mass of iron is made no more self-supporting by being forged into an illimitable chain formed of innumerable infinitesimal links. Do we not realize that the sum of these innumerable links is a sum of zeros, and therefore still zero?

18. *Relics of Primeval Life* (1897), 323.

October 1906
Princeton Theological Review 4:555–58

Review of James Orr,
God's Image in Man
and Its Defacement in the Light
of Modern Denials
(London: Hodder & Stoughton, 1905)

Warfield's consciousness of the conflict between modernist thought and orthodox Christian doctrine—and his impassioned, reasoned defense of the latter—come through clearly in this review. He writes approvingly of the author's balanced effort to present the arguments for Christianity and modernism on the way toward articulating his own Christian anthropology. James Orr (1844–1913) was a minister and professor in the United Presbyterian Church of Scotland (later in the United Free Church) whose most famous book, *The Christian View of God and the World* (1893), presented the kind of biblical and yet culturally comprehensive Calvinism that Princeton theologians also defended. Orr was a trifle less conservative than Warfield on the question of biblical inerrancy, but Warfield turns the tables here by being at this stage somewhat more venturesome than Orr on evolution.

In this review, Warfield again differentiates between evolution as modification and creation as origination; that is, while evolutionary changes can proceed out of the potential that resides within existing material, they cannot give rise to anything totally new. For something new to come into being—such as humans with body and soul in an integral whole—a developmental leap is necessary that requires divine creation. Warfield draws on his experience as a breeder to illustrate these issues. For our purposes, it is noteworthy that Warfield maintains the strict necessity of divine creation for the origin of humanity, while he does not rule out a role for providentially superintended evolution in the emergence of the human body. In making this argument he returns to the strict definitions of "evolution" and "creation" that he developed in his 1901 article.

D r. Orr's Stone Lectures were listened to in Princeton with great pleasure. Their publication in this handsome volume will carry to a wider audience their fine exposition of the fundamentals of Christian anthropology and their vigorous protest against a tendency, apparently growing among us, "to wholesale surrender of vital aspects of Christian doctrine at the shrine of what is regarded as the modern view of the world." What renders this protest most valuable is that it is particularly directed against weak evasions of the issue raised by the conflict between the Christian view of the world and that "congeries of conflicting and often mutually irreconcilable views" which is commonly spoken of as the "modern view." Dr. Orr has the courage to recognize and assert the irreconcilableness of the two views and the impossibility of a compromise between them; he also undertakes the task of showing that the Christian view is the only tenable one in the forum of science itself. That he accomplishes this task with distinguished success is the significance of the volume.

The material is divided into six lectures. In the first of these the issue is stated, and the actual irreconcilability of the two views demonstrated. The biblical doctrine of God, man and sin is set sharply over against the evolutionary view, the exaggerations sometimes found on both sides are cleared away, and the residuary conflict made plain. The second lecture, proceeding to details, sets the Bible and the new views of the nature of man over against one another, and shows that no scientific facts really endanger the Bible doctrine that man differs in kind and not merely in degree from the lower creatures. In the third lecture it is shown that the extreme evolutionary theories have broken down before the advance of knowledge, and that, on the data of science itself, man is to be viewed as the product not of nature but of a higher cause that has intruded into nature. The fourth lecture extends this argument with especial reference to the mental nature of man. In the fifth lecture the great question of sin is grappled with, and the biblical view of sin as a racial fact [that is, a fact that encompasses the whole human race] rooted in voluntary action on the part of the creature is powerfully commended. Finally, in the sixth lecture, the biblical account that death is nonnatural to man and is actually the result of sin is defended, and the bearing of the whole discussion on the entirety of the Christian system is explained. At the end a body of valuable material is collected in a series of appendixes which support, and in some instances advance, the positions taken in the text of the lectures.

What impresses the reader of these admirable lectures most is their fine balance. Neither the statement of the biblical doctrine nor of the modern view, nor their comparison, contains any exaggeration. The two are just calmly set over against one another, and their bases and relations are investigated. Perhaps the most striking feature of the exposition of the biblical doctrine is the just insistence that man is "a being composed of body and soul in a unity not intended to be dissolved." A firm grasp of this element of the biblical doctrine notably clears the air. It not only puts in their right aspects death and the resurrection—the former as the product of sin and the latter as the necessary fruit of redemption from sin, but it also throws the whole question of the origin of man into a new light. It perhaps may not be too much to say that the hinge of the biblical anthropology lies here, and that the argument of Dr. Orr turns upon his clear appreciation of it. Next to this, we are struck perhaps by the searching analysis and account of sin given in the fifth lecture. The question arises, as we read, why sin cannot be characterized, in contradistinction to that love in which the fulfillment of the law consists, as just lovelessness or, in its positive manifestation, hate. This would be only another way—whether a better way or not may be open to question—of reducing sin to the principle of selfishness.

Some striking minor points in Dr. Orr's arguments should also be mentioned. Among these is his suggestion (p. 152) of the impossibility of disparate development of mind and body. From this he infers that it can scarcely be credited that the body of man was formed by the accumulation of insensible variations from a brutish original, and the soul made all at once by a divine fiat for the completed man. Body and mind must go together, and a great brain with a little mind is just as unthinkable as a little brain with a great mind. The argument does not seem to be available, however, against a theory of evolution *per saltum* [by leaps].[1] If under the directing hand of God a human body is formed at a leap by propagation from brutish parents, it would be quite consonant with the fitness of things that it should be provided by his creative energy with a truly human soul.

And this leads us to say that the precise point in the question of evolution is, after all, not whether the new forms proceed from the older ones (either with or without the directing hand of God), but whether the forces concerned in the production of the new forms are all intrinsic in the evolving stuff. Man may breed many varieties of pigeons, fowls, sheep; and the varieties he breeds may often come *per saltum*. But they all find their account in the forces operating in the materials dealt with; man's directing hand cannot be traced in the chain of efficient causes, all of which are discoverable in the evolving stuff. Accordingly, under man's hand we can have nothing but an evolution, an unrolling—a drawing out into new forms of what was potentially present in the evolving material from the beginning.

If this were all that God does, there would be no creation in the case whatever. We do not quite understand, therefore, Dr. Orr's remark on p. 87 (explanatory note 1) to the effect that evolution and special creation are not mutually exclusive, whether as terms or as things. Surely evolution means modification, and creation means origination, and surely modification and origination are ultimate conceptions and mutually exclude one another. You cannot originate by modifying; you cannot modify by originating. Whatever comes by evolution certainly cannot arise by creation, and whatever is created certainly is not evolved. The old definition of creation as the making of something *partim ex nihilo, partim ex materia naturaliter inhabili—ex materia inhabili supra naturae vires aliquid producere*—is certainly the sound one.[2] Unless the thing

---

1. [At a time when Darwin's form of evolution—that is, through natural selection—had fallen from favor, Warfield is exploring, for possible Christian use, theories then being proposed to chart a jerky pace for evolution. These theories might be considered forerunners of what at the turn to the twenty-first century is usually described as punctuated equilibrium.]

2. [In his 1901 article Warfield translated this phrase from the Swiss Reformed theologian Johannes Wollebius, "in part out of nothing, and in part out of preexisting material indeed, but material not itself capable of producing this effect" (see p. 204).]

produced is above what the powers intrinsic in the evolving stuff are capable of producing (under whatever divine guidance), the product is not a product of creation but of providence. And providence can never do the work of creation.

Dr. Orr fully understands this and argues therefore that the apparition of man implies the intrusion of a new cause, that it is a creation strictly so called; and this is what makes the note on p. 87 inexplicable. Let man have arisen through the divine guidance of the evolutionary process; there is, then, no creative act of God concerned in man's production, but only a providential activity of God, unless there has intruded into the process the action of a cause not intrinsic in the evolving stuff, causing the complex product to be something more than can find its account in the intrinsic forces however divinely manipulated. Evolution can never, under any circumstances, issue in a product which is specifically new. Modification is the utmost that it can achieve—origination is beyond its tether.

One of the most pregnant passages in the volume is that (p. 188) in which it is briefly demonstrated that for a moral being to exist in a nonmoral condition is really for it to exist in an immoral condition. We may in the abstract distinguish actions into those that are right, wrong and indifferent. But there are no indifferent acts: in the concrete all acts are good or bad. So we may in the abstract speak of conditions which are moral, nonmoral, and immoral. But for a moral being, a state of nonmorality is a state of immorality. Such a being is either good or bad, never neither good nor bad. This simple demonstration cuts up by the roots the whole Pelagian standpoint.[3]

As we have already pointed out, Dr. Orr's whole treatment of sin is very sane and satisfactory. Only we demur to what seems to us the overemphasis of the fact of heredity taken in the strict sense. We hear indeed of "the representative principle" (p. 277), and the inheritance of death is apparently hung upon it. But the transmission of sin also appears to be hung at least mainly upon the principle of heredity (e.g., pp. 235, 242). This seems to us a

---

3. [Pelagianism, a heresy stemming from the fourth century, holds that humans have the goodness and ability to achieve salvation by their own efforts apart from divine grace.]

mistake and to involve us in many unnecessary difficulties, as e.g., the difficulty of accounting for our inheritance of specifically Adam's first sin (why not Eve's? and why not the sins of all our ancestors?), and the difficulty of accounting for our Lord's failure to inherit sin.

We are burdened with the guilt of Adam's first sin and have received its penalty. Surely that is enough. We do not need to defend the theory of the inheritance of acquired qualities in order to account for our partaking in the penalty of Adam's sin; the principle of representation is enough. We do not need to insist that a son tends to inherit the moral character of his parents, which (on the broad question) certainly is not borne out by common experience. The children of the pious are not uniformly pious nor are those of the vicious uniformly vicious, and assuredly few would contend that the specific forms in which piety and vice are manifested are on the average transmitted. It seems much better, then, to follow what appears to us the simple scriptural presentation, and to say that we partake in Adam's sin because he was our representative, and that he was constituted our representative because he was our father and as such was naturally indicated for that office.

We have in these remarks, we think, noted everything with respect to which we should feel disposed to question even Dr. Orr's modes of developing his subject. Perhaps a query may be placed also against his remarks (pp. 153–54) on the difficulty created for a purely evolutionary theory by the necessity of the production of not a single instance, but of a pair of human beings. We do not feel this difficulty as strongly as Dr. Orr appears to feel it. Why should there be a pair? Nothing is more common in the experience of breeders than the origination of a new type through an individual sport. And what is the difficulty of obtaining a pair or more of the same fundamental type? *Ex hypothesi* the new variation is slight, and that implies the coexistence of many individuals of almost equal advantages. And nothing is commoner in the experience of breeding than the production from the same parentage of a succession of individuals of the same or nearly the same sporting characters.

Perhaps also a query may be placed over against the strong statement (p. 257) to the effect that "there is not a word in Scripture to suggest that animals . . . came under the law of death for man's sin." The problem of the reign of death in that creation which was cursed for man's sake and which is to be with man delivered from the bondage of corruption, presses on some with a somewhat greater weight than seems here to be recognized.

But these are matters of no importance to the march of the general argument of the book. The book is a distinct contribution to the settlement of the questions with which it deals, and to their settlement in a sane and stable manner. It will come as a boon to many who are oppressed by the persistent pressure upon them of the modern point of view. It cannot help producing in the mind of its readers a notable clearing of the air.

October 1908
Princeton Theological Review 6:640–50

Review of Vernon L. Kellogg,
Darwinism Today: A Discussion of Present-Day Scientific Criticism of the Darwinian Selection Theories, together with a Brief Account of the Principal and Other Proposed Auxiliary and Alternative Theories of Species-Forming
(New York: Henry Holt, 1907)

Vernon Lyman Kellogg (1867–1937) was professor of entomology at the University of Kansas and Stanford University, where the future president Herbert Hoover was one of his students. In 1920 he became permanent secretary of the National Research Council. His work on silkworms was a pioneering effort in genetics; he published many works on evolution, entomology, and general biology. A longtime advocate of pacifist eugenics, Kellogg (the author of, among other volumes, *Military Selection and Race Deterioration*) was critical of a strictly selectionist Darwinism and warmed to various non-Darwinian evolutionary mechanisms.

Warfield was clearly appreciative of the scope of Kellogg's synthesis, which ranged widely over an immense range of nonselectionist evolutionary proposals currently on offer. Indeed, these were sufficiently extensive to practically overcome classical Darwinism during the early decades of the twentieth century. To Warfield, many of these latest theories were highly speculative and materialistic and seemed to do little more than attest to the increasing intellectual disarray of evolutionary theory. Certainly he did seem to show some sympathy for the vitalistic doctrines coming from some of the German biologists. But in general he found them unsatisfactory. Besides, he was critical of the antiteleological bias pervading Kellogg's exposition and emphatically contended that causal-mechanical explanations were not incompatible with design. Warfield continued to be disheartened by what he saw as an unfortunate tendency towards philosophical naturalism in some scientific circles.

A book like this has long been greatly needed, and this ever increasing need is admirably met by this volume. Of course, Professor Kellogg writes from his own point of view, and he would not be human if he did not leave some things to be desired. Readers of his book should supplement it by reading also some such book as Rudolf Otto's *Naturalism and Religion,* as readers of Otto's book should certainly supplement it by reading Professor Kellogg's [see pp. 257–65 for Warfield's 1909 review of Otto]. If what Otto has to say, for example, on teleology and the relation of teleology to mechanical explanations of phenomena will help the reader to correct Professor Kellogg's unreasonable objection to all that he calls mystical in our worldview, Professor Kellogg will on the other hand give him a far richer knowledge of, if not a deeper insight into, the great debate which has been going on of late on the factors and processes of the development of organized forms. No one can have been unaware of this debate or of the gradual modifications it has been working in the attitude of the scientific world to the traditional Darwinian conceptions. But the general reader has lacked adequate guidance to an exact estimate of the drift of the discussion, and has been liable to be left in a state of mental confusion or to be unduly swayed by the latest advocate of a special line of theory he may have chanced to read. A comprehensive survey of the whole field of the debate from the hand of a competent guide is what he has needed. And this is what Professor Kellogg has given us in this volume.

Professor Kellogg wisely begins at the beginning—with a lucid account of what evolution means in general, and what that particular theory of evolution known as Darwinism really is. And he rightly finds the differentiation of Darwinism, specifically so called, in the selection theories—or, let us say, so that we may keep our eyes fixed on the real pivot of it all, in the theory of natural selection. Keeping this central point well in sight, he next gives his readers a careful and clear account, in no way glozing [i.e., glossing over] its extent or its seriousness, of the widespread revolt of biological investigators during the last few decades against the principle of natural selection—against ascribing to it the whole work of species-forming, and even at times against ascribing to it any effectiveness or capacity for species-forming. Having thus exhibited the attack on Darwinism in its full reach and force, he next, with equal care and fullness, recounts the defense which has been made of it—a defense sometimes very strong, but always involving certain concessions which go to modify or even to transform the role which is ascribed to natural selection in the molding of forms. This leads naturally to a survey of the new theories of species-forming which have been suggested, whether as auxiliary to the theory of natural selection, designed to supply its deficiencies, or as alternative to it, designed to supplant it.

This survey has not been carried through without betraying Professor Kellogg's own predilections; the volume naturally closes, therefore, with a chapter on "Darwinism's Present Standing" in which the results of the debate are summed up and Professor Kellogg's own conclusions outlined. These conclusions may be briefly stated in these two sentences: "Darwinism, as the all-sufficient, or even most important causo-mechanical factor in species-forming, and hence as the sufficient explanation of descent, is discredited and cast down"; and "Darwinism, as the natural selection of the fit, the final arbiter in descent control, stands unscathed, clear and high above the obscuring cloud of battle." That is to say, Professor Kellogg recognizes in natural selection a true cause actually working in nature; the stream of descent is subjected to the control of natural selection, so that when we look at the whole course of development, we see it moving on under its guidance. But he recognizes also that natural selection works on the stream of descent rather than produces it, and accounts for the general channel in which it flows rather than for itself, whether in its main character or many of its minor characteristics. He evidently conceives himself as standing midway between the contending extremes, allowing to natural selection a most important function in species-forming, but denying to it the omnipotence which the Neo-Darwinians are prone to ascribe to it.

The place of Darwin in the history of the evolutionary theories is determined by the fact that he first pointed to a *vera causa* [a true cause], actually working in the world, to which could be plausibly ascribed the production of the various forms which occur in the animated universe. The essence of his suggestion consisted in the very simple proposition that if multitudes more beings are born into the world than can possibly live in it, it will be inevitable that those which are least fitted to live in it will be crowded out, which will result naturally in the survival of the fittest in each generation. Thus there will come about the gradual molding of organized beings to fit their environment. The strength of the theory lies in its simplicity and its apparent appeal to nothing but recognized facts. We all know that overproduction is the law of life. We all know that no two individuals are precisely alike. We are all prepared to allow that in the struggle for existence which seems inevitable in these circumstances it will be the fittest among these unlike individuals which survive. We are equally prepared to admit that, as like begets like, the fittest will reproduce in their offspring their fitnesses. Who, then, can deny that in the course of innumerable generations going on thus, very considerable modifications from the original stock might be produced? Is there not given here, then, an adequate account of the whole course of development of animate forms?

Certainly the theory looks very simple and convincing. But as soon as we transfer it from the region of imaginary construction to that of fact, difficulties arise. Many of the objections which have been urged against it seem to us, to be sure, to be little justified. These are largely directed against its consistency or completeness as a logical construction. From this point of view, however, as it seems to us, the theory is unassailable. When, for example, it is objected—as it has been persistently objected—that it provides only for the survival of the fittest, not for the production of the fittest; that it leaves unexplained the whole matter of the cause of variation and particularly of the causes of the actual variations which occur; that it has no account to give of the opportune appearance of the variations needed, or of the repeated consecution of variations in the same direction in the line of actual descent—and the like, the mark seems to us to be completely missed. The Darwinian theory does not need to concern itself with the origin of the fittest, the cause of variation, the causes of the specific variations which occur, or their opportuneness or consecution. It is logically complete in the simple postulates of variation, struggle for existence, the survival of the fittest. If we admit, as all must admit, that no two individuals are ever exactly alike, then we must admit that some of these individuals are more fit to exist than others; that is given in the very fact of difference. We need not concern ourselves with how the fitness arises; relative fitness is inherent in the mere fact of difference. Neither need we concern ourselves with the objection that relative fitness in some particulars in a given individual may be offset by relative unfitness in other particulars. To estimate in these circumstances which organism is on the whole most fit to survive might puzzle us; it cannot puzzle nature, which acts simply along the line of the resultant. Wherever two individuals exist, it is inevitable that one will be fitter than the other; wherever thousands or millions of individuals, generically alike, come into being, there necessarily exist among them some, few or many, who will be fitter than the rest. And if these thousands or millions of individuals come into being in such circumstances that the great majority of them must needs be crowded out, the survival of the fittest seems certain; and as this process goes on through generation after generation, the line of descent must follow the line of relative fitness.

Logically unassailable as the theory is, however, as soon as we presume that this process has actually gone on, we find ourselves faced with many difficulties. The difficulties are important—or let us frankly say, as it seems to us, are destructive of the theory. But they do not lie against the logical completeness (and therefore the plausibility) of the theory, but rather against its actual working power. It may be suspected that it is often an underlying sense of these factual difficulties, subtly modifying the objector's point of view as to the conditions of the problem to be solved, which accounts for the pressing of the (really ineffective) logical difficulties.

These real difficulties raise such questions as these: What reason is there to believe that the struggle for existence in animate nature is severe enough to eliminate in each generation all but the fittest to survive? What reason is there to suppose that the differences by which (as we all must agree) individuals are discriminated from one another are great enough to form telling factors in the struggle for existence, even supposing it to exist in the rigor which the theory postulates? What reason is there to suppose, even if the variations are great enough to furnish a handle for selection and the struggle for existence is severe enough to weed out all but the fittest in each generation, that this process, continued from generation to generation, will result in any great modification of type, and the successive generations will not instead fluctuate around a center, as variation itself fluctuates around this center, and thus on the whole the type remain stationary? Or if there is marked on the whole an increasing divergence from the original type as the line of descent advances through the fittest of each generation—a general divergence on the whole amid much fluctuation (which seems the most that, on the theory, can possibly be postulated)—what reason is there to suppose that this divergence could advance very far in the time at disposal? And above all, what reason is there to suppose that this slowly increasing divergence produced by the survival in each generation of only the fittest—through the many fluctuations to this side and that which, on the hypothesis, must occur—could in the time at disposal produce the infinite variety of animate forms which have actually come into being? Or, to put the question in its sharpest form, could not only bridge the gulf which separates the amoeba from man, but bridge it by a steady upward advance—upward, that is, not merely in the sense of ever more and more perfect adjustment to the environment, nor even in the sense of progress from homogeneity to heterogeneity, to ever greater complexity of structure, but measured by an absolute standard of value? For this is what has really happened, if the paleontological record has anything at all to tell us; and it has happened, if any trust at all can be placed in the calculations of the physicists, with a rapidity which confounds thought. The formal completeness of the logical theory of Darwinism is fairly matched, therefore, by its almost ludicrous actual incompetence for the work asked of it.

Of course, this has become ever more and more apparent as time has passed, and workers in the relevant fields of research have escaped somewhat from obsession with the specious plausibility of the selection theory and looked more squarely in the face of the problems to be solved. Here and there, no doubt, as was inevitable, there has been a disposition exhibited to gloze its inefficiency, and to cure its defects by ineffective remedies. A recent instance of this is noted by Prof. Kellogg, when he records (p. 55) Prof. Ray Lankester's appeal to the properties of radium as offsetting the physicists' calculations as to the time available for the possible existence of life on the earth.[1] If, Prof. Lankester argues, the sun contained a fraction of one percent of radium, that would offset its estimated loss of heat and, "upsetting all the calculations of the physicists," give us the thousands of millions of years which are needed (on the Darwinian hypothesis) "to allow time for the evolution of living things." When men catch at straws like this to buttress their theories, it becomes clear what a strawy foundation they are building on.

Nor would the concession of the thousands of millions of years needed (but not obtained) relieve the difficulties of the case, which have led biologist after biologist to suggest supplementary theories designed to meet the failure of the main theory in this or that aspect of it, or, in ever increasing numbers as time has gone on, to propose alternative theories, and in extreme instances to assume an attitude of opposition to the doctrine of descent altogether. Thus De Vries's theory of mutations may be supposed to be ultimately due to the feeling that natural selection must have marked variations to work on, Eimer's theory of orthogenesis to the feeling that some account must be given of the advance of development along a straight line, and Nägeli's theory of a principle of perfection in organisms to the recognition of the steady advance of the line of evolution towards something that looks very much like a goal.[2]

1. [Sir Edwin Ray Lankester (1847–1929), British zoologist and friend of Charles Darwin, demonstrated the absurdity of Lamarck's theory of the inheritance of acquired characteristics.]
2. [Hugo Marie De Vries (1848–1935), Dutch botanist, rediscovered Mendel's laws of inheritance and developed the mutation theory of evolution which states that normal parents can give birth to mutant offspring, thus beginning a new species. This helped to fill in gaps in Darwin's theory, but also altered it. Theodor Gustav Heinrich Eimer (1843–98), Swiss zoologist and professor at Tübingen, opposed natural selection, instead positing orthogenesis, the idea that variation in organisms is directional and occurs due to a law inherent within the organism itself. Karl Wilhelm von Nägeli (1817–91), Swiss botanist, argued that evolution may occur in jumps. Denying that the environment plays a significant role in variation, he also suggested that evolutionary changes are teleological.]

The result of it all is that Darwinism, specifically so called—
that is, as a particular theory accounting for the differentiation of
organic forms—stands today not merely, as Prof. Kellogg somewhat too gently puts it (p. 5), "seriously discredited in the biological world," but practically out of the running. Even the most extreme Neo-Darwinians (like Weismann) have been compelled to
supplement it by auxiliary theories which altogether change its
complexion. It is quite true also, on the other hand, that nothing
has come to take its place; as Prof. Kellogg truly puts it (p. 375),
"these bitter antagonists of selection are especially unconvincing
when they come to offer a replacing theory, an alternative explanation of transformation and descent." The real state of the case
seems to be that the deficiencies of the Darwinian hypothesis
have come to be widely recognized and numerous suggestions
have been made which severally provide for, or seek to provide
for, this or the other of these deficiencies. But no one of these will
serve any better than Darwinism itself serves—possibly not even
so well as Darwinism serves—as a complete causo-mechanical
explanation of the differentiation of organic forms. Each severally
and all in combination (so far as they can be combined) still leave
something, and something essential, to be desired. The problem
still presses on us. Though a great variety of suggestions are being
made to solve it, it remains as yet unsolved.

What most impresses the layman as he surveys the whole
body of these evolutionary theories in the mass is their highly
speculative character. If what is called science means careful observation and collection of facts and strict induction from them of
the principles governing them, none of these theories have much
obvious claim to be scientific. They are speculative hypotheses
set forth as possible or conceivable explanations of the facts. This
is fully recognized by Prof. Kellogg:

> What may for the moment detain us, however, is a reference to the
> curiously nearly completely subjective character of the evidence for
> both the theory of descent and natural selection. . . . Speaking by and
> large we only tell the general truth when we declare that no indubi-
> table cases of species-forming by transforming, that is, of descent,
> have been observed; and that no recognized case of natural selection
> really selecting has been observed. . . . The evidence for descent is of

satisfying but purely logical character; the descent hypothesis explains completely all the phenomena of homology,[3] of paleontological succession, of ontogeny,[4] and of geographical distribution; that is, it explains all the observed facts touching the appearance of organisms in time and place on this earth and the facts of their likenesses and unlikenesses to each other. . . . The evidence for the selection theory . . . also chiefly rests on the logical conclusion that under the observed fact of overproduction, struggle is bound to occur; that under the observed fact of miscellaneous variation, those individuals most fortunate in their variations will win in the struggle; and finally, that under the observed fact of heredity, the winners will transmit to their posterity their advantageous variations, all of which interacting facts and logically derived processes will be repeated over and over again, with the result of slow but constant modification of types, that is, formation of new species (pp. 18, 92, 394).

What is thus true of the theory of descent in general and the specific theory of selection put forward to account for this descent is equally, and often far more true of the auxiliary and substitutionary theories which have been suggested to fill out the deficiencies of the latter or to supplant it (pp. 382, 391). These are often hyperspeculative theories which have only this to recommend them to our consideration—that *if* they be conceived to represent fact, they may supply an explanation of the facts of observation. Thus far, there is no other reason than this for supposing them to represent fact. And it is obvious that a vivid imagination may supply many competing theories of this hypothetical sort and all of them prove subsequently to have no basis whatever in reality. The lay reader may be excused if, reading over the outlines of these several theories, he is oppressed with a sense of their speculative character, in a word, of their unreality.

For ourselves we confess frankly that the whole body of evolutionary constructions prevalent today impresses us simply as a vast mass of speculation which may or may not prove to have a kernel of truth in it. All that seems to us to be able to lay claim to

3. [Homology: (1) similarity often attributable to common origin; (2) likeness in structure between parts of different organisms due to evolutionary differentiation from the same or a corresponding part of a remote ancestor.]

4. [Ontogeny: the development or course of development of an individual organism.]

be assured knowledge in the whole mass is that the facts of homology and of the paleontological record suggest that the relation of animate forms to one another may be a genetic one. As soon as we come to attempt to work out for ourselves a theory of the factors and process of the differentiation of these forms, we are in the region of pure speculation and can claim for our constructions nothing more than that the facts leave them tenable. Whether they ought to be held as well as are capable of being held, we seem to lack all direct evidence.

The next thing that most strongly impresses the lay reader is the amazing zeal which is exhibited by our biological workers for these speculative theories. It is not merely that every man has his theory and sets great store by it, however speculative it may be. It almost seems at times that facts cannot be accepted unless a causo-mechanical theory be ready to account for them. This looks amazingly like basing facts on theory rather than theory on facts.

Professor Kellogg himself is no stranger to this state of mind. He is at least repeatedly telling us that this or the other contention is unacceptable because no causo-mechanical theory explaining its operation is forthcoming. It almost seems at times as if our biological investigators are on the lookout for causo-mechanical theories rather than facts. And, let us note well, it is a causo-mechanical theory alone that satisfies them. There must be no mysticism involved; we had almost said no mysteries. The biological workers seem to say to us that nature is as plain as a book and has no secrets which are intrinsically secrets, but only secrets in the sense that they are not yet found out. But above all, they not only seem to say but, if we are to take Prof. Kellogg for an example, do say that in our explanations there must be no loophole left for the intrusion of even directive forces from without.

Thus Prof. Kellogg will condemn a theory out of hand if it involves the recognition—or the suspicion—of the working in animate nature of forces deeper—or higher—than physicochemical ones. Accordingly, the Neo-Vitalism which is playing its part in the biological circles of Germany is set aside with a bare word.[5]

5. [Neo-Vitalism was a movement, particularly in German biology, returning to the idea of a mystical life force that animates all organic forms and cannot be examined by ordinary laws of physics and chemistry.]

"Bütschli has well pointed out," we read, "that Neo-Vitalism is really only a return to the old 'vital principle' belief, and that we are now, and have been ever since our practical giving up of the vital principle notion, making steady progress in the explanation of life-forms and life-functions on strictly mechanical and physico-chemical grounds" (pp. 226–27).[6] Even when it is introduced "under a pseudo-scientific guise," therefore—as, no doubt, for instance by Driesch, who in positing "an extra-physico-chemical factor" (which he calls "psychoid") is yet careful to represent it as "an attribute of, or essential kind of potentiality pertaining to, organized living substance"[7]—the assumption of the interworking into the phenomena of organic life of anything above psychochemical forces is treated as out of the question. The whole animate universe is to be explained on the basis of these forces alone, and no theory of it is even to be taken into serious consideration which is not ready with a causo-mechanical explanation on these grounds. Here is a chance sentence, for example, which seems to indicate in a word the settled point of view of Professor Kellogg himself certainly and apparently of those whom he naturally represents: "Nägeli's automatic perfecting principle is an impossibility to the thoroughgoing evolutionist seeking for a causomechanical explanation of change" (p. 387).

This amounts, it will be seen, to a definitely polemic attitude—of a rather extreme kind—towards teleology. It is true, of course, that teleological language is sometimes employed. In the immediate context of the sentence just quoted, for instance, Professor Kellogg speaks of the occurrence of "determinate or purposive

6. [Otto Bütschli (1848–1920), German zoologist, pioneered in the field of cytology, a branch of biology dealing with the structure, function, multiplication, and life history of cells. Focusing particularly on invertebrates and protoplasm, he suggested that the properties of living protoplasm could be explained on physicochemical grounds.]

7. [Hans Adolf Eduard Driesch (1867–1941), German biologist and philosopher, advocated a vitalist philosophy of development which postulated nonmechanistic agencies. On the basis of experiments dividing sea urchin eggs, he rejected the mechanistic outlook and proposed instead the existence of an "agent-outside-the-machine" as he developed a theory of entelechy to explain organic development. "Entelechy" is a hypothetical force not demonstrable by scientific methods; in some vitalist doctrines it is believed to regulate and direct the development and functioning of an organism.]

change." But this is only an instance of that personifying language which is the bane of naturalistic writers. What he means is that "the simple physical or mechanical impossibility of perfect identity between process and environment in the case of one individual and process and environment in the case of any other" will automatically produce such a variety in individuals as will result in "the change needed as the indispensable basis for the upbuilding of the great fabric of species diversity and descent." That is to say, he is here saying only that the simple fact of unlikeness between individuals—so that no two individuals are precisely alike—provides materials for selection to work on and precludes the necessity—on Darwinian ground—of inquiring into the causes of variation or seeking out a principle of orthogenesis. There will always be "a fittest" at hand. We have already pointed out the sense and limits in which this contention is valid. What is here interesting us is that this is all that Dr. Kellogg means by "determinate or purposive change."

His polemic attitude towards all real teleology in the evolutionary process—to the intrusion into it of the guidance of purpose, properly and not abusively so called—we will not say is betrayed, it is expressed, over and over again in this volume. In criticizing the type of theory represented by Nägeli and Korschinsky[8] which assumes "a special tendency towards progress" in the organism—"an inner directive force," an "inner law of development"—for instance, Professor Kellogg writes (p. 278):

> It is needless to say that but few biologists confess to such a belief. However much in the dark we may be regarding the whole great secret of bionomics, however partial and fragmentary our knowledge of the processes and mechanism of evolution, such an assumption of a mystic, essentially teleological force wholly independent of and dominating all the physicochemical forces and influences that we do know and the reactions and behavior of living matter to these influences which we are beginning to recog-

8. [S. Korschinsky, Russian botanist, argued that evolution could not be explained mechanically but required a progressive tendency inherent within the organism. Thus Korschinsky was moving toward a teleological position. Refusing to limit himself to a single evolutionary model, he argued for what he called "heterogenesis."]

nize and understand with some clearness and fulness—such a surrender of all our hardly won actual scientific knowledge in favour
of an unknown, unproved, mystic vital force we are not prepared
to make. As Plate well says, such a theory of orthogenesis is opposed, in sharpest contrast, to the very spirit of science.[9]

Again (p. 376): "Modification and development may have been
proved to occur along determinate lines without the aid of natural
selection. I believe they have. But such development cannot have
an aim; it cannot be assumed to be directed towards advance;
there is no independent progress upward, i.e., towards higher
specialization. At least, there is no scientific proof of any such capacity in organisms. Natural selection remains the one causo-
mechanical explanation of the large and general progress towards
fitness, the movement towards specialization, that is, descent as
we know it." Still again, criticizing von Kölliker[10] (p. 350): "He included in his general theory of heterogenesis a basic plan of progressive evolution. Such a conception has in it too much onto-
genic orthogenesis; it is too redolent of teleology for present-day
biology."

Teleology itself is seen, then, to be the *bête noire* of biology as
represented by Professor Kellogg. "Certainly," we are told
(p. 375), "no present-day biologist is ready to fall back on the
long-deserted standpoint of teleology and ascribe to heterogenesis or orthogenesis an autodetermination towards adaptiveness
and fitness." "Definitely directed variation" he may with Weismann allow to exist (p. 199), "but not predestined variation running on independently of the life conditions of the organism as
Nägeli . . . has assumed" (cf. 381). As he expresses it with the polemic edge well turned out in another place (p. 377): "Nor can any
Nägelian automatic perfecting principle hold our suffrage for a
moment unless we stand with the theologists on the insecure ba-

9. [Ludwig Hermann Plate (1862–1937), German zoologist and defender of
Darwin. Believing that natural selection was insufficient to explain all evolutionary factors, he allowed for the inheritance of acquired characteristics to modify
natural selection.]
10. [Rudolf Albert von Kölliker (1817–1905), Swiss anatomist and physiologist, taught in Würzburg for over fifty years. He did important work in cell theory
and embryology and postulated that evolution could occur in leaps as well as at a
gradual pace.]

sis of teleology." That is to say, the ultimate objection to Nägeli's principle of perfection is that it is too much like teleology, the teleology of the theologists. In other words, the scandalon [i.e., offensive scandal] is precisely teleology in any form. Now all this is very depressing. The antiteleological zeal of Mr. Darwin is well known; the vigor with which—as, for instance, in his correspondence with Asa Gray—he repelled the intrusion of teleology into his system betrays his fundamental thought. The antiteleological implication of Darwinism taken in its strictness—when it becomes a system of pure accidentalism—is obvious. But it could have been hoped that by now we had got well beyond all that. Some lack of general philosophical acumen must be suspected when it is not fully understood that teleology is in no way inconsistent with—is, rather, necessarily involved in—a complete system of natural causation. Every teleological system implies a complete causo-mechanical explanation as its instrument. Why, then, should the investigators of the causo-mechanical explanation array themselves in polemic opposition to the very conception of governing purpose? Above all, why should they make their recognition or nonrecognition of teleological factors the test of the acceptability of theories? This gives the disagreeable appearance to the trend of biological speculation—we do not say of biological investigation—that it is less interested in science for science's sake, that is, in the increase of knowledge, than it is in the validation of a naturalistic worldview; that it is dominated, in a word, by philosophical conceptions not derived from science, but imposed on science from without.

Of course, there are many workers in the biological, as in other scientific fields, to which this will not apply. And it may well be contended that the drift of thought among investigators in these fields is precisely towards the recognition of the mystery of life and life processes, of their inexplicability on purely physicochemical grounds, of the necessity of the assumption of the working of some higher directive force in the advance of organic development—in a word, towards just that vitalism and teleology which Professor Kellogg rejects, not as excluded by observed fact or by proved theory, but as inconsistent with the scientific spirit—which seems as much as to say that teleology is to be dismissed because of its *a priori* philosophical attitude. In the meanwhile, however, it seems clear that much of our scientific thought is still under the control of a very definite antiteleological (which is as much as to say atheistic, for teleology and theism are equipollent [i.e., equivalent] terms) prejudice. We should be sorry to close on a note of blame even so desultory a notice of a book so competent and so informing. After all, the book is not an antiteleological treatise; and though its allusions to the hypothesis of teleology in organic nature are disturbing, they are only allusions. What the book undertakes to do is to "present simply and concisely the present-day standing of Darwinism in biological science, and to outline the various auxiliary and alternative theories of species-forming which have been proposed to aid or to replace the selection theories." And this it does well, with thorough knowledge, with sufficient fullness, and with adequate exactness. Professor Kellogg exhibits here great skill in expounding and much penetration in criticizing the several views which have been advanced, and commends his own views to us by their moderation and balance. He impresses us as a safe guide to the history both of evolutionary speculation and of biological research. Readers desiring to know the present state, whether of knowledge or of opinion, in this sphere of research cannot do better than to resort to his comprehensive and readable volume.

October 1908
Princeton Theological Review 6:650–53

Review of George Paulin,
No Struggle for Existence:
No Natural Selection.
A Critical Examination
of the Fundamental Principles
of the Darwinian Theory
(Edinburgh: T. & T. Clark, 1908)

While Warfield comments on this apparently unknown author's "diffuseness of expression," he generally concurs with George Paulin's
critique of Darwinism and Malthusian population theory. In contradiction to these theories, Warfield points to the dearth of fossil evidence for intermediate stages of development and the apparent lack
of intense struggle in the animal world for survival of the fittest; instead, nature exists in a relatively balanced state. He concludes by referring to the "speculative character" of what is accepted by many
as science, and turns the tables on evolutionists by suggesting that
Darwinism itself rests on an implied miracle.

We have not had the fortune to meet with other writings by
Mr. George Paulin and are entirely ignorant of his personality.[1] He
speaks of himself as of one advanced in years, and his manner of
writing seems to accord with this description, characterized as it
is at once by a certain ripeness of tone and by a certain diffuseness

---

1. [Warfield is not alone in his ignorance about Paulin, for search in many
standard biographical and bibliographical reference works has turned up nothing
about him.]

of expression. The matter of his book is highly speculative in character and divides itself into two extended arguments—the one in refutation of the Darwinian theory of natural selection, the other in rebuttal of the central contention of Malthus's *Essay on Population.*[2] Unity is secured by the identity of the governing principle in the two theories which are examined.

Mr. Paulin appears to ascribe a venturesome novelty to his assault on the core of the Darwinian hypothesis. This somewhat astonishes us, for he seems almost to imagine that he is the first, or among the first, to arraign the conceptions of the struggle for existence and survival of the fittest. Readers who are unaware of the widespread revolt from these conceptions among recent scientific investigators should read at least the three chapters on "Darwinism Attacked" in Professor Vernon L. Kellogg's *Darwinism Today.* Meanwhile, Mr. Paulin's apparent lack of acquaintance with these labors of his fellow workers gives to his strictures on the Darwinian hypothesis the value of an independent criticism. The hundred and twelve pages which he devotes to this criticism, diffuse and speculative as they are, and now and then somewhat heated, are nevertheless quite effective—chiefly because they lay stress on certain broad considerations which, apart from all details, appear to be fatal to the Darwinian construction.

Neither the paleontological record nor the present state of the animate universe is such as it would be were the Darwinian hypothesis true. If the Darwinian hypothesis were correct, there would necessarily have existed, in the slow formation of types through infinitesimal changes, innumerable intermediate stages; and the several types would inevitably melt insensibly into one another. Vastly more of the unfit would have died than of the fit. How is it that the record is free from these intermediate types? How have the rocks selected for our inspection only the few fit for preservation in their remains and destroyed all trace of the immensely more numerous unfit?

2. [Thomas Robert Malthus (1766–1834), an Anglican clergyman and political economist, published his controversial *Essay on the Principle of Population* in 1798. In it he asserted that population when unchecked grows geometrically, while means of subsistence increase only arithmetically. Malthus contended that the difference in the two rates of growth leads to overpopulation and consequently to overcrowding, starvation, and disease.]

If the Darwinian hypothesis were correct, again, all nature, in the terrible struggle for existence which is its nerve, would hang ever at the starving point. It does not. The average animal is a well-to-do animal. Why do not the starving multitudes that are unfit swarm around the surviving few that are fit? They do not. On the Darwinian theory, nature should be one vast charnel house. It is not. It is a happy hunting ground. "We behold only the survivors—vigorous, healthy and happy survivors. But where is the struggle for existence? Where are the dying and the dead?" (p. 17). Starvation is not the normal plane of animal existence. On the contrary, in a district stocked from immemorial time, the numbers of animals inhabiting it will be constant at just the point at which they can be comfortably supplied with their proper food (p. 53). This is what we call the balance of nature, and it seems to maintain itself indefinitely without visible struggle. An internecine struggle such as Darwin pictured as the inevitable state of animal nature—and on the inevitableness of which he built his whole theory—simply never exists, as is open to the observation of everybody. And what survives from generation to generation is obviously not a few hard-pressed "fittest," but the normal somewhat pampered "average."

The examination of the Malthusian theory, which occupies the second half of the volume, is somewhat more labored, but scarcely so effective as the criticism of the Darwinian theory which precedes it. Mr. Paulin's argument here, too, is that the struggle for existence, which is the nerve of Malthusianism also, is not in point of fact a characteristic of human existence, and never can become its characteristic. Population, in his view, is automatically governed by the labor market, and follows inevitably, therefore, the fluctuations in the means of sustenance. In times of plenty, men marry early and the birth rate is large; in times of stringency, men marry correspondingly late and the birth rate is small. Thus the population is regulated by the means of sustenance, and the struggle for existence never comes off. These views Paulin supports by elaborate statistical tables designed to show that the birth rate follows closely the fluctuations of the labor market, so that the population abides steadily at the mark at which sustenance is provided according to the standard of living in vogue. A curious corollary is that large emigration, acting as a

new demand for men, stimulates productivity and does not de-
plete a nation, and the same is true of the maintenance of a large
standing army. The rule is, according to Mr. Paulin, that every
people will produce all the men it can support and use—and no
more; and this automatically.

The most abiding impression which the reader receives from
discussions like these is of the highly speculative character of
what we commonly speak of as physical science. The whole construction which we know as Darwinism is obviously pure speculation—and speculation which, as is coming more and more fully
to be realized nowadays, has little to support it in actual nature.
The warnings of men like Virchow against running so recklessly
ahead of observation have been, and no doubt will continue to
be, generally disregarded.[3] So zealous is the human mind for explanations that a plausible explanation is readily accepted, although the actual state of things loudly cries out against it.

Mr. Paulin's own experience curiously illustrates the ineradicable habit of the human mind to proceed on mere assumptions. He
wrote his book as a convinced evolutionist who had his quarrel
only with the Darwinian conception of the factors of evolution.
But before he got it published, grave doubt attacked him as to the
validity of this assumption. The immense length of time required
for the evolutionary process, the entire lack in the paleontological
records of intermediate forms to bridge the gulf, and the sudden
appearance of finished fish, bird and mammal types among het-
erogeneous organisms, the general evidences of design in nature—and such like considerations—invaded his thought with
new energy and threw him suddenly into doubt as to his lifelong
conviction. "If I be asked in what conclusion, then, do I rest," he
confesses with some pathos, "I can only answer, in this, that I
know nothing. The way of God in creation baffles me by its mystery. Of the mode of evolution Nature tells us nothing" (p. xix).
Though the doctrine of special creation "does not recommend itself" to Paulin, and he is "unable to accept it," he admits that the

3. [Rudolf Ludwig Karl Virchow (1821–1902), German pathologist, is considered the founder of modern pathology and was a leader in the movement toward
scientific medicine. He regarded Darwinism as a tentative hypothesis and refused
to accept any single-cause theory of origins.]

argument is logically in its favor, and that it presents no new difficulties not already found in the origin of life.

Thus, as he sends out the book which he has written to show that the fundamental basis of Darwinism is pure assumption, he is compelled to pause and confess that the foundations of his own thought have revealed themselves to him as pure assumption also. *Ignoramus* [we do not know], he cries; and apparently also, *ignorabimus* [we will not know]. This only does he feel sure of—God; and "that the Deity did not intervene to suspend the regular operation of the forces of Nature with a view to prevent the preservation of intermediate forms, while He suffered them to preserve those finished forms which are contained in the geological record" (p. xx). That is to say, Darwinism implies a miracle. And while he is prepared to believe in miracles—or rather does not quite see how he can escape believing in them, if not in the special creation of types of animate existence, at least in the origin of life—he is decidedly unprepared to believe in the special miracle which Darwinism implies. He does not quite know what is true, but he seems to himself to know quite conclusively that Darwinism is not true. It would seem that we must take this as Mr. Paulin's final word to us, and it seems to us far from an unsatisfactory word.

January 1909
Princeton Theological Review 7:106–12

Review of Rudolf Otto,
Naturalism and Religion,
trans. J. Arthur Thomson and Margaret R.
Thomson, ed. W. D. Morrison
(New York: G. P. Putnam's Sons; London:
Williams and Norgate, 1907)

Warfield clearly appreciates this critique of naturalism and defense of a religious worldview, although he parts ways with Otto's theological and philosophical outlook. Warfield particularly focuses on Otto's anti-Darwinian argument that a theory of descent does not inherently rule out teleology; rather, the existence of developmental mechanisms may in fact be the means through which divine purpose is fulfilled. In passing it should be noted that Warfield was sensitive to the weaknesses in what has come to be called "evolutionary epistemology," the application of natural selection to the generation of scientific ideas themselves. Rudolf Otto (1869–1937), a German Protestant, taught theology at Breslau and Marburg. His *Idea of the Holy* (1917, Eng. trans. 1923) introduced the term "numinous" to describe what he considered to be a common human experience of the divine.

D r. Otto is introduced by his English editor to his new audience as "a thinker who possesses the rare merit of combining a high philosophic discipline with an accurate and comprehensive knowledge of the science of organic nature." The appearance of the name of Professor Thomson on the title page of the book as translator may be taken as an additional guarantee of the scientific competency of the author.[1] The book itself fully meets the expectations so aroused. We do not, indeed, share the author's philosophical standpoint; and still less can we homologate [i.e., approve] the theological conceptions which may occasionally be read between the lines. But there can be no question that the book is ably thought and attractively written, or that its author is exceptionally well informed on the current scientific discussion in Germany and exceptionally well equipped to expound it alike in its details and in its general drift. As a result we have in the book an admirable survey of recent German speculation on the origin and nature of the world and man, and a strong and convincing defense of the right of religion in the face of modern thought.

Dr. Otto calls his book *Naturalism and Religion* and explains its purpose as "in the first place, to define the relation, or rather, the antithesis, between the two; and, secondly, to endeavor to reconcile the contradictions, and vindicate against the counterclaims of naturalism the validity and freedom of the religious outlook" (p. 1). Or, as he somewhat more crisply expresses it at a later point, "to define our attitude to naturalism, and to maintain in the teeth of naturalism the validity and freedom of the religious conception of the world" (p. 278). The real subject of the book is, therefore, naturalism; and its real purpose is to assert over against naturalism the right of religion. Its primary purpose, in other words, is polemic rather than constructive. It is less concerned with the positive exposition and development of the religious conception of the world than with the vindication of the right of a religious conception of the world.

Of course Dr. Otto has not written so much without suggesting what, in his view, the religious conception of the world includes. He has even formally outlined and briefly expounded and even argued its elements. But neither the strength nor the mass of the book is given to it, but is expended rather on a careful critical survey of current forms of naturalism, with a view to exhibiting its essential failure. From our point of view the value of the book is immensely increased by this circumstance. For Dr. Otto's philosophical and

1. [John Arthur Thomson (1861–1933), Scottish biologist and professor of natural history at the University of Aberdeen, was particularly interested in correlating science and religion.]

even theological conceptions would necessarily dominate his positive construction of the worldview to which he would give the name of religious. And, as we have already explained, we do not particularly care for Dr. Otto's philosophical or theological views. But in his exposition and criticism of naturalistic theories he is moving on ground common to all who would cherish a religious worldview of any sort. And here we can follow his lucid expositions and his trenchant criticisms with unalloyed satisfaction.

Dr. Otto's philosophical standpoint is that of a convinced Kantian idealism, or perhaps we ought rather to say he is a disciple of that mixed product of Kant and Jacobi, Jacob Friedrich Fries, who has lately been disinterred in Germany and given at least some semblance of renewed vitality.[2] Although he doubtless transcends Fries's antiteleological view of nature, some slight echo of it may perhaps be detected in his willingness to admit that a direct study of nature will not yield a teleological view of it. The Friesian leaven is more in evidence, however, in Otto's view of religion as rooted primarily in a sense of mystery, upon which he then engrafts, to be sure, the sense of dependence in which religion centers, and the conception of teleology in which, we may say, it culminates. The peculiar extension he gives to the implications of the feeling of dependence, deriving from it the assurance not only that man, the subject of this ineradicable and surely not misleading feeling, is a contingent being, but that so is the whole world itself, has, perhaps, its roots in the same idealism. The external world, which is our creation, can scarcely be less dependent than the beings whose creation it is.

2. [Immanuel Kant (1724–1804), German philosopher, suggested that space and time exist only as forms of human knowing rather than as things with external, noumenal relations. Denying the sufficiency of mechanistic causes to explain organic entities, he affirmed that God had created the world. The German philosopher Friedrich Heinrich Jacobi (1743–1819) defended feeling and faith as valid forms of theoretical knowledge. He was repelled by the rationalism of Spinoza and believed that certain truths, such as the knowledge of God, are found in a person's inner consciousness, and are endangered when subjected to the rationalizing processes of the mind. Jacob Friedrich Fries (1773–1843), German philosopher and physicist, was a disciple of Kant who attempted to merge Kantian philosophy and Newtonian physics. Opposed to religious and vitalistic explanations of the universe, he affirmed the necessity of a scientific psychology as a foundation for epistemology.]

One gets the impression that Professor Otto's objection to naturalism turns less on the obliteration by naturalism of the distinction between matter and mind than on naturalism's attempt to work this obliteration the wrong way about. The external world from which naturalism would explain mind, he would rather explain from mind. And so it comes about that as the argument runs on it seems almost to become rather a plea for spiritualism than for what we commonly speak of as a religious interpretation of the world. Its thesis almost appears to be summed up in the striking and strikingly true remark (p. 283) that "mental science, from logic and epistemology up to and including the moral and aesthetic sciences, proves by its very existence, and by the fact that it cannot be reduced to terms of natural science, that spirit can neither be derived from nor analyzed into anything else."

At this point, however, we are a little puzzled by the rushing in of another current of Dr. Otto's thought, which almost sweeps away this spirit, the substantial existence of which he seems to have so firmly established. We must not talk, it seems, of its "substantial nature" (p. 330)—that is a matter of entire indifference (p. 331); what concerns us is only "its incomparable value" (p. 331). "What lives in us . . . is not a finished and spiritual being . . . but something that develops and becomes actual very gradually" (p. 298). Whence it comes . . . who can tell? Or whither it goes? All we know of it is, lo! it is here. And that it is the manifestation of something that is. "There is no practical meaning in discussing its 'origin' or its 'passing away,' as we do with regard to the corporeal. Under certain corporeal conditions it is there, it simply appears. But it does not arise out of them. And as it is not nothing, but an actual and effectual reality, it can neither have come out of nothing nor disappear into nothing again. It appears out of the absolutely transcendental, associates itself with corporeal processes, determines these and is determined by them, and in its own time passes back from this world of appearance to the transcendental again" (p. 358). Is this only another way of saying that "the soul that rises with us, our life's star, hath had elsewhere its setting, and cometh from afar"?[3] Or does it, as we much doubt,

3. [The quotation is from William Wordsworth, "Ode. Intimations of Immortality from Recollections of Early Childhood" (1807).]

mean much more than this? Decidedly Dr. Otto's philosophy needs watching. And we may be glad it does not form the staple of his book but only lies in its background.

What forms the staple of his book is the exposition and criticism of naturalism. Naturalism, he tells us, exists in two forms, naive and speculative. And speculative naturalism entrenches itself in two great contentions, the one embodied in the Darwinian doctrine of evolution, the other in the mechanical theory of life. To the exposition and criticism of these two great contentions of naturalism Dr. Otto accordingly devotes himself. To the Darwinian theory chapters 4 to 7 (pp. 85–186) are given; to the mechanical theory of life, chapters 8 to 11 (pp. 187–359). The discussion in both cases is full, the exposition clear, the criticism telling.

In dealing with the Darwinian theory, Dr. Otto very properly distinguishes between the theory of descent in general and the specific form given this theory by Darwin's hypothesis of the indefiniteness of variations and the survival of the fittest in the struggle for existence. The former, he points out, has maintained its ground, or perhaps we may even say has strengthened its stakes. Dr. Otto intimates, almost as a matter of course, his own adhesion to it. The latter, on the contrary, has become in the estimate of wide circles, not merely suspect, but even disproved. Dr. Otto intimates that he himself will have none of it. But it is precisely in this peculiarly Darwinian theory of natural selection that the virus of naturalism in current evolutionary speculation is prominent.

The theory of descent is in no sense specifically Darwinian; it is far older than Darwin and remains the conviction of multitudes who are definitely anti-Darwinian. What is specifically Darwinian is the appeal to the factors of overproduction, indefinite variation, struggle for existence and consequent elimination of the unfit and the survival of the fittest as containing in themselves the true account of the modifications which have produced the multitudinous forms of life. Thus teleology was reduced to an illusion and suitability substituted in its place; utility became the one sufficient creator of all that is living. The present widespread dissatisfaction with, and even rejection of, this account of organic development may be taken as at the same time, therefore, a refu-

tation of the naturalism which underlies it, because it is an exhibition of the inadequacy of mere utility to account for all things.

As investigation has gone on, it has become clearer and clearer
to numerous students of the subject that variations do not occur
indifferently in every direction, but turn up opportunely. As
Du Bois-Reymond expressed it in his vivid way, nature's dice are
loaded: not accidentalism but purpose rules her acts.[4] Like the
lesser organism of the individual being, the greater organism of
the animate world grows along fixed lines by definite steps to determined ends. Natural selection may have a part to play in the
process, but it is in wider and wider circles coming to be believed
that it is a very subordinate part. It can work on only what is
given it; and it does not seem to have indefinite variations in every direction to work on, but, rather, very definite variations in
one direction. The goal attained is, therefore, not determined by
it, but by the inherent tendency of the developing organism. So,
at least, an increasing number of students of nature are coming to
think.

Dr. Otto's method is marked by a very large infusion of the
concessive spirit. He betrays no tendency to drive antitheses into
contradictions, and he does not permit the cause of teleology in
nature to be identified with the extremest anti-Darwinian opinions. On the contrary, he is quick to point out that purpose has no
quarrel with means and can live, therefore, under the strictest
reign of law. It is not law which is fatal to purpose, but chance.
Nay, says he, "absolute obedience to law and the inexorableness
of chains of sequence are, instead of being fatal to 'teleology,' indispensable to it." "When there is a purpose in view," he argues,
"it is only where the system of means is perfect, unbroken, and
absolute, that the purpose can be realized, and therefore that intention can be inferred" (p. 83). Accordingly, therefore, he considers it possible to embrace in a teleological interpretation "the

4. [Emil Heinrich Du Bois-Reymond (1818–1896), German electrophysiolo-
gist, was raised in an orthodox Pietist home but rejected his father's beliefs and
became a determined opponent of all nonmechanistic viewpoints, especially vitalism. Arguing that forces cannot exist apart from matter, he advocated a strict
materialism and applauded Voltaire for applying Newton to the human sciences,
even while he acknowledged that science cannot answer certain transcendental
questions.]

whole system of causes and effects, which, according to the Darwin-Weismann doctrine, have gradually brought forth the whole diversity of the world of life, with man at its head." For why may not this be looked upon "as an immense system of means," intricate no doubt, but working to its end with inevitable necessity— which may therefore be the manifestation of intention (p. 151)?

At a later point, when dealing with the mechanical theory of life, he reverts to the same line of remark to show that mechanism has in it nothing inconsistent with purpose (pp. 222–23). Mechanism may be only the way in which purpose realizes itself. Of course, the danger here is that we may fall thus into a deistic conception of the method of what we theologically call "providence." But this does not seem necessary, even when the whole of what we call nature is conceived as a machine. Though the guiding hand of purpose be conceived as everywhere and at all times immediately operative, nevertheless the whole account of the several phenomena would be found in the efficient, not in the final causes. In no case are the final causes to be conceived as additional efficient causes producing with them a resultant effect. They are and remain only final causes and operate only through and by means of the efficient causes. Accordingly, each phenomenon finds its whole account when considered in its efficient causes severally. It is therefore indifferent to purpose whether the events which occur under its government occur as products of mechanical or free causes. "Providence," then, which is but another way of saying "purpose," is as consistent with a mechanical theory as with any other theory of life, because purpose is not discerned in the separate phenomena but in their combination. Romanes was quite right, therefore, when he regretfully said of his earlier mistake in ruling purpose out of the universe: "I had forgotten to take in the whole scope of things, the marvelous harmony of the all."

Dr. Otto is anxious that his readers shall not make the analogous mistake of supposing that because a thing is caused it is therefore not intended. He does not imagine, of course, that in this vindication of teleology in relation to mechanism he has done all that is necessary to validate the religious view of the world. He rightly supposes, however, that he has by it done something to remove some current objections to the religious view of the world, for there are still some who imagine that when they say mechanism they deny purpose. How far the alleged mechanism rules is another question.

The most striking feature of Dr. Otto's method is, however, his employment of exposition as argument. His book thus becomes a mirror of current thought on the subjects with which he is dealing. The inherent weakness of the Darwinian construction of the factors of evolution, for example, he exhibits less by direct argument of his own against it than by a running exposition of the course of evolutionary thought in latter-day Germany. The first impression the reader gets from this survey is of the uncertainty of the conclusions which are from time to time announced. He soon perceives, however, that amid the apparent confusion there is a gradual and steady driftage in one direction, and that that direction is away from Darwin's conceptions. Whatever in the end he may come to think of Darwin's theory in its application to nature, he receives a strong impression that it is fairly illustrated in this section of human research and thought.

Here are certainly exhibited indefinite variation in all directions, struggle for existence, and—let us hope—the survival of the fittest. It may become us to bear in mind, to be sure, that the survival of the fittest is not quite the same as the survival of the true. It may be only the survival of the theory that fits in best with the presuppositions and prejudices of the times. Nevertheless, truth is strong; and we can scarcely doubt it will (finally) prevail. And one gets the impression that, in this case, what seems likely to prevail in the meantime is the truth, and that this truth is hostile to the antiteleological schematization of Darwin and, indeed, to his whole construction of the main factors of evolution.

Indeed, it seems at times as if the new investigators were inclined to react from natural selection a shade too violently and, not content with assigning *Darwinismus* to the *Sterbebett* [deathbed], were determined to deny to natural selection not only any real effectiveness or capacity for species-forming, but even reality itself. Prof. Otto avoids this extreme. He not only recognizes its operation in nature as a *vera causa* [an actual cause], but points out that its obvious reality and actual working are the main cause of the attractiveness of the theory which found in it the one great agency in species-forming (pp. 156–57). Nevertheless, he holds firmly with the more recent thought, which discovers for it only a very subordinate role to play in nature; and he points out with great clearness that its dethronement and the substitution for it of theories of evolution dominated by the recognition of inherent tendencies in the organism and progression along right lines definitely relegate naturalism too to the *Sterbelager* [place of death], so far as it had entrenched itself in the doctrine of evolution.

In dealing with the mechanical theory of life, Professor Otto employs much the same method which he uses in dealing with the doctrine of evolution. Here, too, he avoids dogmatism and relies largely on the effect a mere tracing of the history of research is fitted to produce. For the progress of investigation has been away from the mechanical view of life. We have lived to see the dawn of a new age of vitalism, and even where the name is scouted and the thing deprecated, the edges of the old mechanical theory have become very frayed. On the basis of present-day thought, Dr. Otto is justified in emphasizing the mystery of life and in pointing decisively to the supremeness of mind, so making way for the religious view of the world from this point of sight also.

Enough has doubtless been said to manifest the high value we place on Dr. Otto's discussion. It would be difficult to find elsewhere in such brief compass so full and lucid a survey of the recent German literature on evolution and the nature of life. And it would be, we are persuaded, impossible to find another work of such compressed form in which the failure of naturalism as a theory of the world is more tellingly argued.

April 1909
Princeton Theological Review 7:329–30

Excerpt from a review of James Hastings, ed.,
Encyclopaedia of Religion and Ethics, vol. 1, *A–Art*
(New York: Scribner; Edinburgh:
T. & T. Clark, 1908)

Warfield's lengthy review of this important reference work includes a long paragraph on its treatment of "Abiogenesis" and "Adaptation." In it he questions the logic of evolutionary theory that postulates both abiogenesis (spontaneous generation) and adaptation. For him abiogenesis suggests that an organism must be from the outset perfectly adapted to its environment since it is presumably generated by that environment; why then should there be development to higher forms? James Hastings (1852–1922), Scottish clergyman and editor, compiled several notable reference works, including the *Dictionary of the Bible,* the *Dictionary of Christ and the Gospels,* and the *Dictionary of the Apostolic Church.*

. . . It gives the reader an odd impression, we may remark in passing, to turn over a few pages and read the article "Adaptation" in close conjunction with that on "Abiogenesis."[1] Evolution, we learn, is simply a process of adaptation. The fittest in every generation survives; that is to say, there is a constant progress towards more perfect adaptation. Why, then, one may well ask, has there not been a tolerable adaptation attained long ago? Or, remembering abiogenesis, we may rather ask, Why was there not a perfect adaptation from the beginning? If the

---

1. [Abiogenesis: strictly, the origination of living organisms from lifeless matter.]

living organism is in the first instance the spontaneous production of the environment, it is inconceivable that it should not begin by being in perfect adaptation to it. How could the environment produce an organization out of adaptation to itself? And
starting thus in perfect adaptation to its environment, how
could the living organism ever get out of this adaptation to the
environment of which it is not only at the start but throughout
merely the expression? From start to finish the environment is
but the mold in which the organism is cast, and the cast surely
must repeat the features of the mold. If the mold changes, the
cast changes with it; that is all. And it is not so much a question
of adaptation, which implies a certain independence of mold
and cast, as of simple reproduction. The evolutionary idea here
resembles very closely what we read of Alice in the Looking
Glass, who, we remember, had to run with all her might just to
keep standing still.

And here another difficulty faces us. This living organism
which is in the first instance the spontaneous product of its environment and must therefore begin in perfect adaptation to its
environment—of which it is indeed but the expression; and
which ever continues but the product of its environment and
should therefore steadily express its environment and change
only as it changes that it may abide in complete adaptation to
it—does nothing of the sort. On the contrary, it from the beginning spurns the slime (of which it is just the expression) and
soars upwards and advances steadily to higher and higher
things! That is what has happened. The law of development of
organic forms has not been to ever closer and closer adaptation
to the environment. They began (abiogenesis being postulated)
in perfect adaptation to the environment. The law of their development has been to ever fuller, richer, more elevated manifestations of what looks very much like a new thing with forces
all its own, which struggles with its environment and conquers
it, and which ends, indeed, by adapting its environment to itself.
This is not the behavior of crystals, say, which form themselves
in pools of evaporating sea-water, and dissolve again and reform
afresh as the water is alternately diluted by the rain or wasted
by the sun—but never stand over against the mother-water and
insist on going their own way. It is all very puzzling—on the

postulates of the thoroughgoing evolutionism of Mr. Clodd, which Mr. Clodd tells us is the doctrine (unuttered or expressed, we may suppose) of all biologists.[2] . . .

2. [Edward Clodd (1840–1930) was a corresponding member of the Société d'Anthropologie de Paris and vice-president of the Folklore Society at the time he wrote the article on abiogenesis. An English banker and author, he moved from a Baptist background to Congregationalism of a liberal bent to agnosticism by 1887. Clodd embraced Darwinism, and his popular works on religion and evolution earned him the friendship of such people as Thomas Henry Huxley and Herbert Spencer.]

January 1911
Princeton Theological Review 9:1–25
(reprinted from *WBBW,* 9:235–58)

On the Antiquity and the Unity of the Human Race (excerpts)

In this important academic essay, Warfield goes back over some ground he had previously covered concerning the best way to read the genealogies of Genesis, expands on his earlier discussion of the era's scientific evidence for the age of the earth, and defines the close connection between his views of evolution and his convictions about central teachings of Scripture. The essay's argument that the age of the earth is irrelevant to theology repeats the argument from his 1903 essay, "The Manner and Time of Man's Origin" (pp. 211–29). The part of that argument dealing with the genealogies of Genesis is not repeated here, since it mostly reprises what Warfield wrote in that earlier essay. The section treating current scientific proposals about the age of the earth and of humanity is, however, printed here, since in that section Warfield testifies to his ongoing reading of scientific literature by adding considerably to what he had published eight years earlier. (Annotations are provided here for the scientific authorities whom Warfield added in 1911; for those incorporated from his 1903 paper, see that earlier essay.)

There are two reasons why Warfield takes pleasure in the recent scientific literature. First, although he does not feel that cosmological age is a critical theological matter, he nonetheless is pleased that, as he interprets the matter, science has reduced the time postulated for the existence of the earth and of humanity. Warfield sees a consequent reduction in tension between biblical and scientific conclusions. The second reason that Warfield takes pleasure in recent scientific literature has to do with the era's theories of evolution. He concludes that scientists have mostly given up Darwin's mechanism of natural selection and have moved increasingly to theories of evolution by saltation (or leaps, mutations). Warfield heralds this as a positive step because theories of saltation, though still evolutionary, pose fewer difficulties for Bible believers than do Darwinian theories requiring vastly more time.

The final section of this essay presents Warfield's arguments concerning the unity of the human species. Unlike the age of the earth,
Warfield feels a unified humanity is a matter of utmost theological
importance—if there is no human unity, there is no triumphant redemption of humanity through the work of Christ. Racial pride, he
also notes, has often been the motive for denying the unity of the
human race. Warfield's discussion of this matter is highlighted by a
brief but thorough canvassing of the many pre-Adamite theories
that had pictured the existence of humans before Adam.[1] It also features what Warfield held to be the conclusions of contemporary evolutionary theory supporting the unity of humankind.

In a combination that became rare after Warfield's era, this essay
represents a stiff form of Calvinist theological conservatism along
with a nearly complete openness to some kinds of carefully qualified
evolutionary theory.

The fundamental assertion of the biblical doctrine of the origin of
man is that he owes his being to a creative act of God. Subsidiary
questions growing out of this fundamental assertion, however,
have been thrown from time to time into great prominence, as the
changing forms of current anthropological speculation have seemed
to press on this or that element in, or corollary from, the biblical
teaching. The most important of these subsidiary questions has
concerned the method of the divine procedure in creating man. Discussion of this question became acute on the publication of Charles
Darwin's treatise on the *Origin of Species* in 1859, and can never sink
again into rest until it is thoroughly understood in all quarters that
evolution cannot act as a substitute for creation, but at best can supply only a theory of the method of the divine providence. Closely
connected with this discussion of the mode of the origination of
man has been the discussion of two further questions, both older
than the Darwinian theory, to one of which it gave, however, a new
impulse, while it has well-nigh destroyed all interest in the other.
These are the questions of the antiquity of man and the unity of the
human race, to both of which a large historical interest attaches,
though neither of them can be said to be burning questions of today.

1. On the extensive, varied history of pre-Adamitism, see David N. Livingstone, *The Preadamite Theory and the Marriage of Science and Religion,* Transactions
of the American Philosophical Society 82.3 (Philadelphia: American Philosophical
Society, 1992), with pp. 62–64 especially on Warfield.

The question of the antiquity of man has of itself no theological significance. It is to theology as such a matter of entire indifference how long man has existed on earth. It is only because of the contrast which has been drawn between the short period which seems to be allotted to human history in the biblical narrative, and the tremendously long period which certain schools of scientific speculation have assigned to the duration of human life on earth, that theology has become interested in the topic at all. There was thus created the appearance of a conflict between the biblical statements and the findings of scientific investigators, and it became the duty of theologians to investigate the matter. The asserted conflict proves, however, to be entirely factitious. The Bible does not assign a brief span to human history; this is done only by a particular mode of interpreting the biblical data, which is found on examination to rest on no solid basis. Science does not demand an inordinate period for the life of human beings on earth; this is done only by a particular school of speculative theorizers, the validity of whose demands on time exact investigators are more and more chary of allowing. As the real state of the case has become better understood, the problem has therefore tended to disappear from theological discussion, till now it is fairly well understood that theology as such has no interest in it.

It must be confessed, indeed, that a prima facie view of the biblical record of the course of human history readily gives the impression that the human race is of comparatively recent origin. It has been the usual supposition of simple Bible readers, therefore, that the biblical data allow for the duration of the life of the human race on earth only a paltry six thousand years or so; and this supposition has become fixed in formal chronological schemes which have become traditional and have even been given a place in the margins of our Bibles to supply the chronological framework of the scriptural narrative. The most influential of these chronological schemes is that which was worked out by Archbishop Ussher[2] in his *Annales Veteri*

2. [The Irish Protestant James Ussher (1581–1656) was professor of theology at Trinity College, Dublin, and appointed archbishop of Armagh in 1624. An intense student of Scripture, he developed his chronology using only biblical data. Owing to its long-standing presence in the marginal notes of the Authorized (King James) Version, the dating of creation at 4004 B.C. attained authoritative status for many, including some creationists today.]

et Novi Testamenti [Annals of the Old and New Testament] (1650–54),
and it is this scheme which has found a place in the margin of the
Authorized English Version of the Bible since 1701. According to it
the creation of the world is assigned to the year 4004 B.C. (Ussher's
own dating was 4138 B.C.), while according to the calculation of Pétau[3] (in his *Rationarium temporum* [Reckoning of time]), the most influential rival scheme, it is assigned to the year 3983 B.C. On a more
careful scrutiny of the data on which these calculations rest, however, they are found not to supply a satisfactory basis for the constitution of a definite chronological scheme. These data consist largely,
and at the crucial points solely, of genealogical tables; and nothing
can be clearer than that it is precarious in the highest degree to draw
chronological inferences from genealogical tables. . . .

[From this point Warfield mostly repeats the exposition on biblical genealogies that appeared in his 1903 essay.]

. . . The question of the antiquity of man is accordingly a
purely scientific one in which the theologian as such has no concern. As an interested spectator, however, he looks on as the various schools of scientific speculation debate the question among
themselves; and he can scarcely fail to take away as the result of
his observation two well-grounded convictions. The first is that
science has as yet in its hands no solid data for a definite estimate
of the time during which the human race has existed on earth.
The second is that the tremendous drafts on time which were accustomed to be made by the geologists about the middle of the
last century and which continue to be made by one school of
speculative biology today have been definitively set aside, and it
is becoming very generally understood that man cannot have existed on the earth more than some ten thousand to twenty thousand years.

That speculation during the first three-quarters of the nineteenth century estimated the age of the habitable globe in terms
of hundreds of millions of years was a result of the manner of
looking at things inculcated by the Huttonian geology. It was under the influence of this teaching, for example, that Charles Dar-

3. [Denis Pétau (also known as Dionysius Petavius, 1583–1652) was a French
Jesuit theologian and patrologist. His work on world chronology, *Rationarium temporum* (1633), was later used by Jacques Bossuet for his *Discours sur l'historie uni-
verselle.*]

win in 1859 supposed that 300 million years were an underestimate for the period which has elapsed since the latter part of the Secondary Age.[4] In reviewing Mr. Darwin's argument, Professor Jukes in his *Student's Manual of Geology* remarked on the vagueness of the data on which Darwin's estimates were formed, and suggested that the sum of years asserted might with equal reasonableness be reduced or multiplied a hundredfold: he proposed therefore 3 million and 30 billion years as the minimum and maximum limits of the period in question. From the same fundamental standpoint, Professor Poulton in his address as president of the Zoological Section of the British Association for the Advancement of Science (Liverpool, September 1896) treats as too short from his biological point of view the longest time asked by the geologists for the duration of the habitable earth—say some 400 millions of years. Dwelling on the number of distinct types of animal existence already found in the Lower Cambrian deposits, and on the necessarily (as he thinks) slow progress of evolution, he stretches out the time required for the advance of life to its present manifestation practically illimitably. Taking up the cudgels for his biological friends, Sir Archibald Geikie[5] chivalrously offers them all the time they desire; on his own behalf, however, he speaks of 100 million years as possibly sufficient for the period of the existence of life on the globe. These general estimates imply, of course, a very generous allowance for the duration of human life on earth; but many anthropologists demand for this period even more than they allow. Thus, for example, Professor Gabriel de Mortillet[6] reiterates his conviction that the appearance of man on earth cannot be dated less than two hundred and thirty thousand years ago, and Professor A. Penck[7] would agree with this estimate, while Dr. A. R. Wallace has been accustomed to ask more than double that period.[8]

4. *Origin of Species,* 1st ed., p. 287.
5. Address as president of the Geological Section of the British Association, Dover meeting, September 1899—*Science* for October 13, 1899.
6. *Revue Mensuelle* of the Paris School of Anthropology, for January 15, 1897.
7. Silliman Lectures at Yale for 1908. [Albrecht Penck (1858–1945), German geologist and geomorphologist, did a thorough study of Alpine glaciation along with significant studies of uplift and erosion.]
8. *Nature,* October 2, 1873, pp. 462–63; see also *Darwinism* (1889), 456.

These tremendously long estimates of the duration of life on
earth and particularly of the duration of human life are, however,
speculative and, indeed, largely the creation of a special type of evolutionary speculation—a type which is rapidly losing ground among
recent scientific workers. This type is that which owes its origin to
the brooding mind of Charles Darwin; up to recent times it has been
the regnant type of evolutionary philosophy. Its characteristic contention is that the entire development of animate forms has been
the product of selection, by the pressure of the environment, of infinitesimal variations in an almost infinite series of successive generations; or, to put it rather brusquely but not unfairly, that chance
plus time are the true causes which account for the whole body of
differentiated forms which animate nature presents to our observation. Naturally, therefore, heavy drafts have been made on time to
account for whatever it seemed hard to attribute to brute chance, as
if the issuing of any effect out of any conditions could be admitted
if only the process of production were slow enough.

James Hutton had duly warned his followers against the temptation to appeal to time as if it were itself an efficient cause of effects. "With regard to the effect of time," he said, "though the
continuance of time may do much in those operations which are
extremely slow [and in which] no change, to our observation, has
appeared to take place; yet, where it is not in the nature of things
to produce the change in question, the unlimited course of time
would be no more effectual than the moment by which we measure events in our observations."[9] The warning was not heeded;
men seemed to imagine that, if only time enough were given, effects for which no adequate cause could be assigned might be
supposed to come gradually of themselves. Aimless movement
was supposed, if time enough were allowed for it, to produce an
ordered world. It might as well be supposed that if a box full of
printers' types were stirred up long enough with a stick, the letters could be counted on to arrange themselves in time in the order in which they stand, say, in Kant's *Critique of Pure Reason.*
They will never do so, though they be stirred to eternity.

Dr. J. W. Dawson points out the exact difficulty when he remarks that "the necessity for indefinitely protracted time does not

9. *Theory of the Earth,* 2:205.

arise from the facts, but from the attempt to explain the facts without any adequate cause, and to appeal to an infinite series of chance interactions apart from a designed plan, and without regard to the consideration that we know of no way in which, with any conceivable amount of time, the first living and organized beings could be spontaneously produced from dead matter."[10] Nothing could be more certain than that what chance cannot begin the production of in a moment, chance cannot complete the production of in an eternity. The analysis of the complete effect into an infinite series of parts, and the distribution of these parts over an infinite series of years, leave the effect as unaccounted for as ever. What is needed to account for it is not time in any extension, but an adequate cause. A mass of iron is made no more self-supporting by being forged into an illimitable chain formed of innumerable infinitesimal links. We may cast our dice to all eternity with no more likelihood than at the first throw of ever turning up double sevens.

It is not, however, the force of such reasoning but the pressure of hard facts which is revolutionizing the conceptions of biologists today as to the length of the period during which man has existed on earth. It is not possible to enumerate here all the facts which are cooperating to produce a revised and greatly reduced estimate of this period. First among them may doubtless be placed the calculations of the life period of the globe itself which have been made by the physicists with ever increasing confidence. Led by such investigators as Lord Kelvin, they have become ever more and more insistent that the time demanded by the old uniformitarian and the new biological speculator is not at their disposal. The publication in the seventh decade of the past century of Lord Kelvin's calculations showing that the sun had not been shining 60 millions of years, already gave pause to the reckless drafts which had been accustomed to be made on time; and the situation was rendered more and more acute by subsequent revisions of Lord Kelvin's work, progressively diminishing this estimate. Sir Archibald Geikie complains that "he [Lord Kelvin] has cut off slice after slice from the allowance of time which at first he was prepared to grant for the evolution of geo-

10. *Relics of Primeval Life* (1897), 323.

logical history," until he has reduced it from 40 to 20 millions of years, "and probably much nearer twenty than forty."[11] This estimate of the period of the sun's light would allow only something like 6 millions of years for geological time, only some one-sixteenth of which would be available for the Caenozoic period, of which only about one-eighth or forty thousand years or so could be allotted to the Pleistocene age, in the course of which the remains of man first appear.[12] Even this meager allowance is cut in half by the calculation of Professor Tait.[13] The general conclusions of these investigators have received the support of independent calculations by Dr. George H. Darwin and Professor Newcomb;[14] and more recently still Mr. T. J. J. See of the Naval Observatory at Washington has published a very pretty speculation in which he determines the total longevity of the sun to be only 36 millions of years, 32 of which belong to its past history.[15]

It is not merely the physicists, however, with whom the biological speculators have to do: the geologists themselves have turned against them. Recent investigations may be taken as putting pre-Quaternary man out of the question (the evidence was

11. See n. 5.
12. Cf. the estimates of G. F. Wright, *Records of the Past* (1908), 7:24. He suggests for post-Tertiary time, say, 50,000 years, and adds that, even if this be doubled, there could be assigned to the postglacial period only some 10,000 years.
13. *Recent Advances in Physical Science* (1876), 167–68. [Peter Guthrie Tait (1831–1901), Scottish mathematician and physicist, was a professor of natural philosophy at Edinburgh for over forty years. Tait and James McCosh, Warfield's teacher at Princeton, had been close friends at the Queen's College, Belfast.]
14. [George H. Darwin (1845–1912), English astronomer and son of Charles Darwin, developed the theory that the moon was originally thrown off from the earth. He was also the first to base a cosmology on purely mathematical and physical principles. Simon Newcomb (1835–1909), Canadian-born, became the foremost American astronomer. His planetary theories and astronomical constants dominated the field for over seventy-five years.]
15. Under the so-called planetesimal hypothesis of Professors Chamberlin and Moulton, which does not presuppose a molten sun and earth, these calculations, which proceed on the basis of the cooling-globe hypothesis, are of course without validity. And in recent years a somewhat despairing appeal has been made to the behavior of radium to suggest that all calculations based on rate of waste are valueless. [Forest Ray Moulton (1872–1952), American astronomer and professor at the University of Chicago, collaborated with his professor T. C. Chamberlin in arguing for a planetesimal or spiral-nebula hypothesis of the origin of the solar system.]

reviewed by Sir John Evans in his address at the Toronto meeting of the British Association, August 18, 1897).[16] And revised estimates of the rate of denudation, erosion, and deposition of alluvial matter in deltas or of stalagmitic matter on the floors [of] caves have greatly reduced the exaggerated conception of its slowness, from which support was sought for the immensely long periods of time demanded. The postglacial period, which will roughly estimate the age of man, it is now generally agreed, "cannot be more than ten thousand years, or probably not more than seven thousand" in length.[17] In this estimate both Professor Winchell[18] and Professor Salisbury[19] agree, and with its establishment a great body of evidence derived from a variety of calculations concurs. If man is of postglacial origin, then, his advent upon earth need not be dated more than five or six thousand years ago; or if we suppose him to have appeared at some point in the later glacial period, as Professor G. F. Wright does, then certainly Professor Wright's estimate of sixteen thousand to twenty thousand years is an ample one.

The effect of these revised estimates of geological time has been greatly increased by growing uncertainty among biologists themselves as to the soundness of the assumptions upon which was founded their demand for long periods of time. These assumptions were, briefly, those which underlie the doctrine of evolution in its specifically Darwinian form—in the form, that is to say, in which the evolution is supposed to be accomplished by the selecting, through the pressure of the environment, of minute favorable variations arising accidentally in the midst of minute variations in every direction indifferently. But in the progress of

16. [Sir John Evans (1823–1908) was a British archaeologist and numismatist. A collector of stone and bronze implements as well as ancient coins, his geological and archaeological research helped confirm the antiquity of man in western Europe.]

17. See especially the articles in *Bibliotheca Sacra* 60 (July 1903): 572–82.

18. *American Geologist,* September 1902, p. 193. [Newton Horace Winchell (1839–1914) founded the *American Geologist* with his brother in 1888 and edited it until 1905. He did significant research on glacial geology.]

19. *The Glacial Geology of New Jersey* (volume 5 of the Final Report of the State Geologist), 1902, p. 194. [Rollin Daniel Salisbury (1858–1922), American geologist and geographer, contributed significantly to the field of glaciology, working closely with T. C. Chamberlin, his mentor and colleague.]

biological research, the sufficiency of this natural selection to account for the development of organic forms has come first to be
questioned, and then in large circles to be denied.[20] In proportion,
however, as evolution is conceived as advancing in determined
directions, no matter the source,[21] and in proportion as it is conceived as advancing onwards by large increments instead of by
insensible changes,[22] in that proportion the demand on time is
lessened and even the evolutionary speculator feels that he can
get along with less of it.

He is no longer impelled to assume behind the high type of
man whose remains in the postglacial deposits are the first inti-
mation of the presence of man on earth, an almost illimitable series of lower and ever lower types of man through which gradually the brute struggled up to the high humanity, records of
whose existence alone have been preserved to us.[23] And he no
longer is required to postulate immense stretches of time for the

20. See V. L. Kellogg, *Darwinism Today,* 1907; R. Otto, *Naturalism and Religion,*
1907; E. Wasmann, *Die moderne Biologie und die Entwicklungstheorie* [Modern biology and developmental theory], 3d ed., 1906; James Orr, *God's Image in Man,*
1905; E. Dennert, *Vom Sterbelager des Darwinismus* [On Darwinism's deathbed],
1903. [The Jesuit Erich Wasmann (1859–1931) was a zoologist whose study of insects helped establish ecology at the turn of the century.]

21. That orthogenesis is a fact is much more widely recognized than is the validity of Eimer's special mode of accounting for it. [For information on orthogenesis, Eimer, and De Vries (n. 22), see Warfield's 1908 review of Kellogg's *Darwinism
Today,* n. 2 (p. 243 in the present volume).]

22. The recognition of the reality of these saltations—or "mutations," as De
Vries inadequately terms them—is again largely independent of any particular
theory with reference to them.

23. See Hubrecht in *De Gids* for June 1896; Otto, *Naturalism and Religion*
(1907), 110; Orr, *God's Image in Man* (1905), 134. E. D. Cope, *The Primary Factors of
Organic Evolution* (1896), thinks there is evidence enough to constitute two species
of the genus *homo—Homo sapiens* and *Homo neanderthalensis,* to the latter of which
he assigns a greater number of simian characteristics than exist in any of the
known races of the *Homo sapiens.* But he requires to add (p. 170): "There is still, to
use the language of Fraipont and Lohest, 'an abyss' between the man of Spy and
the highest ape"—although on his own account he adds, surely unwarrantably,
"though, from a zoological point of view, it is not a wide one." In point of fact the
earliest relics of man are relics of *men,* with all that is included in that, and there
lies between them and all other known beings a hitherto unbridged "abyss."
[Julien Fraipont (1857–1910) was a Belgian zoologist and paleontologist. He was
involved in the study of human fossils discovered at Spy (Belgium) by his friend,

progress of this man through paleolithic, neolithic and metal-
using periods, for the differentiation of the strongly marked characteristics of the several human races of man, for the slow hu-
manizing of human nature and the slower development of those
powers within it from which at length what we call civilization
emerged. Once allow the principle of modification by leaps, and
the question of the length of time required for a given evolution
passes out of the sphere of practical interest. The height of the
leaps becomes a matter of detail, and there is readily transferred
to the estimation of it the importance which was formerly attached to the estimation of the time involved. Thus it has come
about that, in the progress of scientific investigation, the motive
for demanding illimitable stretches of time for the duration of life,
and specifically for the duration of human life on earth, has gradually been passing away, and there seems now a very general tendency among scientific investigators to acquiesce in a moderate
estimate—in an estimate which demands for the life of man on
earth not more than, say, ten or twenty thousand years.

If the controversy over the antiquity of man is thus rapidly losing all but a historical interest, that which once so violently raged
over the unity of the race may be said already to have reached this
stage. The question of the unity of the human race differs from
the question of its antiquity in that it is of indubitable theological
importance. It is not merely that the Bible certainly teaches it,
while, as we have sought to show, it has no teaching upon the antiquity of the race. It is also the postulate of the entire body of the
Bible's teaching—of its doctrine of sin and redemption alike—so
that the whole structure of the Bible's teaching, including all that
we know as its doctrine of salvation, rests on it and implicates it.
There have been times, nevertheless, when it has been vigorously
assailed from various motives both within and without the
church, and the resources of Christian reasoning have been taxed
to support it. These times have now, however, definitely passed
away. The prevalence of the evolutionary hypotheses has removed all motive for denying a common origin to the human

---

the geologist Max Lohest (1857–1926). This important discovery in human paleontology helped fix the age of Neanderthal man. Fraipont and Lohest published
their results jointly in 1887.]

race, and rendered it natural to look upon the differences which exist among the various types of man as differentiations of a common stock. The convincing evidences of the unity of the race, now that the motive for denying their conclusiveness has been thus removed, have had opportunity to assert their force. The result is that the unity of the race, in the sense of its common origin, is no longer a matter of debate; and although actually some erratic writers may still speak of it as open to discussion, they are not taken seriously, and practically it is universally treated as a fixed fact that mankind in all its varieties is one, as in fundamental characteristics, so also in origin.

In our natural satisfaction over this agreement between Scripture and modern science with respect to the unity of humanity, we must not permit ourselves to forget that there has always nevertheless existed among men a strong tendency to deny this unity in the interest of racial pride. Outside of the influence of the biblical revelation, indeed, the sense of human unity has never been strong and has ordinarily been nonexistent.[24] The Stoics seem to have been the first among the classical peoples to preach the unity of mankind and the duty of universal justice and philanthropy founded upon it. With the revival of classical ideas which came in with what we call the Renaissance, however, there came in also a tendency to revive heathen polygenism, which was characteristically reproduced in the writings of Blount and others of the deists.[25] A more definite co-Adamitism, that is to say, the attribution of the descent of the several chief racial types to separate original ancestors, has also been taught by occasional individuals such, for example, as Paracelsus.[26] And

24. See H. Bavinck, *The Philosophy of Revelation* (1909), 137ff.

25. [Charles Blount (1654–93), deist and advocate of polygenism—that is, development from more than one source—wrote on a wide range of historical and religious topics. He was a follower of Thomas Hobbes and published a collection of tracts in 1693 which included an attack on the early chapters of Genesis.]

26. [Paracelsus (c. 1493–1541), Swiss physician and alchemist, propounded a Neoplatonic philosophy in which the life of man is regarded as inseparable from that of the universe. He taught that the scriptural "dust" from which man was created was in fact a compound of salt, sulfur, and mercury, and that sickness was caused by the separation of these mystic elements in the body. Good health came from being in harmony with the elements, the stars, and the spirit of the universe.]

the still more definite pre-Adamitism, which conceives man indeed as a single species derived from one stock, but represents
Adam not as the root of this stock, but as one of its products, the
ancestor of the Jews and white races alone, has always found
teachers, such as, for example, Zanini.[27] The advocacy of this
pre-Adamitic theory by Isaac de la Peyrère in the middle of the
seventeenth century roused a great debate which, however, soon
died out, although leaving echoes behind it in Bayle, Arnold,
Swedenborg.[28] A sort of pre-Adamitism which looks upon
Adam as the first real man, rising in developed humanity above
the low, beastlike condition of his ancestors, has continued to be
taught by a series of philosophical speculators from Schelling
down.[29] In our own day George Catlin[30] and especially Alexander Winchell[31] have revived in its essentials the teaching of
de la Peyrère. "Adam," says Professor Winchell, "is descended

27. [Probably Zaninus de Solcia who was charged with heresy in the fifteenth
century for postulating the possibility that other humans, not from Adam, may
exist elsewhere in alternative worlds.]

28. [Isaac de la Peyrère (1594–1676) argued that the Bible contains hints of
pre-Adamitic theory and suggested a scheme of polygenism where Adam is the
progenitor only of the Jews. Pierre Bayle (1647–1706), French philosopher of a
Calvinistic and rationalistic bent, was very influential on both the German and
French Enlightenments and advocated the pre-Adamite theory. Arnold is probably Thomas Arnold (1795–1842), famous headmaster at Rugby and author of historical and religious works. Emanuel Swedenborg (1688–1772), after thirty years
of scientific and philosophical pursuits, experienced a call to become a spiritual
seer. He spent the rest of his life developing his unique theology—although he
never formally left the Lutheran church.]

29. [Friedrich Wilhelm Joseph von Schelling (1775–1854), German philosopher, turned toward the idealistic pantheism of the Romantic school before
branching off into voluntarism—advancing the ideal of the free, creative act of the
artist. Denying the mechanistic theories of much current science, he articulated a
nature philosophy which included a vitalistic theory of evolution.]

30. O-kee-pa, London, 1867; he referred the North American Indians to an
antediluvian species which he called Anthropus Americanus. [George Catlin (1796–
1871), American ethnologist, anthropologist, and artist, traveled widely among
the Indians in North and South America. He wrote an important study, Distribution
of the Races (1870), which suggested multiple origins for human life.]

31. Preadamites, Chicago, 1880. [Alexander Winchell (1824–91), American geologist and brother of N. H. Winchell, devoted a great deal of energy to harmonizing science and Scripture, reviving the pre-Adamite theories of the seventeenth
century, and popularizing theistic evolution. His advocacy of the pre-Adamite
theory resulted in his dismissal from Vanderbilt University.]

from a black race, not the black race from Adam." The advancing
knowledge of the varied races of man produced in the latter part
of the eighteenth and the earlier nineteenth century a revival of
co-Adamitism (Sullivan, Crueger, Ballenstedt, Cordonière,
Gobineau)[32] which was even perverted into a defense of slavery
(Dobbs, Morton, Nott, and Gliddon).[33]

It was in connection with Nott and Gliddon's *Types of Mankind*
that Agassiz first published his theory of the diverse origin of the
several types of man, the only one of these theories of abiding interest because the only one arising from a genuinely scientific impulse and possessing a really scientific basis.[34] Agassiz's theory
was the product of a serious study of the geographical distribution of animate life, and one of the results of Agassiz's classification of the whole of animate creation into eight well-marked
types of fauna involving, so he thought, eight separate centers of
origin. Pursuant to this classification he sought to distribute mankind also into eight types, to each of which he ascribed a separate
origin corresponding with the type of fauna with which each is
associated. But even Agassiz could not deny that men are, despite
their eightfold separate creation, all of one kind; he could not

32. [We have found no information on Sullivan, Crueger, and Cordonière. Johann Georg Justus Ballenstedt, German natural historian, was the author of *Zur
Naturgeschichte des Bernsteins* (Leipzig, 1823). Count Joseph Arthur de Gobineau
(1816–82) was a French social philosopher who advanced the theory known as
Gobinism that blond Aryans from northern Europe constituted a superior race of
humans; a corollary was the inferiority of the Negro and Semitic races.]

33. [Francis Dobbs (1750–1811), Irish parliamentarian who believed that contemporary Anglo-Irish politics indicated an immediate second coming; he supposed that there existed a non-Adamic human race conceived in an intrigue between Eve and the devil. Samuel George Morton (1799–1851), anatomist and
student of anthropology, founded the science of invertebrate paleontology in the
United States. Morton was convinced that the human races were distinguished
by the shape and capacity of their crania as well as by their skin color. Josiah
Clark Nott (1804–73), an American physician and professor of anatomy, jointly
authored *Types of Mankind* (1854) with the British Egyptologist, George Robins
Gliddon (1809–57).]

34. [Jean Louis Agassiz (1807–73), Swiss-born immigrant to the United States
and natural historian at Harvard, was Darwin's leading opponent in America. By
insisting that species are permanent representations of a divine idea, Agassiz became a favorite of conservatives like Charles Hodge, who shared his disagree-
ment with Darwin. Ironically, Agassiz also believed that humanity itself was
made up of multiple species, each the product of divine creation.]

erect specific differences between the several types of man.[35] After advancing knowledge of the animal kingdom and its geographical distribution[36] rendered Agassiz's assumption of eight centers of origination (not merely distribution) a violent hypothesis, the evidence which compelled him to recognize the oneness of man in kind remains in its full validity; and the entrance into the field of the evolutionary hypothesis has consigned to oblivion all theories formed without reference to the unity of man. Even some early evolutionists, it is true, played for a time with theories of multiplex times and places where similar lines of development culminated alike in man (Haeckel, Schaffhausen, Caspari, Vogt, Büchner),[37] and perhaps there is now some sign of the revival of this view; but it is now agreed with practical unanimity that the unity of the human race, in the sense of its common origin, is a necessary corollary of the evolutionary hypothesis, and no voice raised in contradiction of it stands much chance to be heard.[38]

It is, however, only for its universal allowance at the hands of speculative science that the fact of the unity of the human race has to thank the evolutionary hypothesis. The evidence by which it is solidly established is of course independent of all such hypotheses. This evidence is drawn almost equally from every department of human manifestation, physiological, psychological, philological, and even historical. The physiological unity of humanity is illustrated by the nice gradations by which the several

35. Similarly Heinrich Schurtz, while leaving the descent of men from a single pair an open question, affirms that it is a fact that "humanity forms one great unity." [Schurtz (1863–1903) was a German anthropologist who published on Africa and on theories of culture.]

36. It was Wallace's *Geographical Distribution of Animals* [1876] which struck the first crushing blow.

37. [Hermann Schaffhausen (1816–93), German anthropologist and codiscoverer of the Neanderthal skull, was one of the German pre-Darwinian evolutionists. Carl Paul Caspari (1814–92) was a Norwegian Lutheran of Jewish parentage. Baptized in 1838, he became a professor of the Old Testament and was strongly opposed to modern critical scholarship. Karl Vogt (1817–95), director of the Institute of Zoology in Geneva, eventually became a strong supporter of the Darwinian concept of natural selection.]

38. Klaatsch wishes to postulate two distinct stems for man (now mingled together); on his views see Keith in *Nature,* December 15, 1910. [The German anthropologist Hermann Klaatsch (1863–1916) did research on prehistoric skeletons and studied the evolutionary history of man emerging out of primitive stages.]

so-called races into which it is divided pass into one another, and by their undiminished natural fertility when intercrossed. This led Professor Owen to remark that "man forms one species, and . . . differences are but indicative of varieties" which "merge into each other by easy gradations."[39] Physiological unity is emphasized by the contrast which exists between the structural characteristics, osteological, cranial, dental, common to the entire race of human beings of every variety and those of the nearest animal types; this led Professor Huxley to assert that "every bone of a Gorilla bears marks by which it might be distinguished from the corresponding bones of a Man; and that, in the present creation at any rate, no intermediate link bridges over the gap between *Homo* and *Troglodytes*."[40]

The psychological unity of the race is still more manifest. All men of all varieties are psychologically men and prove themselves possessors of the same mental nature and furniture. Under the same influences they function mentally and spiritually in the same fashion, and prove capable of the same mental reactions. They, they all, and they alone in the whole realm of animal existences manifest themselves as rational and moral natures; so that Mr. Fiske was fully justified when he declared that though for zoological man the erection of a distinct family from the chimpanzee and orang might suffice, "on the other hand, for psychological man you must erect a distinct kingdom; nay, you must even dichotomize the universe, putting Man on one side and all things else on the other."[41] Among the manifestations of the psychological peculiarities of mankind, as distinguished from all other animate existences, is the great gift of speech which he shares with no other being; if all human languages cannot be reduced to a single root, they

39. E[benezer] Burgess, *What Is Truth? An Enquiry concerning the Antiquity and Unity of the Human Race,* Boston [1871], 185. [Richard Owen (1804–92), comparative anatomist and vertebrate paleontologist at Cambridge, attempted early in his career to develop a vitalist theory of organic development, building on the French and German models, yet with a sounder empirical basis. Owen was heavily influenced by Darwin's thinking on the breakdown in the "species-variety boundary."]

40. *Evidence as to Man's Place in Nature* (1864), 104.

41. *Through Nature to God* (1899), 82. [John Fiske (1842–1901) was a prominent American philosopher-historian who also wrote extensively on evolution and mythology.]

all exhibit a uniquely human faculty working under similar laws, and bear the most striking testimony to the unity of the race which alone has language at its command. The possession of common traditions by numerous widely separated peoples is only one of many indications of a historical intercommunion between the several peoples through which their essential unity is evinced, and by which the biblical account of the origination of the various families of man in a single center from which they have spread out in all directions is powerfully supported.[42]

The assertion of the unity of the human race is imbedded in the very structure of the biblical narrative. The biblical account of the origin of man (Gen. 1:26–28) is an account of his origination in a single pair who constituted humanity in its germ, and from whose fruitfulness and multiplication all the earth has been replenished. Therefore the first man was called Adam, Man, and the first woman, Eve, "because she was the mother of all living" (Gen. 3:20); and all men are currently spoken of as the "sons of Adam" or "Man" (Deut. 32:8; 1 Sam. 26:19; 1 Kings 8:39; Pss. 11:4; 145:12). The absolute restriction of the human race within the descendants of this single pair is emphasized by the history of the flood in which all flesh is destroyed, and the race given a new beginning in its second father, Noah, by whose descendants again "the whole earth was overspread" (Gen. 9:19), as is illustrated in detail by the table of nations recorded in Genesis 10. A profound religious-ethical significance is given to the differentiations of the peoples in the story of the tower of Babel in the eleventh chapter of Genesis, where the divergences and separations which divide mankind are represented as the product of sin; what God had joined together men themselves pulled asunder. Throughout the Scriptures therefore all mankind is treated as, from the divine point of view, a unit, and shares not only in a common nature but in a common sinfulness, not only in a common need but in a common redemption.

Accordingly, although Israel was taught to glory in its exaltation by the choice of the Lord to be his peculiar people, Israel was not permitted to believe there was anything in itself which differ-

42. See the discussion in the seventh lecture of Bavinck's *Philosophy of Revelation* (1909).

entiated it from other peoples. Indeed, the laws concerning aliens and slaves required Israel to recognize the common humanity of all sorts and conditions of men. What they had to distinguish themselves from others was not of nature, but of the free gift of God in the mysterious working out of his purpose of good not only to Israel but to the whole world. This universalism in the divine purposes of mercy, already inherent in the old covenant and often proclaimed in it, and made the very keynote of the new—for which the old was the preparation—is the most emphatic possible assertion of the unity of the race. Accordingly, not only do we find our Lord himself setting his seal upon the origination of the race in a single pair, and drawing from that fact the law of life for men at large (Matt. 19:4); and Paul explicitly declaring that "God has made of one man every nation of men" and, having for his own good ends appointed to each its separate habitation, is now dealing with them all alike in offering them a common salvation (Acts 17:26–27); but the whole New Testament is instinct with the brotherhood of mankind as one in origin and in nature, one in need and one in the provision of redemption.

The fact of racial sin is basal to the whole Pauline system (Rom. 5:12–14; 1 Cor. 15:21–22), and beneath the fact of racial sin lies the fact of racial unity. It is only because all men were in Adam as their first head that all men share in Adam's sin and with his sin in his punishment. And it is only because the sin of man is thus one in origin, and therefore of the same nature and quality, that the redemption which is suitable and may be made available for one is equally suitable and may be made available for all. It is because the race is one and its need one, Jew and Gentile are alike under sin, that there is no difference between Jew and Gentile in the matter of salvation either, but as the same God is Lord of all, so he is rich in Christ Jesus unto all that call upon him, and he will justify the uncircumcision through faith alone, even as he justifies the circumcision only by faith (Rom. 9:22–24, 28–33; 10:12). Jesus Christ therefore, as the last Adam, is the Savior not of the Jews only but of the world (John 4:42; 1 Tim. 4:10; 1 John 4:14), having been given to this his great work only by the love of the Father for the world (John 3:16). The unity of the human race is therefore made in Scripture not merely the basis of a demand that we recognize the dignity of humanity in all its representatives, of

however lowly estate or family, since all bear alike the image of
God in which man was created, and the image of God is deeper
than sin and cannot be eradicated by sin (Gen. 5:1; 9:6; 1 Cor.
11:7; Heb. 2:5–8); but the basis also of the entire scheme of resto-
ration devised by the divine love for the salvation of a lost race.

So far is it from being of no concern to theology, therefore, that
it would be truer to say that the whole doctrinal structure of the
Bible account of redemption is founded on its assumption that
the race of man is one organic whole, and may be dealt with as
such. It is because all are one in Adam that in the matter of sin
there is no difference, but all have fallen short of the glory of God
(Rom. 3:22–23), and as well that in the new man there cannot be
Greek and Jew, circumcision and uncircumcision, barbarian,
Scythian, bondman, freeman; but Christ is all and in all (Col.
3:11). The unity of the old man in Adam is the postulate of the
unity of the new man in Christ.

January 1914
Princeton Theological Review 12:151–61

Excerpts from Review
of H. Wheeler Robinson,
The Christian Doctrine of Man
(Edinburgh: T. and T. Clark, 1911)

Henry Wheeler Robinson (1877–1945), a Baptist minister and Old
Testament scholar, was principal of Regent's Park College in Britain
from 1920 to 1942. *The Christian Doctrine of Man* was an effort to
provide a Christian anthropology guided by modern understandings.
In that effort Robinson's convictions about what evolution meant
bulked large. As criticism, Warfield reiterated the crucial distinction
he saw between evolution (development from existing forms) and
creation (the production of something new not possible from existing forms). Restating that distinction gave Warfield the opportunity
to state clearly the three cosmic moments where he felt creation, as
the impartation of something new to the physical world, was required: life out of nonlife, personality out of living matter, and the
God-man Jesus Christ out of the stream of humanity.

. . . We have gained immensely, of course, from the growth of
scientific knowledge and in nothing more than in the deeper conception of the orderliness of the world which it has brought us;
but this gain would be dearly bought if it separated us further
from God, and left us in the hands rather of a machine. To be sure
that all the events of nature, and of history as well, are under the
direct control of God cannot give us a piecemeal and erratic
world. Law and God are not contradictories; and if they were, it
were better to choose God than law for our portion.

The chief interest in [the] chapter [bearing the title "The Contributions of Post-Reformation Science and Thought"] culminates, however, in the discussion of evolution, which enters in during this period as a factor of importance in man's thought of man. The current ineptitudes in dealing with this subject reappear here. We cannot speak of evolution as relating "simply to the method of man's creation" (p. 242): evolution cannot *create*—it presents a substitute for creation, and undertakes to show us how man may come into being without being created, by just, as Topsy says, "growing."[1] Nor can we follow when we are bidden to look forward to further evolution with hope for ourselves, especially when this is connected with some thought of personal immortality (pp. 243–44). The doctrine of evolution has no hopeful message for us concerning our individual future; it teaches us to look not beyond death but beyond ourselves for what is more likely than us to approach the longed-for goal. But of this we shall have something to say later. . . .

The difficulties of the evolutionary scheme, taken as a complete account of the universe, seem to culminate in such facts as these: the presence among existences of living beings, among living beings of persons, among persons of the divine-man, Jesus Christ. If evolution itself is called on to give an account of these things, we must posit life as latent in the nonliving, personality as latent in the impersonal, deity as latent in the undivine. The alternative is to suppose that life, personality, the divine are introduced from without—and that is to break away from the evolutionary principle as the sole organon of explanation.

We are not quite sure that Mr. Robinson preserves throughout his discussions complete consistency in this matter. But ordinarily at least he takes his courage in his hands and goes the whole way with the evolutionary demands. We may feel considerable satisfaction as we begin to read this sentence (p. 278): "Whilst all personality is dependent on evolution for the clay of its physical manifestation, all personality must transcend the course of such physical evolution by the inbreathed breath of spiritual life. . . ."

1. [The reference is to the slave girl Topsy in Harriet Beecher Stowe's *Uncle Tom's Cabin,* who, when asked who made her, replied, "I 'spect I grow'd. Don't think nobody ever made me."]

So far it looks as if Mr. Robinson intended to allow for an intrusion from without at the point of the production of personality. But our satisfaction is at once dashed by the addition of this closing clause: ". . . though that breath of God go back to the very beginnings of life." The "breath of God" producing spiritual life was, then, according to Robinson, already present, though no doubt only latently present, through the whole series of nonpersonal living beings. And there is no reason for stopping at the beginnings of life; it must have been equally present, though only latently present, also in the nonliving existences that lie behind life.

Similarly, with reference to Jesus Christ, we read (pp. 279–80): "From such conceptions, it is not far to the recognition of all human personality as the partial manifestation of the preexistent Son of God, i.e., the supranaturalistic element we have recognized in all personality is spiritually akin to the one transcendent manifestation in Jesus Christ." And again (p. 280): "If it be asked how such an Incarnation be conceivable in connection with the acceptance of evolution, the answer is not an appeal to supernatural birth (*necessary* to Augustinianism only), but to the presence of personality in and amid the workings of natural law in the case of every man."[2] The incarnation is, then, not a new beginning except in the sense that every new species is a new beginning; it is a new form taken on by what is old—actually present in the evolving stuff beforehand. Accordingly, Mr. Robinson quotes here, with evident emphasis on the comparison made, Illingworth's words (*Lux Mundi,* 1904 ed., p. 152) to the effect that the coming of Christ "introduced a new species into the world—a Divine man transcending past humanity, as humanity transcended the rest of the animal creation, and communicating His vital energy by a spiritual process to subsequent generations of men."[3] If we read Mr. Robinson aright here, then, he would posit the divinity which was "brought out" in Jesus as already latent in

2. [Robinson implies that only Augustinians, who posit an inheritance of original sin from Adam's fall, required the creation of an entirely New Adam to provide for redemption.]

3. [John Richardson Illingworth (1848–1915) was an English clergyman who applied principles of idealistic philosophy to the Christian faith. His rectory became the center of the Lux Mundi group, whose stated purpose was "to put the Catholic faith into its right relation to modern intellectual and moral problems."]

all personality, in all living beings, in the nonliving existences which lie back of all. Jesus Christ is not an intrusion of the divine into the human race; he is merely a modified man, as man is a modified beast, and a beast is a modified thing. All that is patent in him was latent beforehand not only in us, but in the amoeba and in the seawater. Such a theory has express affinities with Manicheanism and Gnosticism, with their extraction of the spiritual and the divine from entanglement with matter; it brings into clear view the pantheistic background of the evolutionary philosophy (as lucidly expressed by, say, Le Conte), but it is not recognizable as Christian.

Another difficulty which is thrust upon Mr. Robinson by his evolutionism—we have already adverted to it briefly—concerns the outlook for the future. Mr. Robinson strenuously argues for personal immortality, that is, for the immortality of the soul, for, being rather of Plato than of Paul, he has doubts of resurrection (is not "death the natural fate of the bodily organism"?). He cannot be content "with an ultimate philosophy which does not carry up all these values and personality itself into God as their home and source and hope" (p. 287). But on evolutionary ground is this reasonable? Is it even to be desired?

From the evolutionary point of view Christ is a new species as different from present humanity as humanity is different from the beast. From him as starting point a new kind may come into being, a new kind which after a while (it did not happen so with Christ) may win to itself deathlessness. But what of those who lived before this new species had its birth? What of those who have lived since it made its appearance in the world, but have manifestly fallen behind it in the qualities of the new life? What of all mankind up to today, no one individual of whom has been quite a Christ? We might as well confess it frankly—evolution has no hope to hold out for personal immortality. It bids us look forward to an ever bettering race, not to an ever bettering individual. It tells us to see in the individual a stepping stone to a higher individual to come, built up upon its ruins in the survival of the fittest. How can it promise eternal survival to the unfit? And to which of the unfit will it promise it?

If we are to project into eternity the unripe to abide forever, instead of seeing an ever increasing succession of the riper and yet riper, how far down the scale of unripeness does immortality extend? If the merely personal—not yet the divine—has in it the power of an endless life, why not also the merely living—not yet personal? Is not the logic of the matter shut up to this alternative: since from the bottom up all that is to come is latent in the evolving stuff, and hidden in the amoeba itself (or the clod, for the matter of that) there already exists, although not yet manifested, all the divinity that is in the Christ, all is immortal and the spirit that is in every form that ever existed shall live on forever; or else the immortality which crowns all is not attained until the end of the process is reached, which is not yet? We must not permit to pass out of sight the fundamental fact of the evolutionary principle: the goal to which all tends is not to be found in the future of the individual, but in the successors of the individual. On an evolutionary basis, immortality must mean the persistence of the evolving stuff in every higher manifestation, and cannot mean the persistence of the unripe individual itself.

When Mr. Robinson proclaims, then, the immortality of the soul, and of all souls, and indeed the ultimate perfection of every soul—for Mr. Robinson would fain "trust the larger hope" and believe in the ultimate blessedness of all (p. 338)—he is drawing his faith and his high hopes from some other than an evolutionary fountain. And to be perfectly frank we do not see that Mr. Robinson has left himself any fountain from which he can draw them. Evolution coupled with the autonomy of man, with some sense of wrongdoing and ill desert and a more or less vague feeling of the goodness of God, constitutes but a poor basis for any eschatology. In point of fact we cannot form any sure expectation of what is in store for us, unless God has told us of it. Where no authoritative revelation of God is allowed, no express eschatology is attainable.

April 1915
Princeton Theological Review 13:190–255
(reprinted from *WBBW* 5:287–349)

Calvin's Doctrine of the Creation (excerpts)

Although this learned article is cast as a discussion of John Calvin's doctrine of creation, it was unusually decisive for Warfield's own positions on scientific issues about which he had been thinking for his entire adult life. As we noted in the introduction, others have subsequently questioned whether Warfield got Calvin right. This is not a minor issue, yet of far greater importance for Warfield's career is the fact that this monograph carries further so many of the lines of argument he had previously developed.

Most critically, it shows Warfield abandoning the threefold distinction he had established in writing at the turn of the century—providentially supervised evolution, mediate creation, and creation *ex nihilo*. While maintaining his earlier distinction between creation (the production of something new) and evolution (development out of something previously existent), Warfield here concludes that Calvin maintained only creation *ex nihilo* and a fully providential view of development. Moreover, Warfield finds that in his treatment of early Genesis Calvin reserves "creation" only for God's origination of the first world-stuff and for the human soul, with the emergence of everything else, including the human body, being the result of divinely supervised development out of the original material of the first creation. Warfield recognizes that Calvin "had no theory whatever of evolution," but nonetheless concludes that "he teaches a doctrine of evolution." In addition he calls upon the notion of *concursus* to explain how development out of the original world-stuff could be both constantly guided by God and a result of secondary causes.

Warfield never states directly that he embraces this reading of Calvin's teaching as his own view, but the tone of the article certainly points in that direction. If Warfield did embrace such a view, it means that he himself came close to saying that evolution was God's means of creation, a conclusion that he had earlier criticized others for making.

It is not clear what led Warfield to this step. Perhaps it was his intense reading in Calvin that led him to adjust his earlier position. Perhaps changes in evolutionary theory in the period moderated his earlier conclusions about tensions between a conservative understanding of Scripture and full use of modern scientific conclusions. (Those changes he had summarized at length in his review of Kellogg's *Darwinism Today* in 1908 and his 1911 article on humankind.) Perhaps he became convinced that the very high view of providence he saw in Calvin was enough to protect the reality of miracles, an issue which earlier seemed to drive his commitment to mediate creation. Whatever the reason for this development in Warfield's thinking about the natural world, however, this essay stands as one of the most intriguing theological statements of the early twentieth century, for in it a backward-looking recovery of Calvin's theology joins a forward-looking proposal for understanding evolution in a Christian manner.

The text below includes only those portions of Warfield's long essay dealing most directly with the natural world and the human soul. Omitted sections are summarized, the Latin and French originals of Calvin's writings that Warfield quotes in English are deleted, and annotations concerning the authorities Warfield cites on Calvin and theological matters are not as complete as are the annotations elsewhere in this book on scientific figures.

In developing his system, Calvin proceeds at once from the doctrine of God to an exposition of his works of creation and providence (1.14–15 and 16–17).[1] That he passes over the divine purpose or decree at this point, though it would logically claim attention before its execution in creation and providence, is only another indication of the intensely practical spirit of Calvin and the simplicity of his method in this work. Carrying his readers over at once from what God is to what God does, he reserves the abstruser discussions of the relation of God's will to occurrences for a later point in the treatise, when the reader's mind, by a contemplation of the divine works, will be better prepared to read off the underlying purpose from the actual event. The practical end which has deter-

1. [Much of this essay is a discussion of Calvin's *Institutes of the Christian Religion,* which was published in several ever-expanding editions between 1536 and 1560 (the last definitive Latin edition was from 1559). Reference to the *Institutes* is by book, chapter, and paragraph. Warfield also cites many other works of Calvin, mostly from Calvin's collected works, or *Opera omnia,* sometimes abbreviated *Opp.,* which made up fifty-nine volumes in the *Corpus Reformatorum,* published 1863–1900.]

mined this sequence of topics governs also the manner in which the subject of creation, now taken up (chs. 14–15), is dealt with. There is no discussion of it from a formal point of view; the treatment is wholly material and is devoted to the nature of the created universe rather than to the mode of the divine activity in creating it. Even in dealing with the created universe, there is no attempt at completeness of treatment. The spiritual universe is permitted to absorb the attention; and what is said about the lower creation is reduced to a mere hint or two introduced chiefly, it appears, to recommend the contemplation of it as a means of quickening in the heart a sense of God's greatness and goodness (14.20–22).

It is quite obvious, in fact, from the beginning, that Calvin's mind is set in this whole discussion of creation primarily on expounding the nature of man as a creature of God, and all else that he incorporates into it is subsidiary to this. He is writing for men and bends all he is writing to what he conceives to be their practical interests. He does not reach the actual discussion of man as creature, to be sure (ch. 15), until after he has interposed a long exposition of the nature of angels and demons (14.3–12 and 13–19). But this whole exposition is cast in a form which shows that angels and demons are interesting to Calvin only because of the high estimate he places upon the topic for the practical life of man, and it is introduced by a remark which betrays that his thought was already on man as the real subject of his exposition and all he had to say about other spiritual creatures was conceived as only preliminary to that more direct object of interest. "But before I begin to speak more fully concerning the nature of man," he says quite gratuitously at the opening of the discussion (14.3), "something should be inserted *(inserere)* about angels." What he actually says about angels, good and bad, in the amount of space occupied by it, is more than what he says about man; but it stood before his mind, we observe, as only "something," and as something, be it noted, "inserted," before the real subject of his discourse was reached. In his own consciousness what Calvin undertakes in these chapters is to make man aware of his own nature as a creature of God, and to place him as a creature of God in his environment, the most important elements of which he conceives to be the rest of the intelligent creation.

It is not to be inferred, of course, from the lightness with which Calvin passes over the doctrine of creation itself in this discussion that he took little interest in it or deemed it a matter of no great significance. That he does not dwell more fully on it is due, as we have said, to the practical nature of his undertaking, and was rendered possible by the circumstance that this doctrine was not in dispute.[2] All men in the circles which he was addressing were of one mind on it, and there were sources of information within the reach of all which rendered it unnecessary for him to enlarge on it.[3] That he had a clear and firm conception of the nature of the creative act and attributed importance to its proper apprehension is made abundantly plain and is emphasized by his consecration of the few remarks he gives to the topic to repelling assaults upon its credibility that were drawn from the nature of the divine being (14.1–2).

In his conception of creation Calvin definitely separated himself from all dualistic,[4] and especially from all pantheistic[5] elements of thought by sharply asserting that all substantial existence outside

2. See P[ieter] J[ohannes] Muller [b. 1854], *De Godsleer van Zwingli en Calvijn* [On teaching about God from Zwingli and Calvin] (1883), 50–51: "Although the importance of the doctrine of creation is felt by the two reformers, yet we seek in vain in Zwingli as well as in Calvin for a definite theory of creation. . . . The reason why the doctrine of creation was not developed by them in the same degree as that of providence, must no doubt be sought in the fact that this dogma did not at the time give occasion to any polemic." Also, *De Godsleer van Calvijn* [Calvin's teaching about God] (1881), 51: "We cannot think it strange that Calvin, as a Biblical theologian, will know nothing of any other theory of creation than that which is given us in the Scriptures." [The Swiss reformer Ulrich Zwingli (1484–1531) was an important early contributor to the Reformed theological tradition for which Calvin provided the first grand statement.]

3. 1.14.20. He refers his readers to Moses, as expounded particularly by Basil and Ambrose, "since it is not my design to treat at large of the creation of the world." [Basil of Caesarea (d. 379), one of the leading Eastern bishops and theologians in the trinitarian controversies, helped the orthodox view prevail. Ambrose of Milan (339–97) was an influential bishop and theologian of the early church in the West. Ambrose was instrumental in the conversion of Augustine.]

4. See 1.14.3, where he inveighs against "Manichaeus and his sect," who attributed to God the origin of good things only, but referred evil natures to the devil. The sole foundation of this heresy, he remarks, is that it is nefarious to ascribe to the good God the creation of any evil thing; but this is inoperative as "there is nothing in the universe which has an evil nature. . . . Neither the pravity nor the malice of either man or devil, or the sins that are born from them, are of nature, but rather of corruption of nature."

5. See 1.15.5: "To rend the essence of the Creator so that everything should possess a part is the extremity of madness."

of God owes its being to God, that it was created by God out of nothing, and that it came from God's hand very good. His crispest definition of creation he lets fall incidentally in repelling the pantheistic notion that, as he scornfully describes it, "the essence of the Creator is rent into fragments that each may have a part of it." "Creation," he says, "is not the transfusion of essence, but the origination of essence out of nothing."[6] "God," says he again, "by the power of his Word and Spirit created out of nothing the heavens and the earth," that is to say, all that exists, whether celestial or terrestrial.[7]

Firmly stated as this doctrine of creation is, however, so as to leave us in no doubt as to Calvin's conception,[8] the elements of it are little elaborated. There is no attempt, for example, to validate the doctrine of creation *ex nihilo* whether on biblical[9] or on such rational grounds as we find appealed to by Zwingli, who argues that creation *ex materia* implies an infinite series whether the material out of which the creation is made be conceived as like or un-

6. 1.15.5.

7. 1.14.20.

8. See P. J. Muller, *De Godsleer van Calvijn* (1881), 53: "Calvin's doctrine of creation is, in brief, this: God created the world out of nothing in six days through his Word, i.e. through his Son."

9. In his Commentary on Genesis 1:1, however, he does argue that the Bible teaches that creation is *ex nihilo*, the weight of the argument being made to rest on the use of בָּרָא, which he sharply discriminates from יָצַר. See Baumgartner, *Calvin Hebraïsant* (1889), 50–51: "Richard Simon has pointed, as a proof that Calvin was not strong in Hebrew, to the fact that he understands the בָּרָא of Genesis 1:1 in the sense of 'creation *ex nihilo*.' But here again R. Simon has been misled by his party-spirit, for the modern lexicographers are far from pronouncing Calvin's interpretation wrong" (e.g. Gesenius, *Thesaurus*, 1:236). The most recent view will scarcely allow that the specific idea of creation *ex nihilo* is expressed in בָּרָא, but recognizes that the ideas of novelty, extraordinariness, effortlessness are expressed in it, and that thus it may be said to lay a basis for the doctrine in question. See Franz Böhl, *Alttestamentliche Studien Rudolf Kittel zum 60. Geburtstag dargebracht* (1913), 42–60; and Skinner, *Genesis* (1910), 14–15. Calvin does not understand Hebrews 11:3 to refer to creation *ex nihilo*, but to the manifestation of the invisible God in the visible works of his hands: "we have in this visible world a conspicuous image of God; . . . thus the same truth is taught here as in Romans 1:20, where it is said that the invisible things of God are made known to us by the creation of the world, they being seen in his works." This is the burden of the Argument to the Commentary on Genesis 1, and its echoes are heard in *Institutes*, 1.14.1.

like in kind to that which is made from it.[10] As we have seen, Calvin (like Zwingli) does argue, however, that creation in its very nature is origination of essence, so that he would have subscribed Zwingli's declaration: "This is the definition of creation: to be out of nothing."[11] He does not even dwell upon the part which the Son takes in the creating, although he does not leave this important matter unmentioned, but declares that "the worlds were created by the Son" (1.13.7), and that God created the heavens and earth "by the power of his Word and Spirit" (1.14.20); thus he sets the act of creation in its trinitarian relation. Calvin develops this fact, however, in the preceding chapter, where he adduces in proof of the deity of the Son and the Spirit the share they took in creation. There he urges that "the power to create and the authority to command were common to the Father, Son, and Spirit," as is shown, he says, by the words "Let us make man in our image" of Genesis 1:26; he also argues at length from the creation narrative of Genesis and the Wisdom passage in Proverbs, no less than from Hebrew 1:2–3, that it was through the Son that God made the worlds.[12]

10. *Opera Omnia* 4.86ff. Zwingli argues that if the preexisting stuff is the same in kind as the thing created, we have an infinite series of worlds; if of a different kind, we have an infinite series of materials. Hence the world is not *ex materia* [out of matter], but *ex causa* [from a cause], which is as much as to say *ex nihilo*.

11. Ibid., 4.87. He defines creation as "esse e nihilo; vel: esse quod prius non fuit; attamen non ex alio tamquam ex materia" [being from nothing; that is to say, being which was not preceded by anything, being that is not from something else of a material kind].

12. 1.13.24; 1.13.7; see also Commentary on Hebrews 1:2: "By him . . . the world was created, since he is the eternal Wisdom of God, which was the director of all his works from the beginning. Hence too we gather that Christ is eternal, for he must needs be before the world has been made by him." See also Commentary on Genesis 1:3: "Since he is the Word of God, all things have been created by him." And see especially the passage in the first edition of the *Institutes* (1536), at the beginning of the comment on the "second part of the Symbol" (*Opp.* 1.64), where, after declaring on the basis of Hebrews 1 that "since God the Son is the same God with the Father," he is "the creator of the heavens and the earth," Calvin proceeds to explain that the habit of alluding to the Father nevertheless peculiarly as the "creator of the heavens and the earth" is due to "that distinction of properties, already stated, by which there is referred to the Father the *principium agendi* [principle and source of action], so that he himself is indeed properly said to act *(agere),* yet through his Word and Wisdom—yet in his Power." "But," he adds, "that the action in the creation of the world was common to the three per-

On one thing, however, Calvin manages to insist despite the
sketchiness with which he treats the whole subject. This is that
whatever came from the divine hands came from them good. "It
is monstrous," he declares,[13] "to ascribe to the good God the creation of any evil thing," and we may not admit that there is in the
whole world anything evil in its nature,[14] but must perceive that
in all that he has made God has displayed his wisdom and justice.
Wherever evil has appeared, then, whether in man or devil, it is
not *ex natura* [from nature] but *ex naturae corruptione* [from corrupted nature] (1.14.3), not *ex creatione* [from the creation] but *ex
depravatione* [from depravity] (1.14.16). We must beware, therefore, lest in speaking of evil as natural to man, we should seem to
refer it to the author of nature, whether we more coarsely conceive it as in some measure proceeding from God himself or, with
more appearance of piety, ascribe it only to nature. We cannot attribute to God what is in the most absolute sense alien to his very
nature, and it is equally dishonoring to him to ascribe any intrinsic depravity to the nature which comes from his hands.[15]

Calvin expressly disclaims the intention of expounding in detail the story of the creation of the world,[16] and judges it sufficient
to refer his readers to the account given by Moses, along with the
comments perhaps of Basil and Ambrose, for instruction in the
particulars of its history (1.14.20; see also 1.14.1). He lets fall,
however, a few remarks by the way, which enable us to perceive
his attitude towards the narrative of Genesis. Needless to say, he
takes it just as he finds it written. The six days he, naturally, understands as six literal days; and, accepting the prima facie chronology of the biblical narrative, he dates the creation of the world
something less than six thousand years in the past. He does not
suppose, however, that Moses has included in his story anything
like an exhaustive account of all that was created. The instance of

---

sons is made clear by that word (Gen. 1) 'Let us make man in our image and likeness,' by which there is not expressed a deliberation with angels, nor a colloquy
with himself, but a summoning of his Wisdom and Power." See also P. J. Muller,
De Godsleer van Calvijn (1881), 51–52; *De Godsleer van Zwingli en Calvijn* (1883), 53.

13. 1.14.3.
14. Ibid.
15. 1.14.16 and 1.15.1.
16. 1.14.20.

angels, of whose origin Moses gives no history, is conclusive to the contrary. Moses, writing to meet the needs of men at large, accommodated himself to their grade of intellectual preparation, and confined himself to what met their eyes.[17]

On the other hand, Calvin will not admit that the created universe can be properly spoken of as infinite. God alone is infinite; and, "however wide the circuit of the heavens may be, it nevertheless has some dimension."[18] He frankly conceives of the created universe as geocentric,[19] or more properly as anthropocentric. "God himself," he declares, "has demonstrated by the very order of creation that he made all things for the sake of man."[20] For, before making man, "he prepared everything which he foresaw would be useful or salutary for him" (1.14.22). It was "for human use that he disposed the motions of the sun and stars, that he filled the earth, the waters, the air with living creatures, that he produced an abundance of all kinds of fruits which might be sufficient for food—thus acting the part of a provident and sedulous father of a family and showing his wonderful goodness towards us" (1.14.2).

Even in so rapid a sketch, Calvin finds it sufficiently important to pause to deal with two difficulties which arise out of the consideration of the infinitude of God in connection with his creative work. These concern the relation of the idea of creation to that of eternity on the one hand, and the description of the creation as a process on the other. Both of these he treats from a practical rather than a theoretical point of view.

Calvin does not even hint at the metaphysical difficulty which has been perennially derived from the divine eternity and immutability, namely, that a definite creation implies a change in God. Wollebius neatly solves this difficulty with the remark that "creation is not the creator's but the creature's passage from potentiality to actuality."[21] The difficulty to which Calvin addresses him-

17. 1.14.3.
18. 1.14.1.
19. See the Argument to the Commentary on Genesis 1: "The circle of the heavens is finite, and the earth, like a little globe, is placed in the center."
20. 1.14.22. See also the Commentary on Genesis 3:1: "the whole world which had been created for the sake of man."
21. Johannes Wollebius, *Compendium Theologiae Christianae* (Oxford, 1657), 36.

self is the purely popular one, which, with a view to rendering the idea of a definite act of creation on God's part incredible, asks what God was doing all those ages before he created the world (1.14.1). Calvin's response proceeds in general on the principle of answering a fool according to his folly, although it is directed to the serious purpose of recalling men's minds from fruitless attempts to fathom the mysteries of infinity to a profitable use of the creation narrative as a mirror in which is exhibited a lively image of God.[22] The gist of this response seems to be summed up in a sentence which occurs in the Argument to his Commentary on the first chapter of Genesis—which runs very much parallel to the discussion here. "God," he says, "being wholly sufficient for himself, did not create a world of which he had no need, until it pleased him to do so."

Calvin does not disdain, however, before closing, to advert, under the leading of Augustine,[23] to the metaphysical consideration that there is no place for a question of "time when" in our thought of that act of God by which time began to be. We might as well inquire, Augustine had reasoned, why God created the world *where* he did as why he created it only *when* he did. We may puzzle ourselves with the notion that there is room in infinite space for an infinite number of finite universes as readily as with the parallel notion that there was opportunity in eternal time for the creation of an infinite series of worlds before ours was reached. The truth is, of course, that as there is no space outside of that material world the dimensions of which when abstractly considered constitute what we call space, so there is no time outside that world of mutable existence from which we abstract the notion of succession and call it time. "If they say," reasons Augustine, "that the thoughts of men are idle when they conceive of infinite places, since there is no place beside the world, we reply that, by the same showing, it is vain to conceive of past times of God's rest, since there is no time before the world." Utilizing Augustine's remarks Calvin warns his readers against vainly striving to press "outside of the world" *(extra mundum)* by "the boundaries

22. This point is very fully elaborated in the Argument to the Commentary on Genesis 1, and in the comment on Hebrews 11:3.

23. *City of God* 11.5.

of which we are circumscribed," and exhorts them to seek in "the ample circumference of heaven and earth" and the certainly sufficient space of "six thousand years" material for meditating on the glory of God who has made them all.

The primary matter for us to observe in this discussion is the persistence with which Calvin clings to the practical purpose of his treatise; even in connection with abstruse subjects he confines himself to the "practical use" of them. But it is not illegitimate to observe also the hints the discussion supplies of his metaphysical opinions. His doctrines of space and time are here suggested to us. Clearly, he holds that what we call space is only an abstraction from the concrete dimensions of extended substance, and what we call time is an abstraction from the concrete successions of mutable being. Space and time, therefore, were to him qualities of finite being, and have come into existence and will pass out of existence with finite being. To speak of infinite space or infinite time contains accordingly a *contradictio in adjecto* [contradiction in terms]. . . .

[At this point Warfield takes several pages to defend the idea that, despite appearances, Calvin had a fairly good sense of humor after all. As a few modern students have done, Warfield is able to find more examples of Calvin's cheerfulness, jokes, and injunctions to enjoy life than the stereotype would suggest; see, for example, Richard Stauffer, *The Humanness of John Calvin* (Nashville: Abingdon, 1971).]

. . . That the work of creation should be thought to occupy time was as much a matter of scoffing from the evil-disposed as that it should take place in time. Why should the omnipotent God take six days to make the world? Did he perhaps find it too hard a task for a single effort?[24] This cavil, too, Calvin deals with purely from the practical point of view, not so much undertaking to refute it as recalling men's minds from it to dwell (1) on the condescension of God in distributing his work into six days that our finite intelligence might not be overwhelmed with its contemplation, (2) on the goodness of God in thus leading our thoughts up to the consideration of the rest of the seventh day, and above all (3) on the paternal care of God in so ordering the

24. 1.14.2.

work of bringing the world into being as to prepare it for man before introducing him into it. In drawing the mind thus away from the cavil, Calvin does not, however, fail to meet the difficulty which was adduced. His response to it is, in effect, to acknowledge that God perfected the world by process (*progressus,* 1.14.2), but to assert at the same time that this method of performing his work was not for his own sake, but for ours. Far from being unworthy of God, because "alien from his power,"[25] this progressive method of producing the world illustrates instead his higher attributes—his paternal love, for example, which would not create man until he had enriched the world with all things necessary for man's happiness. Considered in himself, "it would have been no more difficult" for God "to complete at once the whole work in all its items in a single moment than to arrive at its completion gradually by a process of this kind."[26]

It should be observed that in this and similar discussions of the progressive completion of the world, Calvin does not intend to attribute to God what we may speak strictly of as progressive creation. With Calvin, while the perfecting of the world—as its subsequent government—is a process, creation, strictly conceived, tended to be thought of as an act. "In the beginning God created the heavens and the earth"; after that it was not "creation" strictly so called, but "formation," gradual modeling into form, which took place. Not, of course, as if Calvin conceived creation deistically—as if he thought of God as having created the world-stuff and then left it to itself to work out its own destiny under the laws impressed on it in its creation. A "momentary Creator, who has once for all done his work," was inconceivable to him; and he therefore taught that it is only when we contemplate God in providence that we can form any true conception of him as Creator.[27] But he was inclined to draw a sharp distinction in kind be-

25. 1.14.2.
26. 1.14.22.
27. 1.16.1. See also the Genevan Catechism of 1545 (*Opp.* 6:15–16, 17–18) where the question is asked why God is called in the Creed only Creator of heaven and earth, when "tueri conservareque in suo statu creaturas" is "multo praestantius" [to look after and preserve creatures in their proper estate is far more excellent] than just to have once created them. The answer is that this particularizing of creation is not intended to imply that "God so created his works at one

tween the primal act of creation of the heavens and the earth out of nothing, and the subsequent acts of molding this created material into the forms it was destined to take; and to confine the term "creation," strictly conceived, to the former.

Hence in perhaps the fullest statement of his doctrine of creation given us in these chapters (1.14.20) Calvin expresses himself carefully thus: "God by the power of his Word and Spirit created out of nothing *(creasse ex nihilo)* the heavens and the earth, thence produced *(produxisse)* every kind of animate and inanimate thing, distinguished by a wonderful gradation the innumerable variety of things, endowed each kind with its own nature, assigned its offices, appointed its place and station to it, and, since all things are subject to corruption, provided, nevertheless, that each kind should be preserved safe to the last day." "Thus," he adds, "he marvelously adorned heaven and earth with the utmost possible abundance, variety and beauty of all things, like a great and splendid house most richly and abundantly constructed and furnished; and then at last by forming *(formando)* man and distinguishing him with such noble beauty, and with so many and such high gifts, he exhibited in man the noblest specimen of his works."[28]

It is God who has made all things what they are, Calvin teaches; but, in doing so, God has acted in the specific mode properly called creation only at the initial step of the process, and the result owes its right to be called a creation to that initial act by which the material of which all things consist was called into being from nonbeing. "Indigested mass" as it was, yet in that world-stuff was "the seed of the whole world," and out of it that world as we now see it (for "the world at its very beginning was not perfected in the manner it is now seen")[29] has been evoked by pro-

---

time *(semel)* that he afterwards rejects the care of them." On the contrary, he upholds and governs all he has made; and this is included in the idea of his creation of them all. See also the *Confession des Escholiers* of 1559 *(Opp. 9:721–22)* where we read: "I confess that God created the world at once *(semel)*, in such a manner as to be its perpetual governor. . . ."

28. It is worthwhile to observe here how Calvin betrays his sensibility to the glory and beauty of nature (see also 1.5.6; *Opp.* 29:300). See the remarks of E. Doumergue, *Jean Calvin* (1910), 4:105.

29. These phrases occur in the Commentary on Genesis 1.

gressive acts of God; and it is therefore that this world, because evoked from it, has the right to be called a creation.

The distinction which Calvin here draws, it is to be observed, is not that which has been commonly made by Reformed divines under the terms first and second creation, or in less exact language immediate and mediate creation. That common distinction posits a sequence of truly creative acts of God throughout the six days, and therefore defines creation, so as to meet the whole case, as that act "by which God produced the world and all that is in it, partly *ex nihilo,* partly *ex materia naturaliter inhabili* [from preexisting material not itself capable of producing something new], for the manifestation of the glory of his power, wisdom and goodness";[30] or, more fully, as that "first external work of God by which in the beginning of time, without suffering any change, by his own free will, he produced by his sole omnipotent command *immediate per se* [immediately in itself] things which before were not, from simple nonbeing to being—and they were produced either *ex nihilo* or *ex materia* which had afore been made *e nihilo* [from nothing], but was *naturaliter inhabili* [incapable by nature] for receiving the form which, created out of nothing, the Creator now induced into it."[31] It is precisely this sequence of truly creative acts which Calvin disallows; and he so expresses himself, indeed, as to give it a direct contradiction.

Perhaps as distinct a statement of Calvin's view as any is found in his comment on Genesis 1:21, where the term "create" is employed to designate the divine production of the animals of the sea and air, which, according to verse 20, had been brought forth by the waters at the command of God. "A question arises here," remarks Calvin,

30. Wollebius, *Compendium,* 35. [Warfield repeats here phrases he had employed—and approved!—twice before; see his 1901 essay on "Creation, Evolution, and Mediate Creation," p. 204; and his 1906 review of James Orr, p. 233.]

31. Amand. Polanus, *Syntagma theologiae christianae,* Hanover, 1525, v. 2. See also Gisbertus Voetius, *Selectae disputationae theologicae* (1648), 1:554: "Creation may be distinguished . . . into first and second. The first is the production of a thing *ex nihilo,* and in this manner were produced the heavens, the elements, light; and every day there are so produced human souls, so far as they are spiritual in essence. The second is the production of the essential or accidental form in *praesubjecta sed indisposita plane materia* [in matter put in place beforehand but as yet still quite unformed], and that by the immediate operation of the divine power; and in this manner were produced the works of the five days as also many miraculous works in the order of nature as now constituted."

about the word "created." For we have before contended that the
world was made of nothing because it was "created," but now
Moses says the things formed from other matter were "created."
Those who assert that the fishes were truly and properly "created"
because the waters were in no way suitable *(idoneae)* or adapted
(aptae) to their production are only resorting to a subterfuge; for
the fact would remain, meanwhile, that the material of which they
were made existed before, which, in strict propriety, the word
does not admit. I therefore do not restrict "creation" [here] to the
work of the fifth day, but rather say it[s use] refers to (hangs from,
pendet) that shapeless and confused mass which was, as it were,
the fountain of the whole world. God, then, is said to have "created" the sea monsters and other fishes because the beginning of
their "creation" is not to be reckoned from the moment in which
they received their form, but they are comprehended in the universal matter *(corpus, corpore)* which was made out of nothing. So
that with respect to their kind, form only was then added to them;
"creation" is nevertheless a term used truly with respect to the
whole and the parts.

Calvin's motive in thus repudiating the notion of mediate creation is not at all chariness on his part with respect to the supernatural. What he disallows is not the supernaturalness of the production of the creatures which the waters and earth brought
forth, but only the applicability of the term "creation" to their
production. On verse 24 he comments thus: "There is in this respect a miracle as great as if God had begun to create out of nothing these things which he commanded to proceed from the
earth." Calvin's sole motive seems to be to preserve to the great
word "create" the precise significance of to "make out of nothing," and he will not admit that it can be applied to any production in which preexistent material is employed.[32]

This might appear to involve the view that after the creation of
the world-stuff recorded in Genesis 1:1, there was never anything
specifically new produced by the divine power. And this might be
expressed by saying that, from that point on, the divine works
were purely works of providence, since the very differentia of a
providential work is that it is the product proximately of second
causes. Probably this would press Calvin's contention, however, a

32. See n. 9.

little too far; he would scarcely say there was no immediacy in the
divine action in the productions of the five days of creation, or indeed in the working of miracles. But we must bear in mind that his
view of providence was a very high one, and he was particularly
insistent that God acted through means, when he did act through
means, through no necessity but purely at his own volition. Second
causes, in Calvin's view, are nothing more than "instruments into
which God infuses as much of efficiency as he wishes," and which
he employs or not at his will (1.16.2). "The power of no created
thing," says Calvin, "is more wonderful or evident than that of the
sun. . . . But the Lord . . . willed that light should exist . . . before the
sun was created. A pious man will not make the sun, then, either
the principal or the necessary cause of the things which existed before the sun was created, but only an instrument which God uses
because he wishes to; for he could without any difficulty at all do
without the sun and act of himself."[33] The facility with which
Calvin sets aside the notion of mediate creation is then due in no
sense to desire to remove the productions of the five days of creation out of the category of divine products, but is itself mediated
by the height of his doctrine of providence.[34]

33. 1.16.2; see also the Commentary on Genesis 1:3.
34. See [Julius Theodor] Köstlin [1826–1902], *Theologische Studien und Kritiken*
(1868), 427: "In the section of edition 2b (*Opp.* 29:510) on God as the almighty
Creator there should be particularly noted the emphasis with which Calvin maintains, in spite of the mediation of the divine activity through creaturely instruments, yet the dependence of these instruments, and the absolute independence
of God with respect to them. And in ed. 3 (*Opp.* 30:145–46, 150; *Institutes* 1.16.2,
7) there are given still stronger expositions of this. God, says Calvin, bestows on
the instruments powers purely in accordance with his own will, and governs
them; and God could work what he works through them, say through the sun,
just as easily without them, purely by himself. God, he says, in ed. 3, lets us be
nourished ordinarily by bread; and yet according to Scripture, man does not live
by bread alone, for it is not the abundance of food but the divine blessing which
nourishes us; and on the other hand (Isa. 3:1) he threatens to break the staff of
bread." "We have here already," adds Köstlin, "the general premises for the special
use which God, according to Calvin, makes of the Word and of the sacraments
for his saving work." Would anybody but a Lutheran have ever thought of the
means of grace in this connection? Nevertheless, it is not bad to be reminded that
the Reformed doctrine of the means of grace has its analogue in the Reformed
doctrine of providence; it is a corollary of the fundamental notion of God as the
independent One.

It is important further that we should not suppose that Calvin removed the production of the human soul out of the category of immediate creation, in the strictest sense of that term. When he insists that the works of the days subsequent to the first, when "in the beginning God created the heavens and the earth," were not strictly speaking "creations," because they were not productions *ex nihilo*, he is thinking only of the lower creation, inclusive, no doubt, of the human body; all this is made out of that primal indigested mass which sprang into being at the initial command of God. The soul is a different matter, and not only in the first instance, but in every succeeding instance throughout the whole course of human propagation, is an immediate creation *ex nihilo*. Moses, he tells us, perfectly understood that the soul was created from nothing;[35] and he announces with emphasis (*Institutes,* 1.15.5) that it is certain that the souls of men are "no less created than the angels," adding the decisive definition: "now creation is the origination of essence *ex nihilo.*" It is thus with the lower creation alone in his mind that Calvin insists that all that can justly be called by the high name of creation was wrought by God on the first day in that one act by which he created, that is, called into being out of nothing, the heavens and the earth.

It should scarcely be passed without remark that Calvin's doctrine of creation is, if we have understood it aright, for all except the souls of men, an evolutionary one. The indigested mass, including the promise and potency of all that was yet to be, was called into being by the simple fiat of God. But all that has come into being since—except the souls of men alone—has arisen as a modification of this original world-stuff by means of the interaction of its intrinsic forces. Not these forces apart from God, of course; Calvin is a high theist, that is, supernaturalist, in his ontology of the universe and in his conception of the whole movement of the universe. To him God is the *prima causa omnium* [first cause of all], and that not merely in the sense that all things ultimately—in the world-stuff—owe their existence to God, but in the sense that all the modifications of the world-stuff have taken place under the directly upholding and governing hand of God, and find their account ultimately in his will. But they find their ac-

35. Commentary on Malachi 1:2–6 (*Opp.* 44:401).

count proximately in second causes, and this is not only evolutionism but pure evolutionism.

What account we give of these second causes is a matter of ontology—how we account for their existence, their persistence, their action, and the relation we conceive them to stand in to God, the upholder and director as well as creator of them. Calvin's ontology of second causes was, briefly stated, a very pure and complete doctrine of *concursus,* by virtue of which he ascribed all that comes to pass to God's purpose and directive government. But that does not concern us here. What concerns us here is that he ascribed to second causes as their proximate account the entire series of modifications by which the primal indigested mass called heaven and earth has passed into the form of the ordered world which we see, including the origination of all forms of life, vegetable and animal alike, inclusive doubtless of the bodily form of man. And this, we say, is a very pure evolutionary scheme.

Calvin does not discuss, of course, the factors of the evolutionary process, nor does he attempt to trace the course of the evolutionary advance, nor even expound the nature of the secondary causes by which it was wrought. It is enough for him to say that God said, "Let the waters bring forth. . . . Let the earth bring forth," and they brought forth. Of the interaction of forces by which the actual production of forms was accomplished, he had doubtless no conception; he certainly ventured no assertions in this field. How he pictured the process in his imagination (if he pictured it in his imagination) we do not know. But these are subordinate matters.

Calvin doubtless had no theory whatever of evolution, but he teaches a doctrine of evolution. He has no object in so teaching except to preserve to the creative act, properly so called, its purity as an immediate production out of nothing. All that is not immediately produced out of nothing is therefore not created—but evolved. Accordingly his doctrine of evolution is entirely unfruitful. The whole process takes place in the limits of six natural days. For the doctrine to be of use as an explanation of the mode of production of the ordered world, these six days would have to be lengthened out into six periods—six ages of the growth of the world. Had that been done, Calvin would have been a precursor of the modern evolutionary theorists. As it is, he forms only a point of departure for them to this extent—that he teaches, as they teach, that by the instrumentality of second causes—or as a modern would put it, of intrinsic forces—the original world-stuff was modified into the varied forms which constitute the ordered world. This is his account of the origin of the entire lower creation.[36]

Of this lower creation Calvin has, however, as has already been pointed out, very little to say in the discussion of the creature which he has incorporated in the *Institutes* (1.14.20–22). And what he does say is chiefly devoted to the practical end of quickening in our hearts a sense of the glory and perfections of its Maker, whose wisdom, power, justice and goodness are illustrated by it, and of raising our hearts in gratitude to him for his benefits to us. These are the two things, he says, which a contemplation of what is meant by God being the Creator of heaven and earth should work in us: an apprehension of his greatness as the Creator (§ 21) and an appreciation of his care for us his creatures in the manner in which he has created us (§ 22).

More than to suggest this, the scope of his treatise does not appear to him to demand of him, as it does not permit him to dwell on the details of the history of creation—for which he contents himself with referring his readers to the narrative of Genesis, with the comments of Basil and Ambrose. He pauses, therefore, only to insert the comprehensive statement of the elements of the matter which has already been cited, and which asserts that "God by the power of his Word and Spirit created out of nothing the heavens and the earth" and afterwards molded this created material into the ordered world we see around us, which also he sustains and governs; in this world he has placed man, up to whom all the rest has tended and in whom he has afforded the culminating manifestation of his creative power (§ 20). The main items of Calvin's teaching as to the physical universe may therefore be summed up in the propositions that it owes its existence absolutely to the divine

36. H. Bavinck in the first of his Stone Lectures (*The Philosophy of Revelation* [1909], 9–10) remarks: "The idea of development is not a production of modern times. It was already familiar to Greek philosophy. More particularly Aristotle raised it to the rank of the leading principle of his entire system by his significant distinction between *potentia* and *actus*. . . . This idea of development aroused no objection whatever in Christian theology and philosophy. On the contrary, it received extension and enrichment by being linked with the principle of theism." Calvin accordingly very naturally thought along the lines of a theistic evolutionism.

power,[37] that it was created out of nothing, that it was perfected through a process of formation which extended through six days, that it was made and adorned for the sake of man and has been subjected to him, and that it illustrates in its structure and in all its movements the perfections of its Maker. . . .

[At this point in the essay, Warfield, following Calvin, turns to an extensive discussion of the creation of the spiritual universe, a universe which Genesis does not describe in its creation account. Warfield begins with the creation of the angels. He believes that Calvin, taking note that God existed before all creation and that the angels were created *ex nihilo* like the physical universe, concluded that the physical and spiritual universes were created in "one creative epoch"—what Calvin saw as the first day of creation. Subsequent to the first day God did not, technically, create—that is, nothing new came into existence. Days two through six witnessed the activity of God using preexisting matter. Thus Calvin viewed creation as, in a restricted sense, evolutionary. Nothing expressly creative happened subsequent to the initial moment of creation *ex nihilo*. God used and formed what already existed.

[From here Warfield continues by looking at Calvin's treatment of angelic influence. Angels are the agents of God; they are God's hands involved in almost all of God's activity. Warfield, following Calvin, maintains that this does not in the least distance the Creator from active involvement with his creation. Why there are angels is another question, but their existence does not take away from the action of God. Angels neither act in opposition to God nor occupy a necessary intermediary state between God and his creation. Here one can see clearly the idea of *concursus* working in Warfield's analysis: although angels are comprehensive in their activity, God is fully manifesting his redemptive power through them, making him as active as if they were not created or used at all.

[Concluding Warfield's section on the creation of the spiritual universe is an analysis of the angels' counterparts—devils. God

37. Commenting on Ps. 148:5 (*Opp.* 32:434), he remarks: "The pronoun *he* is therefore emphatic, as if the prophet would say that the world is not eternal as profane men dream, nor is produced by some concurring atoms, but this beautiful order which we see suddenly stood forth *(exstitisse)* on the mandate of God." See also *Opp.* 31:327.

created them, like the angels, good, that is, with good natures; but
by their own devices they became corrupt. Here, avers Warfield,
one catches a glimpse of Calvin's theodicy. Evil comes from the
corruption of the creature's will and not from the Creator. God is
neither the author nor abettor of evil. While bound by their wick-
edness to oppose God, the devils, owing to God's providential
government of the universe, yet do nothing outside of God's permission and will. Thus God can control the work of evil without
being responsible for it.

[The article concludes with a discussion of Calvin's view of humanity as created by God. Before treating the creation of the soul,
Warfield argues for a dichotomy (body and soul) rather than a tri-
chotomy (body, soul, spirit), he summarizes Calvin's relatively
slight treatment of the human body, he argues that without sin
the body would have been immortal, he suggests that the human
soul differs from the body in origin as well as nature, and he summarizes Calvin's several arguments for the immortality of the
soul. Then, showing Calvin's commitment to the creation *ex nihilo* of the human soul, Warfield returns to his earlier distinction
between development and creation.]

. . . Now this immortal substance, alternately called soul and
spirit, which constitutes the animating or governing principle in the
human constitution, Calvin is insistent, is an immediate creation of
God. He insists upon this, not merely in opposition to the notion
that it is nothing at all but a mere breath or power, but with equal
strenuousness in opposition to that "diabolical error" which considers the soul a derivative *(traducem)* of the substance of God—seeing that this would make "the divine nature not only subject to
change and passions, but to ignorance also, to depraved desires, to
weakness and every kind of vice . . . rending the essence of the Creator that every one may possess a part of it." No, says he, "it is to
be held as certain that souls are created," and "creation is not transfusion of essence, but the origination of it from nothing" (1.15.5).
This "origination of the soul out of nothing," which alone can be
called creation, he insists on, again, not merely with reference to
the origin of the first soul,[38] but also with reference to every soul

38. See, e.g., Commentary on Malachi 1:2–6 (*Opp.* 44:401): "Moses understands that man's soul was created from nothing. We are born by generation, and
yet our origin is clay, and the chief thing in us, the soul, is created from nothing."

which has come into existence since. It is horrible, says he, that it should be thrown into doubt by men who call themselves Christians, whether the souls of men are a true created substance.[39]

Calvin's doctrine of the creation of the soul is thrown up into contrast, therefore, on the one side with his view that all else which was brought into being during the creative week, after the primal creation of the indigested mass of the world-stuff on the first day, was proximately the product of second causes, and on the other side with his belief in the production of the body by ordinary generation in the case of all the descendants of Adam. The soul of the first man stands out as an exception in the midst of mediately produced effects: it was the one product of God's direct creative power in the process of the perfecting of the creative scheme. And the souls of the descendants of this first man stand out in contrast with their bodily forms: they are in every case also products of God's direct creative activity. In creating souls *(in creandis animis)*, Calvin says, "God does not use the instrumentality of man *(non adhibet hominum operam)*."[40] "There is no need," he says again, "to resort to that old figment of some *(figmentum)* that souls come into being *(oriantur) ex traduce.*"[41] "We have not come of the race of Adam," he says yet again, "except as regards the body."[42] And not only does he thus over and over again through his writings sharply assert creationism as over against traducianism, but he devotes a whole section of the *Institutes* to the question and formally rejects the whole traducian conception.[43]

In its nature, as we have seen, this immortal and yet created essence which vitalizes and governs the human frame is defined by Calvin as percipient substance whose very nature it is to move,

39. *Opp.* 7:180.
40. On Hebrews 12:9.
41. On Genesis 3:6 (*Opp.* 23:62).
42. Sermon on Job 14:4 (*Opp.* 33:660).
43. 2.1.7. Two subordinate points in Calvin's doctrine of creation may be worth noting here. He remarks in passing while commenting on Numbers 16:22 (*Opp.* 25:222) that it may be collected from that passage that each man has his separate soul, and that by this "is refuted the prodigious delusion of the Manicheans that all souls are so infused *ex traduce* by the Spirit of God that there should still be one spirit." He returns often to this. Commenting on Job 3:16 (*Opp.* 33:162) he teaches that God breathes the soul into the creature at the moment when it is conceived in its mother's womb.

feel, act, understand; it is, in a word, characteristically sensibil-ity.[44] When we attend to Calvin's conception of the soul from this point of view, we are in effect observing his psychology; and, of course, he develops his psychology with his eye primarily upon the nature of man in his state of integrity—or rather, let us say, in his uncorrupted condition (1.15.1). "When definitions are to be given," he remarks in another place,[45] "the nature of the soul is ac-customed to be considered in its integrity." He develops his defi-nition also, however, under the influence of a strong desire to be clear and simple. Subtleties in such matters he gladly leaves to the philosophers, whose speculations he has no desire to gainsay as to either their truth or their usefulness; for his purposes, however, which look to building up piety, a simple definition will suffice.[46] It is naturally upon the questions which cluster around the will that Calvin's chief psychological interest focuses. We must, how-ever, leave the whole matter of Calvin's psychology and his doc-trine of the will to another occasion. We must postpone also an exposition of his doctrine of the image of God. A survey of these two topics remains in order to complete our exposition of his doctrine of the creature.[47]

44. *Opp.* 5:184: sensus.

45. *Responsio contra Pighium de Libero Arbitrio* [Response opposing Pighius on the freedom of the will] (*Opp.* 6:285): "It is sufficiently clear that [in Basil's re-marks here under consideration] the nature of the soul is considered in its integ-rity, as it is accustomed to be in giving definitions."

46. A. S. E. Talma, *De Anthropologie van Calvijn* (1882), 43, remarks: "The whole manner in which Calvin deals here (*Inst.,* 1.15.6) with the . . . faculties of the soul is remarkable. The style loses the liveliness, the progress of thought its regularity; and the whole makes the impression that Calvin did not feel fully at home in this field." Talma notes that the discussion of the faculties of the soul is not found in the *Institutes* of 1536, but is already very full in the edition of 1539. (See Doumergue, *Jean Calvin* [1910], 4:109, for Calvin's psychology.)

47. [Warfield never wrote, or at least never published, these later studies on Calvin.]

April 1916
Princeton Theological Review 14:323–27

Review of J. N. Shearman,
The Natural Theology of Evolution
(London: George Allen and Unwin, [1916])

In his 1891 review of John William Dawson's *Modern Ideas of Evolution* Warfield had expressed the hope that Dawson would prepare a "new Paley," that is, a book explaining purpose, design, and teleology from organic, evolutionary ways of looking at the natural world as William Paley's *Natural Theology* (1802) had done for mechanistic, static ways of understanding nature. Warfield's judgment that J. N. Shearman had now produced such a book rested on the argument that order in evolutionary explanations is tantamount to a proof of intelligence; intelligence, in turn, is proof of a designer. As Warfield states it, "Imbedded in the very conception of evolution . . . is the conception of end. . . . Teleology is the very soul of evolution."

Even with evolution now shown to his satisfaction to entail design, Warfield—ever the resolute empiricist—cannot forbear suggesting that research still has not explained how evolutionary mechanisms work. In drawing these conclusions, Warfield was reflecting the scientific judgment of 1916. It would be another fifteen or twenty years until a Neo-Darwinian version of natural selection, based on the application of genetic variation to species development, once again brought back some of Darwin's specific reasoning that in 1916 did not enjoy scientific consensus.[1]

Josiah Nicholson Shearman published this book with Dutton of New York as well as in the London edition Warfield used. Beyond that no further personal information has been found.

1. For the context of this period, see Peter J. Bowler, *The Eclipse of Darwinism: Anti-Darwinian Evolution Theories in the Decades around 1900* (Baltimore: Johns Hopkins University Press, 1983).

In this interesting volume we have an evolutionary Paley. It is a book which was bound to come, and it has come in good form and with convincing force. Mr. Shearman writes with notable simplicity and presents his argument plainly and with great expository skill. He divides his work into four parts. In the first of these he reproduces Paley with only such corrections as the evolutionary point of view compels. This he calls the "common sense argument." In the second part the same argument is restated in a more abstract or philosophical spirit. The third part applies the argument to a number of examples. The fourth part, which is very brief, considers cursorily a few objections. Mr. Shearman is strongest in the direct presentation of his argument. His criticism strikes the reader as sometimes a little overacute, and even sometimes as largely verbal.

The standpoint of the book is that of plain common-sense. The trustworthiness of the human understanding is assumed and confidently built upon. The fundamental proposition asserted is that order means intelligent design, and the whole argument is but the elaboration and illustration of that principle. The attempts which have been made to account for order without mind are surveyed and rejected. The presence of order itself implies mind and that no matter how this order, in point of fact, has come into existence. The point is not by what processes it was brought into existence, but that it is order. Wherever order is produced, there mind has been at work. By whatever processes things may have come to be, if mind is seen in the result, mind must have been at work in their production. Thus the flank of the evolutionist is turned and his evolutionism is shown to be irrelevant to the issue. He may point out the steps and stages through which the product has been produced, but he has not eliminated the action of intelligence from the process so long as the mark of intelligence, order, is discernible in the product. Without intelligence order could not have got into the product.

The main argument turns on the course of evolution itself, which Mr. Shearman has no doubt has been continuously upward. Change as change might not imply design: we can conceive of meaningless change. But change which is at the same time progress cannot be conceived except as intended. Where there is real progress or advance to anything higher or more complex, chance variations will not help and any change that occurs is a proof of design.

The assumption on which this reasoning rests may, of course, be challenged, that, to wit, the course of evolution has been, on the whole, forward. Mr. Shearman himself does not scruple to speak of it as "a continual progress, a steady rise in the scale of being, a constant coming in of new designs, fresh kinds of organisms, more complicated machines." With this understanding of the course of evolution the argument is irrefragable. A captious objector might, it is true, challenge the very idea of advance. What is a "higher" organism? Mr. Shearman appears to use "higher" and "more complex" as synonyms. What reason is there to represent a constant increase in complexity as an advance? Well, there is at least a constant increase in complexity; and every increase in complexity renders it more and more difficult—more and more impossible if the phrase may be pardoned—to attribute the product to mere chance.

And here our attention may pass over from the general course of evolution, which obviously suggests design, to the complexity of organs which have emerged in the course of evolution. We may look at the human eye, or at the pecten's eye;[2] we may look at the mechanism of fertilization in the cuckoopint and the aristolochia,[3] or in the orchids; we may look at the action of insectivorous plants, at the asymmetry of the plaice, at the marvelous arrangements for the flight of birds—to say nothing of the flight of the bats and fossil reptiles, and the insects, all independently developed; we may look at the wonders of instinct. He who can believe that these things have come by mere chance may hopefully set to work stirring up a box of printer's types with a stick in the expectation that he will stir out of them a volume of sonnets. The thing is absurd: you cannot

2. [Pecten: a vascular pigmented membrane in the eye of nearly all birds and many reptiles.]

3. [Cuckoopint: a common European herb with heart-shaped leaves, erect spathe, and short purple spadix. Aristolochia: a large genus of mostly tropical herbs or woody vines with pungent aromatic rootstocks and irregular flowers.]

get more intelligence out of a process in the end, by way of product, than you put into it at the beginning, in the way of design.

So far from evolution being fatal to teleology, it may be fairly argued that teleology is the very soul of evolution, and "the end" is the
only reality which a strictly conceived evolutionism can admit. This
is because of the inherent affiliation of a strictly conceived evolutionism with idealism. The idealist cannot look upon existing things as
real in the full sense because they are to him in a flux; the only reality
is the fixed mental concept. Similarly to the evolutionist (if we may
take Mr. Huxley as an example) the external world is process and
process only; it *is* not, it is rather ever *becoming*. All things are in a perpetual process of change; the only stable thing is the idea to which
the external world is ever more and more approximating.

In this idea, then, alone can be found the true reality; external
things are only progressing more and more to its embodiment in
fact. But this is merely to say that the one real thing is the governing
end towards which all that is tends. This conclusion can be escaped
only by representing evolution not as progressive change, but mere
blind and therefore vagrant change. But this, though it may be
called transformation, scarcely fills out the idea of evolution, especially as that evolution is observed actually at work in the course of
the world's development. In its very idea, evolution involves
change towards a result, a perfecting; and this is the evolution
which a contemplation of the world's development brings to our
observation. It is an unrolling, a realization of something already
present in idea, but not yet embodied in fact. An idea so present is
the very form of an idea which we call an end. Imbedded in the
very conception of evolution, therefore, is the conception of end,
and of an end which is in process of realization; and all that exists
is but a series of stages toward that realization. It is this end that
impresses its law of existence on all the process, and that gives
what reality it has to every stage of the process. A purely materialistic evolution is inconceivable; it would not be an evolution, but a
mere instability—meaningless and vacuous. To give meaning to it
direction must be postulated for it; and when direction is postulated for it, an end towards which it is directed is postulated on the
one side, and a director, directing it to that end, on the other.

We are not saying, of course, that a purely materialistic evolutionism has never been attempted. Men like Haeckel would at

once rise up to confront us, and indeed men like Charles Darwin. Darwin attempted to develop a purely materialistic evolutionism: his system was pure accidentalism, and his whole interest in it turned exactly on that fact. Precisely what he tried to show was that order might be the product of chance; that we might have all the marks of mind before us and yet not be able to infer mind; that we might have, in effect, the results of intelligence without intelligence. That Darwin failed in his effort, we suppose is now fairly universally admitted. But a curious thing has happened. Men desire to retain the conclusion which Darwin reached while they reject the evidence on which Darwin reached this conclusion. Mr. Shearman, for example, tells us that Darwin "brought together reasons for believing that the existing species of animals and plants had their origin by a process of evolution," and that these reasons are "so strong and so forcibly put that the doctrine of evolution is now universally received"; and then adds, "But besides proving the doctrine of evolution, Darwin tries to show how evolution has been brought about, and in this he is less successful." We do not think these two things can be thus separated. What Darwin endeavored to do was to render the idea of evolution credible and acceptable by pointing out a *vera causa* [actual cause] by which it might be—he said, by which it was—effected. The reason which he commended to his readers for believing in evolution lay in his doctrine of natural selection, and he can hardly be said to have proved the former if the latter fails. The discrediting of his doctrine of natural selection as the sufficient cause of evolution leaves the idea of evolution without proof, so far as he is concerned—leaves it, in a word, just where it was before he took the matter up.

And there, speaking broadly, it remains until the present day. If we understand Mr. Shearman, he sits skeptically over against not only Darwin's attempted explanation of the evolutionary process, but all others which have been proposed. He would have us accept the fact that evolution is established, but look upon the several attempts which have been made to explain how it has all come about as only so many plausible speculations. It is a fact, the true explanation of which as yet escapes us. That is to say, Mr. Shearman wishes us to look upon evolution as a bare "law of nature," in his sense of that term. "A great deal," he tells us, has been written in our day about the laws of Nature, and much of it is very wise, and some of it is very foolish. But nothing can be further from the truth than the assertion that Science is wholly devoted to the discovery of laws of nature. Scientific people are like other people in this, that what they want is not laws but explanations. Wherever an explanation is possible it is given, and where no explanation can be found we have to be content with the law. The laws of nature are in reality the mass of unreduced facts which remain when as much as possible has been explained. They are not the triumphs of the scientist but his problems; they measure not our knowledge but our ignorance.

Evolution is, then, if a fact, not a triumph of the scientist but one of his toughest problems. He does not know how it has taken place; every guess he makes as to how it has taken place proves inadequate to account for it. His main theories have to be supported by subsidiary theories to make them work at all, and these subsidiary theories by yet more far-reaching subsidiary theories of the second rank—until the whole chart is, like the Ptolemaic chart of the heavens, written over with cycle and epicycle and appears ready to break down by its own weight. Meanwhile we are to accept evolution as a bare "law of nature"; it is an observed fact—but how it comes about Goodness only knows. Well, it is something to be sure that Goodness knows, and to be solidly assured by Mr. Shearman's convincing argument that it did not come about without Goodness having a hand in it.

We are rather surprised to find Mr. Shearman still operating with the embryonic-recapitulatory theory which was in vogue a generation ago: "all animals, in the course of their development, go through a kind of condensed summary of the history of the race." We have supposed that this notion had been long since exploded. We regret that he has, even as a rebuttal not supposed by himself to be necessary, allowed himself to suggest that imperfections in nature may be accounted for by supposing that not God directly but the angels, acting as his intermediaries, are responsible for the making of these things. But these are little matters. The book is a good book and its argument plainly put and well sustained throughout.

January 1921
Princeton Theological Review 19:148–54

Review of H. Visscher,
Van den Eeuwigen Vrede tusschen Wetenschap en Religie
(On eternal peace between science and religion) (Utrecht: Drukkerij Universitas, 1920); and H. W. van der Vaart Smit, *Professor Visscher's Rectorale Rede* (Professor Visscher's rectoral address) (Baarn: Drukkerij Oranje Nassau, R. K. v. d. Berg, 1920)

It is fitting to end this book with a more general statement by Warfield on theology and science. It came in the last year of his life as a comment on a proposal made by the Dutch theologian, biblical scholar, and religionist Hugo Visscher (1864–1947) in his rector's address at the celebration of the University of Utrecht's 284th anniversary. The occasion afforded Warfield an opportunity to summarize a lifetime's convictions.

In this review, Warfield restates his conviction that "theology is as truly a science as is physical science." He rejects the equation that would link science with intellect and knowledge, while religion is tied only to emotion and faith; he explains why science is as subjective as theology ("the voices of the scientists are not the voice of science"); and he reaffirms in the strongest terms his belief in the physical world as a scene of divine revelation ("Science too is a builder in the kingdom of God. . . . No less truly than religion itself, science is a son of God"). Historically considered, in other words, Warfield ends his life with the commitments he had been given by his theological mentor Charles Hodge.

This review reveals why Warfield was so caught up with the question of evolution throughout his career. Evolutionary theories were
designed to account for facts. For Warfield, Christianity also rested
on facts—especially the creation of the world out of nothing, the incarnation of the Son of God, and the resurrection of that Son from
the dead. In the realm of fact, as Warfield understood fact, science
and theology decidedly intersected. Yet even as theology had rights
over against science, so too did science deserve the greatest respect
from theology. Warfield's convictions about what was at stake in the
relationship of natural facts and revealed facts go a long way toward
explaining why he gave such a great deal of his long and productive
working life to considering the nature of their intersection.

I t is a somewhat exigent position in which a theologian finds
himself when, as rector magnificus of a great university, he faces
"the four faculties" for the purpose of delivering to them his rectoral address. There are many points of view represented among
his hearers; and some of them are quite intolerant of anything
which he, as a theologian, may have to bring before them. In his
rectoral address Professor Visscher has chosen the role of peace-
maker. Looking out upon a hard-bestead world, he bespeaks the
cooperation of all in the pressing task of saving Western civilization from the dissolution with which he appears to think it
threatened.

Professor Visscher seems fairly to groan within himself as he
surveys the social unrest of the day. The times are out of joint.
The whole world is suffering from a one-sidedness of development which has destroyed the spiritual equilibrium—and is not
harmonious growth the condition of social health? True, progress
has hitherto been made, not on a straight line of advance, but as
a ship tacks back and forth in its course. But the leg of *Diesseit-
igkeit* [a focus on life in this world] on which the social ship in our
Western world is now sailing seems to Professor Visscher an in-
ordinately long one, and he trembles lest it should prove that the
ship has lost its bearings and may never get back on the balancing
tack of *Jenseitigkeit* [a focus on the life to come]. Indeed, he does
not wish it to do just this. The leg of *Jenseitigkeit* is itself only a
tack. He wishes the ship to cease all tacking and sail straight onward, in the teeth of whatever wind, directly to its goal.

Why should not science and religion, for example, live in harmony, each contributing its part to the spiritual health of man-

kind? Each has its own sphere, and each has only to keep its own place for the harmony to be complete. And surely their harmonious coworking is a clamant duty of the times.

> For the salvation of Western humanity there rests on science and religion the most pressing call to work in harmony for the regeneration of civilization. Science has the task of subjecting nature to the scepter of reason, in order thus to make it ancillary to the full development of human life. But because of its very nature, it is unable of itself to bring about this ripe result. The happiness of the peoples is not the product of it alone. Quite the contrary. It is social health alone that secures the happiness of the people. And it is religion, which sheds the light of eternity on human life, that is the wellspring of moral strength. Science and religion are the two spiritual powers which in harmonious cooperation can save the peoples of civilization. Or is it possible to save them? If the social movement continues to refuse to take the factor of religion up into itself, the destruction of our civilization is certain, and science, too, will go down in the common ruin.

It is under the impression of so great a need, and with so high a purpose in view, that Professor Visscher undertakes the discussion of the relations of science and religion. He is at bottom pleading for the right of religion to a part in the social development of the day. This plea, however, takes the form of an attempt to show that science, properly conceived and properly presented, cannot possibly invade the field of religion, nor religion the field of science. Thus the discussion becomes formally a discussion of the relations of science and religion, and much is very richly and much is very wisely said of the relations of these two spiritual forces to one another as they have actually wrought in the life of mankind.

The discussion suffers somewhat, however, from a vacillation in the use of the terms, which it would be no doubt difficult to avoid in any case with terms so loose and general—too loose and general to lend themselves to exact discriminations. It is so managed, moreover, that it seems at times on the point of becoming a discussion of the relations between knowledge and faith, if not between intellect and feeling. It is too obvious to require argument, however, that we cannot out of hand identify, on the one hand, intellect, knowledge and science, and, on the other, emotion, faith and religion. Both science and religion are products of the human spirit, and the human spirit does not function thus in sections. It is, however, the attempt to bring into comparison precisely these two things, science and religion, that works the most mischief. We might bring, say, research and religion into relation, or "science" in some narrowed sense and theology; but "science" in the narrowed sense in which Professor Visscher understands that term and "religion" in the purely subjective sense which Professor Visscher strangely puts upon it move in such different spheres that they are unrelatable—there is no *tertium comparationis* [meeting place for comparison] between things so disparate. You might as well talk of instituting relations between the planet Neptune and the League of Nations.

We have noted that Professor Visscher narrows the conception of "science" for the purpose of his discussion. By it he means merely physical science. But physical science is far from being all the science there is. There is, for example, as we have suggested, theology. Theology is as truly a science as is physical science; it is as truly a product of the intellect; it deals as truly with facts; it is as truly a knowledge. It is theology, the science, not religion, the life, which should be set in comparison with physical science. The thrusting of religion, so understood, into its place has the effect of depriving it of—or at least of obscuring—its fact-content. Of religion it may be possible to say—what could not be said of theology—that it is only a manner (perhaps only an emotional manner) of looking at facts which science alone has to deal with as facts, so that science and religion cannot possibly come into conflict. It is science alone which determines facts, while it is the sole function of religion to suffuse these facts, given to it by science, with a glow of transcendental emotion.

It is a melancholy page which Professor Visscher writes under the influence of this point of view, when he attempts to illustrate it by examples. Had he drawn his examples from natural religion, his mistake might have been less glaring. But he draws his examples from revealed religion. The effect is that he seems to require Christianity to surrender to natural science—for it is of natural science alone that he speaks—all question of facts, while it confines itself to a "valuation of them in relation with God." This appears to abolish all supernaturalism from the fact-basis and fact-content of Christianity. For the science to which is assigned the determination of the facts which will be allowed actually to have occurred is defined not only as a science which cannot know anything of God— for whom it has no organ—but a science which can take cognizance of nothing which does not proceed mechanically.

The actual examples considered are drawn from the creation of the world, miracles, answers to prayer, the resurrection of Christ. Of the creation of the world we are simply told that science, which knows nothing of origins and confines itself to the phenomena lying before it, has nothing to do with it. We gather, however, that neither has revelation. It is a mistake to read the creation narrative as a statement of fact; it merely gives expression to the purely religious valuation *(waardeering)* of the cosmos.

For the rest we prefer to transcribe Professor Visscher's own words:

> Lessing declared that "miracle is faith's most darling child."[1] And are not science and miracle in conflict? In point of fact science recognizes no miracle. But that does not yet bring it into conflict with religion. Does the chemist's subjecting bread to exact analysis prevent the pious man from receiving his food from God's hand? Necessity teaches man to pray, and to the petitioner the deliverance comes as an answer to his prayer. Does this forbid a scientific explanation of the occurrence? But let us come to the most critical matter of all. The Crucified One is proclaimed as risen from the grave. Is there any place for resurrection in exact science? Yes; whenever resurrection shall be brought before it as a phenomenon. Not before. And then it will have to investigate resurrection as a physiological problem. But it is precisely here that the difference comes clearly to view. In the world-order of religion, life and death are not conceived as physiological processes, but are religious-ethical values *(waarden)*. The resurrection is for religion an element in the great regenerative process which, by God's creative

1. [Gotthold Ephraim Lessing (1729–81) was a German dramatist and critic during the Enlightenment era. Some of his later writings helped to lay the foundations of Protestant liberalism. Rejecting the idea that an enduring Christian faith could be based on history, he held humanitarianism, truth, and reason to be the highest goals of religion.]

act, is producing out of this world-order a new heaven and a new earth.

Despite the reassuring tone of its closing words, the reader may be pardoned if he receives from this paragraph a very unpleasant impression. There is an appearance at least that the actual occurrence of strictly miraculous events in the foundation of Christianity is denied. Miracles and providential answers to prayer seem to be brought into the same category. The one, as the other, appears to be conceived at best as the product of the concursive action of God; at worst, as only a subjective way of looking at facts wholly natural alike in their nature and in the mode of their production.

And what shall we say of the manner in which the resurrection of Christ is dealt with? Science, we are told, can have nothing to do with it until Christ's resurrection is presented to science as a phenomenon. Is it not precisely as a phenomenon that it lies in the sight of all men—an occurrence in space and time verified by the senses? And has not even the "physiological problem" been adequately determined? Has it not been established on unexceptionable observation that the resurrection body, like that which was laid in the grave, was a body of flesh and bones? When now it is immediately added that life and death are not conceived in the religious world-order as physiological processes, but as religious-ethical values, can we escape a distressed feeling that religion—precisely the Christian religion—is in danger of being politely bowed out of the world of fact? Precisely what characterizes Christianity, however, among the religions is that it is a historical religion, that is, a religion whose facts are its doctrines. Christianity does not consist in a tone of feeling, a way of looking at things—as, for example, the perception of a Father's hand in all the chances and changes of life; rather, Christianity has to tell of a series of great redemptive acts in which God the Lord has actually intervened in the complex of nature and the stream of history in a definitely supernatural manner. If these facts are denied as actual occurrences in time and space, Christianity is denied; if they are neglected, Christianity is neglected. Christianity is dismissed from the world of reality, and evaporated into a sentiment—"an iridescent dream."

We have no wish to be read as asserting that Professor Visscher intends to deny, or is ready to neglect, the series of great redemptive acts of definitely supernatural character which are constitutive of Christianity. We are pointing out only that an impression to that effect is inevitably created by the sharp contrast in which he places science as the only organ of objective reality and religion as moving in a purely subjective sphere. Whatever may be said of religion as a general world-phenomenon native to the spirit of man, that religion which is Christianity is inseparably bound up with its facts, and stands or falls with their objective reality. Any science which leaves no place for these facts as such is not neutral but antagonistic to Christianity, and between that science and this religion there must be not eternal peace but eternal war.

Professor Visscher apparently supposes that he escapes this result by so defining science as to exclude facts of supernatural origin from its ken. Facts of supernatural origin, however, are not different in nature from other facts. There is no reason to suppose that the chemical composition of the wine made at Cana or the physical properties of the loaves and fishes with which our Lord fed the multitudes—or of his resurrection body, for that matter—differed from those of natural wine and bread and bodies. If facts like these have actually occurred in time and space, they necessarily come under the scrutiny of that science whose function is to give an account of phenomena.

Professor Visscher seems, however, to have made a mode of escape for himself: he confines the function of science to pure description. He tells us, it is true, that the knowledge for which this science seeks is a knowledge of relations, and he even declares with some formality that "its object can be nothing else than the world as it presents itself as a system of relations to the knowing subject." When we say relations, however, we have already said metaphysics; and if among the relations determined there is included not merely that of antecedence and consequence, but of cause, we are already embarked on an inquiry which cannot stop short of origins.

Professor Visscher tells us, however, not only that everything which exists behind phenomena lies beyond the sphere of his science, but that this science must repel the conception of a super-

natural, mystical, nonmechanical factor and confine itself to the
world in which everything proceeds mechanically. If he really
means us to understand the science with which he deals after this
fashion—as strictly limited to the world of mechanical causation,
of which it undertakes nothing more than a descriptive account—
it may not be impossible to contend that its failure to take cognizance of the supernatural facts constitutive of Christianity in no
way dismisses them from objective reality. That failure may be
the result merely of the limitations of a purely descriptive science
which does not take cognizance, even descriptively, of the whole
field of objective reality, but only of that portion of this field
which is governed by mechanical necessity. In this case it might
be true enough that "all the results of this exact science are consistent with religion," because the world of religion "is a different
and a wider world than the system of relations which exact science," so conceived, "builds up with immense labor." An eternal
peace may well be declared between the two, a peace bought not
at the cost of religion—the fact-content of Christianity—but at
the cost of science.

Whether this limited conception of science as seeking only a
descriptive account of mechanical reality can be maintained is another question. Certainly, in any case, the science with which
Professor Visscher proclaims religion to be eternally at peace has
never, whether in the limitations which he puts upon it, or in the
perfection which he ascribes to its deliverances, existed on sea or
land. He is not unaware, of course, of the subjective side of science; but he appears to neglect it in the prosecution of his discussion, and to identify the science of which he speaks with the objective system of realities itself, which he apparently imagines to
be perfectly reflected in the human intellect. Thus he seems to
think of science as the pure product of the pure intellect of a pure
humanity working purely. We shall get no such science as that
until the world of reality is reflected in the consciousness of the
perfected humanity of the completed palingenesis.[2] The science
and religion of perfected humanity will of course be in harmony.

2. [Palingenesis: a term that Warfield borrowed from the Dutch theologian
Abraham Kuyper; literally "renewal by rebirth," it signifies the life or destiny
growing out of Christian faith or the new birth.]

What we have in the meantime, however, is only the distorted reflection of reality in warped intellects, dimmed by imperfections and clouded by prepossessions.

Could we listen directly to the teaching of that "beautiful Maiden bearing the torch of enlightenment" to whom Professor Visscher introduces us, we should of course yield to it instant and complete obedience. But this "calm-eyed science" is not to be encountered in the marketplace, and is not to be met with in the Rialto [i.e., a commercial exchange]. She speaks to us only in the voices of her servants, and each of them has his own, shall we say, personal equation. After all is said, the voices of the scientists are not the voice of science. And no inability which religion—the Christian religion—may show to live in peace with the one can argue disharmony with the other. No more here than elsewhere can millennial conditions be anticipated. There is no conflict between science and religion; they are not only, as Professor Visscher declares, two expressions of our spiritual life, but two revelations of God. But conflict between science and religion will continue so long as we toil and moil in the present distress; they are only expressions of our spiritual life, and in these days of our tribulation our spiritual life is faulty in all its expressions. It is only when that which is perfect is come that, here too, imperfection shall put on perfection.

There is no help for it, then; science and religion must just strive together until both the one and the other lie perfect in the minds of the perfected. In principle, there is no conflict between them; actually, the conflict is without cessation. There is no menace in this struggle. What would be ominous would be if the struggle should cease, especially if it should cease through either one or the other losing heart or selling its soul for a patched-up peace. We take it that the gist of Professor Visscher's address is to call on religion to recognize science's right to exist, to call on science to recognize religion's right to exist. If we may so read it, we shall all heartily echo the call. Of course neither will wait for the permission of the other to exist. Whether we accord them permission or not, both exist side by side, not only in the social organism, but in every man's own soul. The problem is their adjustment to one another. In the soul of the individual and in the community of mankind alike, the adjustment can be attained only through conflict. As they wrestle together, each is more and more purified and perfected; each grows ever stronger. Now the one may seem to get the advantage; now the other. But through the struggle both push steadily onward. The advance is a zigzag progress, but it is ever advance. At the end lies the goal, the goal not of one, but of both; then the struggle ceases because both emerge from it perfect. Science too is a builder in the kingdom of God, and along with religion advances its coming. No less truly than religion itself, science is a son of God, and works as he has taught it how.

It is not surprising that the ambiguities of Professor Visscher's treatment of his theme have caused distress to those who have been accustomed to look to him for guidance and support. Acute expression is given to this distress in the remarks by Dr. van der Vaart Smit. As he reads the address, it dismisses from Christianity the whole element of direct supernaturalism. We cannot deny that there is much justification for such an interpretation of it. It is true, moreover, that Professor Visscher seems to impose on himself with the phrase "exact science," that he conceives too narrowly of science as purely materialistic-mechanistic, that he has forgotten theology in his absorption with religion. Still we hope that the intended meaning of the address is not that which Dr. Smit finds in it.

Professor Karl Heim contributed to the *Studies on Systematic Theology* presented a year or two ago to Theodor von Haering on his seventieth birthday a very interesting sketch of the history of the doctrine of "The Double Truth."[3] In it he tells the story of a young instructor at the University of Paris in 1247, John Brescain by name, who, holding a professorship alike in the faculty of arts and the faculty of theology, thought it right to teach Averroism in the one, with its denial of individual immortality and the resurrection, and Christianity in the other, with its affirmation of both.[4] His case proved not to be singular: at the university a

3. [Karl Heim (1874–1958) was a Lutheran theologian who endeavored to build a bridge between theology and the natural sciences. Theodor von Haering (1848–1928) was professor of New Testament at the University of Tübingen and a conservative of the Ritschlian school.]

4. [Averroes (Ibn-Rushd, 1126–98) was a Muslim physician and philosopher from Cordoba whose most important writings were his *Commentaries on Aristotle*.]

whole party developed that declared that such things were true *secundum fidem catholicam* [according to the catholic faith] but not *secundum philosophiam* [according to philosophy], as if, says the Episcopal Rescript, *sunt duae contrariae veritates* [there could be two contrary truths]. We are not insinuating that Professor Visscher holds to the doctrine of the double truth, or lives under its shadow; but we think that the state of mind at the University of Paris in the thirteenth century may afford us a not unsuggestive parallel to such a complete disassociation of science and religion as Professor Visscher seems to wish to carry through.

His teachings concerning the complete separation of God from the world and the unity of the human intellect (there is only one intellect in which all humans share) reached Catholic Europe in the early thirteenth century. Averroism became a proscribed subject at the University of Paris in 1277 after some members of the faculty of arts were accused by the church of teaching what is known as the doctrine of double truth, that is, asserting that "some things are true according to philosophy but not according to the Catholic faith, as though there were two contradictory truths." Scholars who published works against Averroism included Albertus Magnus and Thomas Aquinas.]

Select Bibliography

While selecting from a range of works that treat Warfield directly, this bibliography attempts to be comprehensive for secondary treatments of his scientific views. For further bibliography on Warfield generally, see Mark A. Noll, ed., *The Princeton Theology, 1812–1921* (Grand Rapids: Baker, 1983), 321–34; on the broader contexts of Hodge's and Warfield's scientific concerns, see the bibliography appended to Charles Hodge, *What Is Darwinism? And Other Writings on Science and Religion* (Grand Rapids: Baker, 1994), 171–74.

Aucker, W. Bryan. "Hodge and Warfield on Evolution." *Presbyterion: Covenant Seminary Review* 20 (Fall 1994): 131–42.

Buswell, James O., III. "Warfield and Creationist Anthropology: A Rejoinder to Paul H. Seely." *Journal of the American Scientific Affiliation* 18 (Dec. 1966): 117–20.

Cornelius, Donald Murray. "The Theological Reaction of Charles Hodge, B. B. Warfield, and James Orr to Charles Darwin's Theory of Evolution." M.C.S. thesis, Regent College, Vancouver, 1982.

Fuller, Daniel P. "Benjamin B. Warfield's View of Faith and History." *Bulletin of the Evangelical Theological Society* 11 (Spring 1968): 75–83.

Gerstner, John H. "Warfield's Case for Biblical Inerrancy." In *God's Inerrant Word*, edited by John Warwick Montgomery, 115–42. Minneapolis: Bethany, 1974.

Gundlach, Bradley John. "The Evolution Question at Princeton, 1845–1929." Ph.D. diss., University of Rochester, 1995.

Hoefel, Robert J. "B. B. Warfield and James Orr: A Study in Contrasting Approaches to Scripture." *Christian Scholar's Review* 16.1 (1986): 40–52.

Hoffecker, W. Andrew. "Benjamin B. Warfield." In *The Princeton Theology,* edited by David F. Wells, 65–91. Grand Rapids: Baker, 1989.

———. *Piety and the Princeton Theologians.* Phillipsburg, N.J.: Presbyterian and Reformed, 1981.

Illick, Joseph E., III. "The Reception of Darwinism at the Theological Seminary and the College at Princeton, New Jersey." *Journal of the Presbyterian Historical Society* 38 (1960): 152–65, 234–43.

Johnson, Deryl Freeman. "The Attitudes of the Princeton Theologians toward Darwinism and Evolution from 1859–1929." Ph.D. diss., University of Iowa, 1968.

Kerr, Hugh T. "Warfield: The Person behind the Theology." Lecture at Princeton Theological Seminary, 1982.

Lamoureux, Denis Oswald. "Between 'The Origin of Species' and 'The Fundamentals': Toward a Historiographical Model of the Evangelical Reaction to Darwinism in the Fifty Years." Ph.D. diss., Toronto School of Theology, 1991.

Lane, A. N. S. "B. B. Warfield and the Humanity of Scripture." *Vox Evangelica* 16 (1986): 77–94.

Letis, Theodore P. "B. B. Warfield, Common-Sense Philosophy, and Biblical Criticism." *American Presbyterians* 69 (1991): 175–90.

Livingstone, David N. "B. B. Warfield, the Theory of Evolution and Early Fundamentalism." *Evangelical Quarterly* 58 (Jan. 1986): 69–83.

———. "Darwinism and Calvinism: The Belfast-Princeton Connection." *Isis* 83 (1992): 408–28.

———. *Darwin's Forgotten Defenders: The Encounter between Evangelical Theology and Evolutionary Thought.* Grand Rapids: Eerdmans; and Edinburgh: Scottish Academic Press, 1987.

———. "The Idea of Design: The Vicissitudes of a Key Concept in the Princeton Response to Darwin." *Scottish Journal of Theology* 37 (1984): 329–57.

———. *The Preadamite Theory and the Marriage of Science and Religion.* Transactions of the American Philosophical Society, vol. 82, part 3. Philadelphia: American Philosophical Society, 1992.

———. "Situating Evangelical Responses to Darwin." In *Evangelicals and Science in Historical Perspective,* edited by David N. Livingstone, D. G. Hart, and Mark A. Noll, 193–219. New York: Oxford University Press, 1999.

Marsden, George M. "A Case of the Excluded Middle: Creation versus Evolution in America." *Nature* 305 (Oct. 13, 1983): 571–74.

———. "The Evangelical Love Affair with Enlightenment Science." In Marsden, *Understanding Fundamentalism and Evangelicalism,* 122–52. Grand Rapids: Eerdmans, 1991.

———. *Fundamentalism and American Culture.* New York: Oxford University Press, 1980.

Meeter, John E., and Roger R. Nicole. *A Bibliography of Benjamin Breckinridge Warfield, 1851–1921.* Nutley, N.J.: Presbyterian and Reformed, 1974.

Moore, James R. *The Post-Darwinian Controversies: A Study of the Protestant Struggle to Come to Terms with Darwin in Great Britain and America, 1870–1900.* Cambridge: Cambridge University Press, 1979.

Noll, Mark A., ed. *The Princeton Defense of Plenary Verbal Inspiration.* New York: Garland, 1988.

———. *The Princeton Theology, 1812–1921: Scripture, Science, and Theological Method from Archibald Alexander to Benjamin Warfield.* Grand Rapids: Baker, 1983.

Riddlebarger, Kim. "The Lion of Princeton: Benjamin Breckinridge Warfield on Apologetics, Theological Method and Polemics." Ph.D. diss., Fuller Theological Seminary, 1997.

Roberts, Jon H. *Darwinism and the Divine in America: Protestant Intellectuals and Organic Evolution, 1859–1900.* Madison: University of Wisconsin Press, 1988.

Rogers, Jack B., and Donald K. McKim. *The Authority and Interpretation of the Bible.* San Francisco: Harper & Row, 1979.

Sandeen, Ernest R. *The Roots of Fundamentalism: British and American Millenarianism, 1800–1930.* Chicago: University of Chicago Press, 1970.

Seely, Paul H. "The Antiquity of Warfield's Paper on the Antiquity of Man." *Journal of the American Scientific Affiliation* 18 (March 1966): 28–31.

Smith, Gary S. "Calvinists and Evolution, 1870–1920." *Journal of Presbyterian History* 61 (Fall 1983): 335–52.

Spencer, Stephen R. "A Comparison and Evaluation of the Old Princeton and Amsterdam Apologetics." Th.M. thesis, Grand Rapids Baptist Seminary, 1981.

Sproul, R. C., John H. Gerstner, and Arthur Lindsley. *Classical Apologetics.* Grand Rapids: Zondervan, 1984.

Taylor, Marion Ann. *The Old Testament in the Old Princeton School (1812–1929).* Lewiston, N.Y.: Mellen, 1992.

Torrance, Thomas F. Review of *The Inspiration and Authority of the Bible,* by Benjamin B. Warfield. *Scottish Journal of Theology* 7 (March 1954): 104–8.

Vander Stelt, John C. *Philosophy and Scripture: A Study in Old Princeton and Westminster Theology.* Marlton, N.J.: Mack, 1978.

Warfield, Ethelbert D. "Biographical Sketch." In *Works of Benjamin B. Warfield,* 1:v–ix. New York: Oxford University Press, 1927; Grand Rapids: Baker, 1981 reprint.

Woodbridge, John D., and Randall H. Balmer. "The Princetonians and Biblical Authority: An Assessment of the Ernest Sandeen Proposal." In *Scripture and Truth,* edited by D. A. Carson and John D. Woodbridge, 251–79. Grand Rapids: Zondervan, 1983.

Index

Mark A. Noll is the McManis Professor of Christian Thought and professor of history at Wheaton College. Among his books are *A History of Christianity in the United States and Canada, The Scandal of the Evangelical Mind,* and *Turning Points: Decisive Moments in the History of Christianity.* David N. Livingstone, a fellow of the British Academy, is professor of geography and intellectual history at the Queen's University of Belfast. He has published several books, including *Darwin's Forgotten Defenders: The Encounter between Evangelical Theology and Evolutionary Thought* and *The Geographical Tradition.* Together they have edited Charles Hodge's *What Is Darwinism? And Other Writings on Science and Religion* (Baker, 1994) and (with D. G. Hart) *Evangelicals and Science in Historical Perspective* (Oxford University Press, 1999).